So you want to

BE A COMPUTER PROGRAMMER

JAMES E. MILLER

Printed in the United States of America.

ISBN: 978-0-615-87277-3

Table of Contents

Preface v

Chapter 1 Problems Definition 1

Chapter 2 Problems 15

Chapter 3 Programming Language BASIC 183

Chapter 4 Programming Language FORTRAN 227

Chapter 5 Programming Language Pascal 265

Chapter 6 Programming Language C 299

Chapter 7 Programming Language C++ 333

Preface

Success in computer programming requires the same basic set of skills that are required for success in any discipline: a keen interest, dedication, patience and perseverance. The successful computer programmer has a desire to solve any programming problem encountered, and may also enjoy learning the syntax of different programming languages. The purpose of this book is to challenge the student with a large set of programming problems and introduce the student to five different programming languages.

This text includes over 300 problems which have been collected over a period of thirty years. These problems were collected for the purpose of using them in computer problem solving competitions. As a professor of mathematics and computer science at Transylvania University in Lexington, Kentucky, I supervised teams of Transylvania students who competed in university computer problem solving competitions. I also planned and conducted, with other university faculty, staff and students, computer problem solving competitions for high school students. Each competition presented five problems from the set provided in this text and twenty-five to forty teams of four students each were given four hours to test their skills of writing and coding algorithms, and solving as many of the problems as possible. The team solving the most problems with fastest time in the four-hour time limit was the winner of the competition.

In the early 80s, when I first started conducting computer competitions for high school students, the computer languages used to code and execute the coded algorithms were BASIC and FORTRAN. Over the next thirty years the computer languages Pascal, C and C++ became available, and were also used. In many cases, the students at the competitions were given the opportunity to code in the language of their choice. The problems presented in this text can be solved in any of the above languages; however, some problems may be easier to solve in some languages than others.

To assist the reader in testing, reinforcing or building programming skills, a primer of the languages FORTRAN, BASIC, Pascal, C and C++

has been included. To test your code you will need an interpreter or compiler for your language. The compilers can be purchased at many bookstores, and test versions for most of the compilers can be found on-line, free of cost. The programming language primers included in this text were developed and used for one week academic camps with computer emphasis for high school students. These camps were held at Transylvania University during the summers for the past thirty years.

I have had the pleasure of teaching mathematics and computer science courses at Transylvania University for over forty years. I have taught most mathematics courses from basic math through complex analysis, and have also developed and taught computer courses from basic language courses through compiler construction courses. I recently published a book on Numerical Analysis (*Elementary Theory & Application of Numerical Analysis* – Dover Publication 2011) and a book on Compiler Construction (*Compiler Construction A Practical Approach* – The Clark Group 2009). These two books as well as this current book (*So You Want to be a Computer Programmer*) were some of the products of my teaching and service as a college professor over a forty-year span.

I am grateful to my many outstanding students and colleagues at Transylvania University for their assistance in making this work possible. Finally, I am most grateful to my wife, Betty, for being so understanding during the time that I have spent in the pursuit of sharing knowledge.

Dr. James E. Miller
Lexington, Kentucky
jmiller@transy.edu

CHAPTER 1

Problems Definition

The purpose of this chapter is to give a brief overview of the 333 problems detailed in Chapter 2.

1. A program to input three integers, then find and output the greatest common divisor of the three integers. **(Pg. 15)**
2. A program to input a set on numbers, then find and output the average of all the numbers that are multiples of 3 or ending in 7. **(Pg. 15)**
3. A program to use the sieve of Eratosthenes to find prime numbers. **(Pg. 16)**
4. A program to find and list all words found in a text message. **(Pg. 16)**
5. A program to input a mathematical expression in reverse Polish, then calculate and print its numeric value. **(Pg. 17)**
6. A program to use a given mathematical expression to approximate PI.
7. A program to convert decimal numbers to rational fractions. **(Pg. 18)**
8. A program to input a set of numbers, then find and print a frequency distribution for the set. **(Pg. 18)**
9. A program to input a text message, then print the characters of each word in reverse order of input. **(Pg. 19)**
10. A program to input an integer of at most four digits, then find and print all permutations of the integer. **(Pg. 19)**
11. A program to input a number in base 7, then output the number in base 16. **(Pg. 20)**
12. A program to find, and then use, the smallest base possible to add two integers. **(Pg. 20)**
13. A program to take two arrays of numbers in ascending order, then combine into a third array that is in ascending order. **(Pg. 20)**

14. A program to calculate the "change" needed for the purchase of an item. **(Pg. 21)**
15. A program that inputs an integer, then determines if it is defective, perfect or abundant. **(Pg. 21)**
16. A program to find all two digit integers with the property that their squares can be divided into two, two digit integers, whose sum is the given integer. **(Pg. 22)**
17. A program to print a specified pattern. **(Pg. 22)**
18. A program to count the squares of a tablecloth that Erno the ant travels. **(Pg. 22)**
19. A program to input a sequence of integers, then find and print each run of integers. **(Pg. 23)**
20. A program to input a grid of cities and distances, then find and print the distance from city X to city Y. **(Pg. 24)**
21. A program to input a positive integer, then determine if prime or Fibonacci or both. **(Pg. 24)**
22. A program to input a sequence of numbers, and then find how many times a number is strictly larger than the one just before it. **(Pg. 25)**
23. A program to add large integers (integers as long as 20 digits). **(Pg. 25)**
24. A program to calculate a memory address for a character string. **(Pg. 26)**
25. A program to input a set of numbers, then calculate the average for a unique subset of the input. **(Pg. 26)**
26. A program to determine if a given number is the sum of exactly three numbers from a given set of numbers. **(Pg. 27)**
27. A program to compress and decompress textual data. **(Pg. 27)**
28. A program to add the digits of any three digit integer. **(Pg. 28)**
29. A program to score a bowling game. **(Pg. 28)**
30. A program to take an integer and convert to a palindrome. **(Pg. 30)**
31. A program to find the average of numbers from a list that has special properties. **(Pg. 30)**
32. A program to simulate the "game of clock patience". **(Pg. 31)**
33. A program to compute the number of frames a bowler made spares and the number of frames the bowler made a strike. **(Pg. 32)**
34. A program to input an array of elements, then find and output the largest and the smallest element. **(Pg. 32)**
35. A program to input sets of four numbers, then find and output the largest element of each set and the largest element of all sets. **(Pg. 32)**
36. A program to find and print all prime numbers less than 500. **(Pg. 33)**

37. A program to input an integer, then find, and print the integer is perfect or not perfect. **(Pg. 33)**
38. A program to create a table of x and f(x) for a given function f(x). **(Pg. 33)**
39. A program to compute the miles per gallon for a fleet of cars. **(Pg. 34)**
40. A program to calculate a function for a particular value if defined differently at x=a, x<a and x>a. **(Pg. 35)**
41. A program to calculate the cost of electricity. **(Pg. 35)**
42. A program to input identification numbers and names of individuals then prints the names in alphabetical order and identification numbers in numeric order. **(Pg. 35)**
43. A program to find and print the ages of individuals given the month and year they were born. **(Pg. 36)**
44. A program to input a list of positive numbers, then finds and prints the largest and how many times it occurred. **(Pg. 36)**
45. A program to print a student's grade report. **(Pg. 36)**
46. A program to input an integer, then find and print the prime factorization of the integer. **(Pg. 37)**
47. A program to input the cost and miles/gallon for two vehicles, then determine which is more cost effective. **(Pg. 38)**
48. A program to determine the amount of money to deposit from age 25 to age 65 to have an income of $25,000 each year during retirement. **(Pg. 38)**
49. A program to evaluate the Hermite polynomial, $H_n(x)$, for given n and given x. **(Pg. 39)**
50. A program to determine the grains of wheat requested from the king by the inventor of chest. **(Pg. 39)**
51. A program to determine the terminal date, given the beginning date and the number of days to pass. **(Pg. 39)**
52. A program to play the game of chest against the computer. **(Pg. 40)**
53. A program to find one root of a 5th degree polynomial. **(Pg. 40)**
54. A program to evaluate a Legendre polynomial, $P_n(x)$, for given n and given x. **(Pg. 40)**
55. A program to calculate the total distance traveled by a bouncing ball. **(Pg. 41)**
56. A program to input a word, then rearrange the characters of the word to alpha order. **(Pg. 41)**
57. A program to input the names and grades of students, then print the names and grades in alphabetic order by student name. **(Pg. 41)**

58. A program to input a square array of elements, then determine if the elements form a magic square. **(Pg. 42)**
59. A program to input a list of numbers, then print the numbers and also list with each number below average, average, or above average. **(Pg. 43)**
60. A program to input a list of student names with GPA, and then print in order by student name and in order by GPA. **(Pg. 44)**
61. A program to determine how far from a wall a student will have to be in order to see a tower that is behind the wall. **(Pg. 44)**
62. A program to determine tax due given income amount and tax table and number of exemptions. **(Pg. 45)**
63. A program to translate a sentence, given a translation table. **(Pg. 46)**
64. A program to input a text message, then find and list each word and the number of times the word was found. **(Pg. 46)**
65. A program to input a set of points that make a polygon, then find and print the perimeter of the polygon. **(Pg. 48)**
66. A program to determine how long it takes to mow a lawn. **(Pg. 49)**
67. A program to determine which type of light bulb gives most lumens per dollar value. **(Pg. 49)**
68. A program to use the bubble sort to arrange a set of numbers in order from low to high and show the number of exchanges necessary. **(Pg. 50)**
69. A program to input three possible sides of a triangle and determine if they could form a triangle. **(Pg. 50)**
70. A program to input a year and then determine if that year was a leap year. **(Pg. 50)**
71. A program to calculate the month and the day of the year, given a number that represents the day of the year and a number that represents the year. **(Pg. 50)**
72. A program to determine the loss or gain from sales of ice cream. **(Pg. 51)**
73. A program to compute the odds that at least two people from a group of size n will have the same birthday. **(Pg. 51)**
74. A program to compute the effective rate of interest on money when the rate is compounded annually. **(Pg. 52)**
75. A program to evaluate n such that $2^{(n-1)} <= x < 2^n$ for a given x. **(Pg. 53)**
76. A program to determine the eventual cash value of an annuity. **(Pg. 53)**
77. A program to count in any base b, where b<=10. **(Pg. 53)**
78. A program to generate the first N rows of Pascal's triangle. **(Pg. 54)**

79. A program to count the number of words and sentences that are in a paragraph. (**Pg. 55**)
80. A program to convert Roman numerals to equivalent integers. (**Pg. 55**)
81. A program to translate English to Pig Latin. (**Pg. 55**)
82. A program to convert base 2 (binary) numbers to base 10 (decimal). (**Pg. 56**)
83. A program to find the greatest common divisor of two numbers using the Euclidean algorithm. (**Pg. 56**)
84. A program to perform a "Crap Simulation game". (**Pg. 56**)
85. A program to determine the closeness of binary vector. (**Pg. 57**)
86. A program to use the "Method of Least Squares" to determine the relationship of two variables. (**Pg. 57**)
87. A program to simulate the toss of a coin. (**Pg. 58**)
88. A program to input two positive integers less than 10000, then prints one line for each number K between those two given numbers. Each line contains 12 numbers. The first number in a line is the K for that line and each number after the first is the "Ziel" of the one before. (**Pg. 59**)
89. A program to input a text message, then count the number of words with one character two characters, etc. (**Pg. 59**)
90. A program to play "guess the number" – with a twist. (**Pg. 60**)
91. A program to calculate the number of ways a number of dollar bills can be converted into change. (**Pg. 60**)
92. A program to have the computer guess a number between 1 and 100 inclusive that is entered. (**Pg. 61**)
93. A program to perform fractional arithmetic. (**Pg. 61**)
94. A program to perform simple arithmetic with Roman numerals. (**Pg. 62**)
95. A program to find perfect squares by calculating the product of 4 consecutive integers. (**Pg. 62**)
96. A program to simulate the roll of four dice. (**Pg. 62**)
97. A program to determine if a given point lies within a specified circle. (**Pg. 63**)
98. A program to find all three digit integers with the property that the some of the cube of the digits give the number. (**Pg. 63**)
99. A program to determine "mathematical mistakes" such as 16/64 = 1/4; where the result is obtained by striking out the 6. (**Pg. 63**)
100. A program to input a decimal number X, then print the rational numbers of form p/q greater than or equal to X where p and q are integers from 1 to 10 inclusive. (**Pg. 64**)

101. A program to find all two digit palindrome primes. A prime number is a palindrome prime if it is also a prime when its digits are reversed. **(Pg. 64)**
102. A program to divide coconuts between three soldiers shipwrecked on a desert island. **(Pg. 64)**
103. A program to find the square root of a number by Newton's method. **(Pg. 65)**
104. A program to estimate the world's population assuming a given death rate and a given birth rate. **(Pg. 65)**
105. A program to print checks for a small business. **(Pg. 66)**
106. A program to find the "least common multiple" of three numbers. **(Pg. 66)**
107. A program to determine the money lost from a "game of chance". **(Pg. 67)**
108. A program to calculate a frequency distribution for a set of integers. **(Pg. 67)**
109. A program to calculate a date following a given date. **(Pg. 67)**
110. A program that plays the game of HANGMAN. **(Pg. 68)**
111. A program to determine if two positive integers are relatively prime. **(Pg. 68)**
112. A program to compute C(n,r), the combination of n items taken r at a time. **(Pg. 69)**
113. A program to determine the probability of outcome for the roll of two dice. **(Pg. 69)**
114. A program to translate an arithmetic expression. **(Pg. 69)**
115. A program to find a ship with doctor aboard which is closest in time to a given ship. **(Pg. 70)**
116. A program to determine the best move in a tic-tac-toe board. **(Pg. 70)**
117. A program to input five integer pairs representing a poker hand and evaluate the poker hand. **(Pg. 71)**
118. A program to simulate the "game of life". **(Pg. 72)**
119. A program to input a list of integers, then find the longest consecutive run of increasing value integers in the list. **(Pg. 74)**
120. A program to input nine lines of character data, then find the letter which makes up the biggest BLOCK of characters. **(Pg. 47)**
121. A program to determine the EDGE of a two-dimensional pattern. **(Pg. 75)**
122. A program to determine the cost of printing a book. **(Pg. 76)**
123. A program to handle the billing procedures for Junko-Rent-A-Car. **(Pg. 76)**
124. A program to compute the monthly service charge on a bank checking account. **(Pg. 77)**
125. A program to read a text message and then print a list of all the words. **(Pg. 78)**
126. A program to compute the relative frequencies for the days the thirteenth of the month falls. **(Pg. 78)**

127. A program to evaluate an applicant's credit worthiness. (Pg. 78)
128. A program to calculate the optimum theater ticket price. (Pg. 80)
129. A program to simulate a rabbit population over time. (Pg. 80)
130. A program to calculate the frequency of each vowel in some English text. (Pg. 81)
131. A program to find roots to quadratic equations. (Pg. 82)
132. A program to find all possible strings of length k from k distinct characters. (Pg. 82)
133. A program to find all integer solutions to the equation Ax + By – Cz = D. x,y and z restricted range. (Pg. 82)
134. A program to find the average and number closest to the average for a set of numbers. (Pg. 82)
135. A program to input a sequence of numbers, then find if the sequence is monotonic increasing or monotonic decreasing. (Pg. 83)
136. A program to compute bonuses for salespeople who qualify. (Pg. 83)
137. A program to compute the inner product of two matrices. (Pg. 84)
138. A program to extract numbers embedded in a line of text. (Pg. 84)
139. A program to calculate the factorials for integers. (Pg. 84)
140. A program to input a set of numbers, then calculate the mean, median and mode. (Pg. 85)
141. A program to input a string of characters, and then find all palindromes in the string. (Pg. 85)
142. A program to input an n x n matrix, then determine if it is symmetric. (Pg. 85)
143. A program to input the numerator and denominator of a fraction, then output the fraction reduced to lowest terms. (Pg. 85)
144. A program to input the coefficients of two linear equations, then determine if the equations represent parallel line, interesting lines or coincident lines. (Pg. 85)
145. A program to find and output all perfect numbers between 1 and 10,000. (Pg. 86)
146. A program to output an n x m array of asterisks. (Pg. 86)
147. A program to find and output a multiplication table. (Pg. 86)
148. A program to score the "paper-rock-scissors" game. (Pg. 86)
149. A program to determine additional state tax owed. (Pg. 87)
150. A program to accept a character string and remove all blanks. (Pg. 87)
151. A program to calculate the cost of telephone calls. (Pg. 88)
152. A program to determine and list individual digits of an integer. (Pg. 88)

153. A program to determine if an integer is divisible by 9 by considering the sum of the digits of the integer. **(Pg. 88)**
154. A program to calculate the interest on money that is compounded daily. **(Pg. 88)**
155. A program to scan a sentence and replace all multiple occurrences of a blank with a single occurrence of a blank. **(Pg. 88)**
156. A program to input an integer and then determine various properties of the integer. **(Pg. 89)**
157. A program to input a positive real number then finds and outputs the number of digits to the left and right of the decimal point. **(Pg. 89)**
158. A program to find the largest value, the smallest value, and the sum of the input data. **(Pg. 89)**
159. A program to input a positive integer, then find and print all divisors. **(Pg. 89)**
160. A program to input two arrays, and from these two form a third array. **(Pg. 89)**
161. A program to input a sentence, then count the number of one letter words, two letter words, etc. **(Pg. 90)**
162. A program to input a character string, then find the length of the string and other properties. **(Pg. 91)**
163. A program to add, subtract and multiply a pair of matrices. **(Pg. 91)**
164. A program to input a sentence, then find the number of words, and average word length. **(Pg. 91)**
165. A program to calculate the day of the week given the month, day and current year. **(Pg. 91)**
166. A program to compute the accumulated balance on a fixed deposit at the end of each interest period. **(Pg. 91)**
167. A program to simulate stacks by using an array with 10 numbers. **(Pg. 92)**
168. A program that identifies the modal value in an array. **(Pg. 93)**
169. A program that adds, subtracts, multiply and divides fractions. **(Pg. 93)**
170. A program to generate a table of statute miles, nautical miles, and kilometers. **(Pg. 93)**
171. A program to approximate e^x by summing the expression $(1 + x/1! + x^2/2! + \dots)$. **(Pg. 93)**
172. A program to find integer solutions to the equation $a^2 + b^2 = c^2$. **(Pg. 94)**
173. A program to determine if two words come from the same base alphabet. **(Pg. 94)**
174. A program to approximate the value of PI using the value of C (circumference of a circle) and the value of R (the radius of a circle). **(Pg. 94)**

175. A program to find a series of consecutive positive integers whose sum is 100. **(Pg. 94)**
176. A program that finds six-digit numbers which can be split into two parts of three digits each and when the two numbers are added and the sum squared, you get the original number. **(Pg. 95)**
177. A program to find a four-digit number such that the sum of the fourth power of its digits gives the number. **(Pg. 95)**
178. A program that finds two five-digit numbers that between them use the digits 0 through 9 once each, such that the first number divided by the second is equal to 9. **(Pg. 95)**
179. A program that simulates deque manipulation. **(Pg. 95)**
180. A program to determine "Latin Squares". **(Pg. 95)**
181. A program that compares strings for equality. **(Pg. 96)**
182. A program to determine and print any three digit number in words. **(Pg. 96)**
183. A program to simulate a two player dart game. **(Pg. 96)**
184. A program to create a circular list. **(Pg. 97)**
185. A program that counts the number of anagrams from a list of words. **(Pg. 97)**
186. A program to determine why a matrix of elements is not quite a Magic Square. **(Pg. 98)**
187. A program that works with a grid of 0's and 1's that represent the pixels for a black and white picture. **(Pg. 99)**
188. A program to make the bubble sort more efficient. **(Pg. 101)**
189. A program to simulate a serial communication controller. **(Pg. 101)**
190. A program to analyze data. **(Pg. 103)**
191. A program to reformat data. **(Pg. 103)**
192. A program to search for a given string with permutations. **(Pg. 105)**
193. A program to analyze the "Peasant and Wizard" problem. **(Pg. 106)**
194. A program to analyze two strings to see if one string is a subset of the second string. **(Pg. 106)**
195. A program to check for pattern matching. **(Pg. 106)**
196. A program to automate bowling handicaps. **(Pg. 108)**
197. A program to input a binary tree pattern and then output all words represented in each pattern tree. **(Pg. 109)**
198. A program to find integers with special properties. **(Pg. 110)**
199. A program to multiply large integers. **(Pg. 110)**
200. A program to evaluate constant integer expressions. **(Pg. 110)**
201. A program to convert decimal numbers into another base. **(Pg. 111)**

202. A program to find a selected average of a set of numbers. **(Pg.111)**
203. A program to remove blanks and vowels from a string. **(Pg. 111)**
204. A program to find perfect numbers imbedded in a matrix. **(Pg. 111)**
205. A program to test keyboard skills. **(Pg. 112)**
206. A program to simulate a turtle versus a rabbit race. **(Pg. 112)**
207. A program to solve a linear equation that has literal input. **(Pg. 113)**
208. A program to print squares and then place digits within squares. **(Pg. 113)**
209. A program to determine the minimum amount of paint to cover a given surface. **(Pg. 114)**
210. A program to determine the number of roofing bundles to cover a roof. **(Pg. 114)**
211. A program to determine the amount of paint needed to paint a water tower. **(Pg. 114)**
212. A program to print a table of values for a given function. **(Pg. 115)**
213. A program to print a bar graph for a given set of integers. **(Pg. 115)**
214. A program to simulate the "BUZZ" party game. **(Pg. 115)**
215. A program to find integers whose squares have special properties. **(Pg. 116)**
216. A program to input a list of names with identification numbers, then print the names in alphabetical order with given number. **(Pg. 116)**
217. A program to input a string, then output each character found in the string with the number of times that character appears in the string. **(Pg. 116)**
218. A program to construct a cryptogram for a given message. **(Pg. 117)**
219. A program to take dates in numeric form and place into a single "canonical" form. **(Pg. 118)**
220. A program that will score a T/F exam. **(Pg. 118)**
221. A program that will take an integer as input, then find all primes less than or equal to the integer. **(Pg. 119)**
222. A program that encrypts messages. **(Pg. 119)**
223. A program that finds the first N twin prime pairs. **(Pg. 120)**
224. A program that evaluates exam scores. **(Pg. 120)**
225. A program that computes the value of the user's holding of one stock. **(Pg. 121)**
226. A program to print words for telephone numbers. **(Pg. 122)**
227. A program to calculate an employees pay. **(Pg. 123)**
228. A program to find numbers with the property that they are equal to the sum of each digit of the number raised to the power of the number of digits in the number. **(Pg. 123)**

229. A program to change ordinal numbers to Roman numerals. **(Pg. 124)**
230. A program to determine if a string of digits contains a repeated string of digits. **(Pg. 124)**
231. A program to find all permutations of four characters. **(Pg. 125)**
232. A program to count selected words found in an input stream. **(Pg. 125)**
233. A program to evaluate fractions that are input in character mode. **(Pg. 126)**
234. A program to translate Morse Code. **(Pg. 126)**
235. A program that will translate your weight on earth to your weight on the planets. **(Pg. 127)**
236. A program to compute the average of "legal" exam scores. **(Pg. 127)**
237. A program to print "Parkside Triangles". **(Pg. 128)**
238. A program that spell-checks a text message. **(Pg. 129)**
239. A program that calculates the speed of a race in feet/second and in meters/second. **(Pg. 129)**
240. A program that determines the "best buy" house cost. **(Pg. 129)**
241. A program that calculates the cost of telephone calls. **(Pg. 130)**
242. A program that inputs a real or decimal number, then determines the number of digits to the left of the decimal point. **(Pg. 130)**
243. A program that generates Morse Code. **(Pg. 130)**
244. A program that evaluates a poker hand. **(Pg. 131)**
245. A program that creates nested rectangles. **(Pg. 132)**
246. A program that converts decimal integers to binary numbers. **(Pg. 133)**
247. A program that converts decimal numbers to rational fractions. **(Pg. 133)**
248. A program that gets numbers from character strings. **(Pg. 133)**
249. A program for calculating a bank balance. **(Pg. 134)**
250. A program to determine the height of "Mount Mongo" and to determine how long it will take the "Texarkana Clone" to reach its summit. **(Pg. 135)**
251. A program to test numbers to see if they are "perfect". **(Pg. 136)**
252. A program to translate text to Braille. **(Pg. 136)**
253. A program for individual and team scoring. **(Pg. 137)**
254. A program to calculate population growth and population decline. **(Pg. 138)**
255. A program to simulate the operation of a furnace under the control of a thermostat. **(Pg. 139)**
256. A program to simulate the population of pine bark beetles in pine trees. **(Pg. 140)**
257. A program to find all prime palindromes between two given numbers. **(Pg. 141)**

258. A program to simulate the "Game of Life". (**Pg. 141**)
259. A program to encode and decode text messages using the "Beaufort method of Cryptology". (**Pg. 142**)
260. A program to convert money from one currency to another currency. (**Pg. 143**)
261. A program to score a diving competition. (**Pg. 143**)
262. A program to determine the number of rabbits born over a given interval of time. (**Pg. 144**)
263. A program to perform some two dimensional array work. (**Pg. 144**)
264. A program to tally postal service charge by department. (**Pg. 145**)
265. A program to draw a line given one point and the slope of the line. (**Pg. 146**)
266. A program to determine the location of a new factory given a set of criteria. (**Pg. 146**)
267. A program to find the "best match for a date" given a set of criteria. (**Pg. 147**)
268. A program to create a new string from old string. (**Pg. 149**)
269. A program to evaluate known trigonometric functions that are given in character mode. (**Pg. 149**)
270. A program to find the grandparent from a list of children and grandchildren. (**Pg. 150**)
271. A program to simulate the "Like Birth Month" problem. (**Pg. 151**)
272. A program to calculate a racer's relative position every 10 minutes of the race. (**Pg. 151**)
273. A program to separate even and odd numbers from an input stream. (**Pg. 152**)
274. A program to find all four values, velocity, distance, acceleration, and time given two of the values. (**Pg. 152**)
275. A program to add large integers defined as character strings. (**Pg. 152**)
276. A program to work with "Fibonacci like" series. (**Pg. 153**)
277. A program to count in any base less than or equal to 16. (**Pg. 153**)
278. A program to find the area between a cube and a sphere. (**Pg. 154**)
279. A program to print a square of specified size. (**Pg. 154**)
280. A program to find the solution to linear and quadratic equations. (**Pg. 154**)
281. A program to print the letter V of various sizes. (**Pg. 155**)
282. A program to find super palindromes. (**Pg. 155**)
283. A program to list all triplets (groups of size 3) that can be selected from a group of size N. (**Pg. 156**)
284. A program to find the median and all numbers greater than the median from a list of numbers. (**Pg. 156**)

285. A program to find the average and all numbers greater than the average from a list of numbers. **(Pg. 157)**
286. A program to compute the cost of a "Live Psychic Party Line Call". **(Pg. 158)**
287. A program to remove particular characters and punctuation from a line of text. **(Pg. 158)**
288. A program to check for proper moves for the Knight in a chess game. **(Pg. 158)**
289. A program to calculate the number of days between two input dates. **(Pg. 159)**
290. A program to find the average of the absolute difference between adjacent numbers of the set. **(Pg. 160)**
291. A program to implement a "beeper" for a TV show. **(Pg. 160)**
292. A program to determine the number of tiles needed to roof a house. **(Pg. 161)**
293. A program to test to see if three points lie on a straight line. **(Pg. 162)**
294. A program to calculate the percentage of scores correct on an exam. **(Pg. 163)**
295. A program to place the words of a sentence in alphabetical order. **(Pg. 164)**
296. A program to find the unique numbers from a list of numbers. **(Pg. 164)**
297. A program to add two large integers, either or both could be longer than the max integer. **(Pg. 165)**
298. A program to calculate the interior angle of a regular polygon of N sides. **(Pg. 165)**
299. A program to draw a line given two points. **(Pg. 165)**
300. A program to find the row and column with largest sum for a two dimensional array. **(Pg. 166)**
301. A program that places words in designated places of a text after it has been entered ("Mad- Libs") program. **(Pg. 167)**
302. A program that finds the ending point given the starting point (x,y) and instructions of how to move. **(Pg. 167)**
303. A program that takes a number given in text mode and writes in numeric mode. **(Pg. 167)**
304. A program to build "magic squares". **(Pg. 168)**
305. A program that performs bit mapping as a method of reducing storage. **(Pg. 169)**
306. A program that performs as a multi-base calculator (base 2 through 10). **(Pg. 170)**
307. A program that calculates the number of days needed to climb a mountain if you climb up x feet each day and slide down y feet each night. **(Pg. 170)**
308. A program that generates a calendar for any given year. **(Pg. 171)**

309. A program to generate palindromes. **(Pg. 172)**
310. A program to calculate the contraction in length of an object due to its speed. **(Pg. 172)**
311. A program to sort elements in a two dimensional array. **(Pg. 172)**
312. A program to find the nth Fibonacci number. **(Pg. 173)**
313. A program to implement a money change machine. **(Pg. 173)**
314. A program that compresses data. **(Pg. 174)**
315. A program to score Olympic competitions. **(Pg. 175)**
316. A program to convert a date in numeric form to text form. **(Pg. 175)**
317. A program to determine if a number is divisible by 3 using the sum of digits rule. **(Pg. 175)**
318. A program to sort numbers by the second digit of the number. **(Pg. 176)**
319. A program to compare segments of two strings to see if they are the same. **(Pg. 177)**
320. A program to compare someone's weight on earth and weight on the planets. **(Pg. 177)**
321. A program to rotate the elements of a two dimensional array. **(Pg. 177)**
322. A program to combine two fractions. **(Pg. 178)**
323. A program to find the distance traveled by a bouncing ball. **(Pg. 178)**
324. A program to count the number of times each character (a/z) appears in a text message. **(Pg. 179)**
325. A program to find a palindrome nearest to a given number. **(Pg. 179)**
326. A program to evaluate mathematical expressions given in character mode. **(Pg. 179)**
327. A program to determine the next number in a sequence of numbers. **(Pg. 180)**
328. A program to create a bar chart for a set of numbers. **(Pg. 180)**
329. A program to get numbers embedded in text, adds the numbers, and prints their sum. **(Pg. 181)**
330. A program to find and output the factorial of numbers 1 through 10. **(Pg. 182)**
331. A program to find and output the mean, median, and mode of a set of numbers. **(Pg. 182)**
332. A program to test a string of characters to see if a palindrome. **(Pg. 182)**
333. A program to find the average of a subset of a given set of numbers. **(Pg. 182)**

CHAPTER 2

Problems

1. Write a program that accepts three integers, then finds and prints the one largest positive integer that divides each of them evenly.
   Input: 36,54,18

   Output: 18

   Make your input/output conversational type.

2. Write a program to input a set of numbers then find and print the average of all numbers that are multiples of 3 or ending in 7. If a number satisfies both then add it twice. The number 0 will terminate the input and is not considered a multiple of 3. Round the output to the nearest integer, which is a multiple of 3 or ends in 7. If the result to be rounded is halfway between two such integers, round up.
   Input: 17
   3
   14
   33
   0

   Output: 18

3. There are many methods in which one could find only prime numbers. The method used in this program is known as the sieve of Eratosthenes. Here is a description of this method. List the integers from 2 to N (N <= 1000). Starting at 2, mark out every second value following 2. Then mark out every 3rd value after 3. Continue this process with subsequent integers. At the beginning of each marking process skip integers that have been marked out -- for example, 4 will be marked out when it is reached, so do not mark out every fourth value (this was done when every second value was marked out). List all values that are left in your list; these will be primes. Also list those that were candidates to be marked out at least three different times.

   Input: 20

   then:

2	3	4	5	6	7	8	9	10	11	12	13	14	15	16	17	18	19	20
		X		X		X		X		X		X		X		X		X
				X			X			X			X			X		
						X				X				X				
								X										

   Output: PRIMES: 2,3,5,7,11,13,17,19

   Candidates to be marked out at least 3 times: none
   Make your input/output conversational type.

4. Write a program to input lines of English text and print a list of all the words (more than one character in length) that occur in the lines. The words appear in the list in the same order that they appear in the lines. Each unique word will appear only once in the list. The text may be punctuated with periods, commas, question marks, colons, and semi-colons; the punctuation marks do not appear in the list. Assume the input lines are at most 60 characters in length, and a delimiter of ** terminates all lines of input. No hyphenated words will be included. Use conversational input/output.

Input: The best attack to a problem is a structured approach.**

Output: The
best
attack
to
a
problem
is
a
structured
approach.

5. Write a program to input an expression in reverse Polish notation then calculate and print a value for the expression. You can assume that:
   1. The expression is at most 40 characters in length.
   2. Only single digit whole numbers appear in the expression.
   3. Only the operators (+) and (-) appear in the expression.
   4. An * will terminate the input string.

   For infix notation (standard) the operator appears between two operands

   3 + 5

   In reverse Polish the operator appears to the right side of the operands

   3 5+

   Examples:

INFIX	REVERSE POLISH
3+5-7	3 5+7-
2-7+9	2 7-9+
1+4-6+9	1 4+6-9+

   All operations are performed from left to right.
   Make your input/output of conversational type.
   An example of input and output follows:

   Input: 3 5+*

   Output: 8

6. PI (3.14159265 ...) can be approximated by the expression:
   PI = 4 * (1 - 1/3 + 1/5 - 1/7 + 1/9...)
   Sum the first N terms (N <= 10000) of the above to approximate PI. Sum the expression from left to right and from right to left. The sum from right to left should give more accuracy. Give output for both sums.

   Input: Number of terms to sum? 9999

   Output: Approx. for PI (summing right to left) is: 3.141493
   Approx. for PI (summing left to right) is: 3.141321

7. Write a program to input a positive decimal constant then write it as a quotient of two positive integers reduced to lowest terms.

   Input: 23.78
   Then 23.78 = 2378/100 = 1189/50

   Output: numerator 1189
   denominator 50

8. Write a program to input a set of numbers then find and print a frequency distribution for the numbers. The number 99.9 will be used to terminate input and will not be one of the unique numbers. The output will be in order from high frequency to low frequency and if a tie in frequency occurs then the larger number is to be printed first.

   Input:
   88.67
   32.40
   14.77
   88.67
   32.40
   32.40
   99.9

   Output:

unique number	frequency
32.40	3
88.67	2
14.77	1

The input will be through an input statement and both input and output will be of conversational type with output headings.

9. Write a program that inputs a message then prints the characters of each word in the message in reverse order. Assume no punctuation, a maximum of 40 characters including blanks and all upper case characters.
Input:
HELP ME SOLVE THIS PROBLEM

Output:
PLEH EM EVLOS SIHT MELBORP

10. Input a positive integer, at most four digits in length, and then print all permutations of the number. Duplicates will be printed only once. Print the output from low number to high number.
Input: 1253

Output:
1235
1253
1325
1352
1523
1532
2135
2153
2315
2351
2513
2531
3125
3152
3215
3251
3512
3521

5123
5132
5213
5231
5312
5321

11. Input a number given in base 7, then output the number in base 16.

Input: 323

Output: A4

The input will be a positive integer and less than or equal to 32666.

12. Mathematical operations are most commonly performed using decimal arithmetic. The binary (base 2) has only the symbols 0 and 1; the base 5 systems have 0,1,2,3, and 4. Assume that we want to use the smallest base possible to add two numbers. For example, given 3241 and 13, we would use base 5. Write a program to input two numbers then determine the smallest base possible and add the two numbers using that base.

Input: 1245
3212

Output: The smallest possible base is: 6
The sum is: 4501

13. The numbers of a one-dimensional array called A have been placed in a DATA statement (behind the letter A) in ascending order. Since the contents of A-array may vary from run to run, a signal number of 0 has been placed at the end. The 0 is not part of the A-array. The numbers of another one-dimensional array called B have been set up similarly. A sample of the data follows:

```
800 REM *********DATA MODULE**********
810 DATA A, 7,18,26,31,37,43,0
820 DATA B, 9,14,35,47,52,58,63,0
```

The A and B arrays will usually be of different lengths. Write a BASIC program which will read in the A and B arrays and merge them together into a new long array C, which is also in ascending order. Print the letter C on one line, then the elements of C five per line. If the number of elements of C is not a multiple of 5, do not print 5 elements on the last line. (Do not use a sort routine. The A and B arrays will normally be of different length but each will have at least one element and no more than 20 elements.)

Output for above input: C
7 9 14 18 23
26 31 35 37 43
47 52 58 63

NOTE: Spacing of output will be up to the programmer.

14. Print the exact change received from a purchase costing P dollars if an amount D is presented to the salesclerk. Assume that D is at most $100. If D<P then go to the input statement again. The change should be given using the largest possible denominations of bills and coins. For example, if P=17.43 and D=100, the change should be as follows:

		Bills and Coin Denominations	
1	$50 bill	$50	$.05
1	$20 bill	$20	$.25
1	$10 bill	$10	$.10
1	$2 bill	$5	$.05
1	$.50 coin	$2	$.01
1	nickel(s)	$1	
2	pennies(s)		

The input and output should be of conversational type.

15. An integer is said to be perfect if it equals the sum of all of its factors, except itself. (Thus, 28=1+2+4+7+14 is perfect.) An integer is defective if the sum is less than the number. (Thus, 14 > 1+2+7 is defective.) An integer is abundant if the sum is greater than the number. (Thus, 12< 1+2+3+4+6 is abundant.) Write a program that:
    a. Reads a nonnegative number (integer)

b. Determines whether the number is perfect, defective, or abundant, and prints the result.
c. Repeats steps a) and b) until the number 0 is read.

16. The number 55 has the interesting property that its square can be divided into two, two-digit integers whose sum is 55 that is,

55*55 = 3025
and
55 = 30 + 25

Find all two-digit integers that have this property.

17. Write a program to print the pattern:

```
*
***
*****
*******
*********
*******
*****
***
*
```

where input will be the maximum number of asterisks on one line. For example, the input for this particular diamond would be the number 9. (Assume the input will be odd and less than 50.)

18. Erno the Ant loves picnics, partly because of the food, but mostly because he enjoys walking on the large checkered tablecloths that people always bring. Erno is a fairly methodical walker. He only walks in four directions (North, South, East, and West), and every one of his steps takes him to a square adjacent to the one he is currently on. Erno is also a bit of a travel buff, so when he returns from one of his strolls, he'd like to know how many checkerboard squares he visited. Unfortunately, Erno cannot count very well (ants don't as a rule) so he's come to you for help. Your job is to write a program that will take as input the directions of Erno's steps, and produce as output the number of distinct squares he touched. You are to count the square Erno starts on, and each additional square he steps on that he has not already visited.

Input Format:
Each line of input will represent Erno's walks. A line will consist of a number of direction letters (N, S, E, or W with the usual meanings) followed by a period marking the end of the line. The first character on the line will denote the direction of Erno's first step, the second, and so on. There will never be more than 20 of any one-direction letter on a line (lines will thus never be more than 81 characters long). The last line of input will have a period in column 1. By starting in the center of the cloth Erno will not fall from the table on any of his journeys.

Output Format:
For each line of input (except the end-of-input marker) you should print one line containing the number of distinct squares that Erno visited on that walk.

Input:	**Output:**
N.	2
NSEW.	3
NNWW.	5
.	

(USE ONLY UPPER CASE LETTERS FOR INPUT)

19. Suppose we are given a sequence of numbers such as 1, 3, 8, 9, 4, 12, 25, 24, 17, 19, 30, 35, 28, and 40. Those segments of the sequence that are in non-decreasing order are called runs. Thus, for the sequence given, the runs are:
1, 3, 8, 9
4, 12, 25
17, 19, 30, 35
28, 40

Note that the end of each run (except the last one) is signaled by a step-down – a larger value followed by a smaller one. Write a program to read a sequence of 20 positive numbers (from an input statement), and print each run on a separate line. Runs of length of 1 are to be ignored.

20. The following chart gives the airline distance in kilometers from one city to another.

	Seattle	Los Angeles	Omaha	Miami	Boston
Seattle	0	1540	2220	4430	4060
Los Angeles	1540	0	2090	3820	4250
Omaha	2220	2090	0	2280	2090
Miami	4430	3820	2280	0	2090
Boston	4060	4250	2090	2090	0

Write a program, which will do the following:

1. Read in the kilometers given above and place them into an array.
2. Allow the user to enter the name of the first city and the name of the second city.
3. Print out a statement saying, "THE DISTANCE FROM first city TO second city IS d KILOMETERS", where first city and second city are replaced by the names as given in step (2) and d is replaced by the proper value from the table.

21. Write a conversational style program that will read in a positive integer value and determine the following:
    a. If the integer is a prime number.
    b. If the integer is a Fibonacci number.

Write the program in such a manner that it will execute repeatedly (loop), until a zero value is detected for the input quantity.
Fibonacci numbers are generated by the following:

F(0) = 0 and F(1) = 1
F(n+1) = F(n) + F(n-1), n>=1
A prime number is a number having only itself and one as divisors. (Consider 2 to be the first prime number)

EXAMPLES:

Input: 3

Output: 3 is prime
3 is Fibonacci

Input: 17

Output: 17 is prime
17 is not Fibonacci

22. Input a list of numbers and terminate with 9999 (9999 is not one of your numbers). Determine how many times a number is strictly larger than the one just before it. For example, if the list of numbers is: 17, 3, 19, 27, 23, 25, 9999 the answer will be three (3), because 19 > 3, 27 > 19, and 25 > 23.

23. There is a restriction on the size of integers stored in computer memory. In computers having a 16-bit memory cell the allowed integers range from - 32768 to 32767. Many real-life computations involve the manipulation of large integers. One way of handling larger numbers with computers is to read them into arrays, one digit per array element, and to use special programs to manipulate the array elements. For example, the addition of 1,079,345 and 936,204 can be visualized as:

0000001079345 Array IX
0000000936204 Array IY
0000002015549 Array IZ
Where IZ(1) = IX(1) + IY(1) = 5 + 4 = 9
IZ(2) = IX(2) + IY(2) + Carry from previous addition
= 4 + 0 + 0 = 4

Write a program that uses this technique to add two strings of digits. The input will be two strings (assume each of length 10) containing the characters 0...9 as well as other characters. Suppress (i.e. remove) all non-digit characters then add the two suppressed strings and print the sum.

Input:	**Array 1**	**Array 2**
	1	2
	1	2
	b	c
	c	c
	a	c

a	c
a	2
1	2
1	c
c	c

Hint: 1111
2222

Output: 3333

24. A problem encountered in writing compilers or determining efficient means of storing data on disks is converting a name into a unique or reasonably unique numeric value (hash value). This procedure is called hashing. Several algorithms are used to accomplish this task. One of the simpler methods is to use the numeric expression of each letter in some type of equation. In this problem you are to convert a word into a reproducible integer value between 0 and 500. To get this value, add each ordinal value of a letter times that letters position within the word. Take 65 as ordinal value of A, 66 as ordinal value of B, 90 for Z etc. This could generate a rather large number, which may not be within the required range. To calculate a number within the range, determine the modulus of this large number and 500. The modulus is the remainder when 500 divides the number. For example the number for ACE would be:

$$1 * 65 + 2 * 67 + 3 * 69 \text{ or } 406$$

Write a program to input a name, and print the hash value. Assume each name consist of the characters A through Z only, upper case and at most 8 characters in length. Terminate the input with the word END. Use conversational input and output.

25. A set of numbers is to be entered. Numbers less than 50 are to be doubled and those greater than 50 are to be halved. However, if 50 is the input, no more numbers are to be entered. Calculate the average of these modified numbers, but exclude 50.

Input: 35
66

143
10
49.55
-3.2
73
50

Output: 46.242856

26. Given a number S, we want to find out if it can be expressed as the sum of exactly three different numbers from a given group of numbers. For example, if S is 100, and the group of numbers is 20, 57, 32, 86, 4, 11, 14 then a solution is: 100 = 57 + 32 + 11. If S is 40 and the group is 17, 25, 15, 32, 14, 40, 3 then there is no solution. You must input the number S and the group of numbers where 0 serves as an end-of-input flag. (There will always be at least three numbers and a maximum of 20 numbers in the group, and the trailing 0 is not part of the group.) Thus, the input for the first example above would look like:

    100, 20, 57, 32, 86, 4, 11, 14, 0

    The output from the program should either be a line showing one solution like this:

    100 = 57 + 32 + 11

    or, if there is no solution, a line like this (if more than one solution still print THERE IS NO SOLUTION):

    THERE IS NO SOLUTION

27. In order to save storage space, Flo wants to be able to compress or decompress her textual data as follows:

    For each line she will find out what pair of characters occurs most frequently, and replace that pair with a "*". So that she can restore each line to the original when she reads the line later, she will put a "*" followed by those two characters at the beginning of each line. (She will not have any *'s in the original text and every line will have at least two characters. If several pairs tie as most frequent, then the first pair will be used. Treat a blank character just like any other character.) Write a program which will compress or decompress each line according to whether or not it begins with an *.

Input:

HOW NOW, BROWN COW?
OW H N*, BR*N C*?
NOW IS THE TIME TO THINK
ELEVEN ELVES IN SEVENTH HEAVEN
TRA-LA-LA-LALA, LA-LA LA LA.
HI
*T NOW IS *HE*IME*O*HINK
*VE ELE*N EL*S IN SE*NTH HEA*N
$$

Output:

OW H N*, BR*N C*?
HOW NOW, BROWN COW?
* TH NOW IS *E TIME TO *INK
*VE ELE*N EL*S IN SE*NTH HEA*N
LA TRA--*-*-*, *-* * *.
HI
NOW IS THE TIME TO THINK
ELEVEN ELVES IN SEVENTH HEAVEN

The input will be read from INPUT with each line at most 60 characters in length. The message will be terminated by $$. The output will be the message compressed or decompressed line by line as indicated by the *. The output will follow each line of input.

28. Write a program to add the digits in any three digit integer. For example, if 378 is the input, then 18 (3+7+8) should be printed. The program should reject input values that are: (1) not integers, (2) less than 100, and (3) greater than or equal to 1000.

29. As part of a feasibility study for the design of a scoring computer to operate in conjunction with your employer's automatic pinsetter, you are to develop a program, which will do the scoring for up to

six players bowling on a single alley. The program must operate on data collected at the pinsetter end of the alley so the identity of the bowlers is not known, but it may be assumed that they take their turns in sequence. In each of his ten turns (called frames) a player has up to two shots at the ten pins. If his first shot knocks down all ten, his second shot is not taken, and his score for the frame is 10 points plus the total pins knocked down on his next two shots (from subsequent turns except in the case of the 10th frame when the extra two shots are taken immediately and serve only to determine the point yield of the tenth frame). If the first shot does not knock down all ten pins but the second shot does knock down the remainder, the score is ten points plus the pins knocked down on the next shot. (In the 10th frame this extra shot is taken immediately.) If the two shots of a player's turn leave some pins standing, his score on the turn is the number knocked down. The score sheet is to show the cumulative score for each of the ten frames, horizontally, by player. A line group represents each game; the first line showing the number of players (0 signals end-of-run) and successive lines give the number of pins knocked down on the shots in chronological order. For example, the input group (Player A shots underlined for clarity):

2

5 3 9 1 10 10 8 0 10 0 9 8 2 7 3 6 3 9 1 8 0 10 9 0 8 2 10 10 7

3 10 7 2 9 1 7

0

is to produce the output

FRAME	1	2	3	4	5	6	7	8	9	10	TOTAL
A	8	26	34	43	62	82	102	122	149	168	168
B	20	48	68	84	93	101	110	130	149	166	166

IF BASIC IS USED, THE INPUT CAN BE THROUGH DATA STATEMENTS.

30. Some numbers are palindromes (numbers that read the same from left to right as from right to left). For example, 1221, 373, and 9078709 are all palindromes. It has been speculated that any number can be made into a palindrome by the process of reversing the digits of the number and adding the results to the original number. If the sum is not a palindrome, the process is repeated until one is produced.

Converting 84 to a palindrome involves the steps

```
   84
+  48
  132
+ 231
  363
```

Write a program that converts integers into palindromes. You can assume the input will be two digits in length and the corresponding palindrome output at most 5 digits in length. Example: (input and corresponding output) what is the number? 84. The palindrome is 363. What is the number? 77. The palindrome is 77.

31. Find the sum and average of all numbers in a list that are divisible by 3 or by 11. Terminate the input by entering -1. If a number is both divisible by 3 and 11 count it twice. If no numbers are divisible by 3 or 11, omit the average.

Input: 15
4
66
43
123
7
19
121
54
-1

Output: Sum = 445
Average = 74.16666

32. You are to simulate playing a game of clock patience. A pre-shuffled deck of 52 cards is represented as follows: (IF BASIC IS USED THE INPUT CAN BE READ FROM DATA STATEMENTS)
EACH card is represented by face name and suit where face names are A,2,3,4,5,6,7,8,9,T,J,Q,K and the four suites are S,H,D,C (e.g. AS= ace of spades, 5H= five of hearts, TD = ten of diamonds, and JC = jack of clubs).
Deal the cards, one at a time, "face down" in a clockwise fashion so they would cover the numbers of a standard analog clock. Begin the deal at one o'clock and proceed to twelve o'clock, then place one card in the center of the clock. Continue to deal, in this fashion, from the shuffled deck until all 52 cards are distributed "face down".
After all 52 cards are dealt; begin the game by drawing the top card from the center pile. Place this card "face up" under the pile that corresponds to its face value on the clock. For example, the ace is placed under the pile at the one o'clock position and the next card is taken from this pile. A jack is placed at eleven o'clock, a queen at twelve o'clock, and a king under the center pile. Whenever you place a card "face up" on the bottom of a pile you must remove the top card of that pile and use it as your next card. The game continues in this way until the four kings are turned up and placed in the proper place in the center pile. After each game your program will ask you for input through an input statement. The input will be a number 1 through 13 which specifies the pile to print. The cards for specified pile will be printed on one line. It is not necessary to allow for multiple hands.
SAMPLE INPUT AND OUTPUT:
JS,7C,2H,9D,QD,TD,8H,6C,KD,8C,3C,3D,5S
AD,4C,AC,QH,9C,5H,8D,TC,7H,2C,3S,JC,KH
9H,5C,2S,4H,4S,6S,TS,4D,KS,7D,8S,QC,6H
AH,JH,3H,6D,5D,2D,KC,JD,TH,9S,AS,QS,7S

INPUT OF 2 WILL GIVE OUTPUT OF
2H 2S 2D 7C

INPUT OF 8 WILL GIVE OUTPUT OF
8S 8D 6C TC

33. Write a program that inputs the number of pins a bowler knocked down with each ball he threw during a game. There are 10 frames in a game. If it takes a bowler two balls to knock down 10 pins in a frame (a spare), his score for that frame is 10 plus the number of pins he knocks down on his next ball. If it takes him only one ball to knock down 10 pins in a frame (a strike), his score is 10 plus the number of pins he knocks down on his next two balls. If he gets a spare or strike in the tenth frame, he gets to roll the necessary 1 or 2 extra balls. If he doesn't knock down all 10 pins in a frame (a miss), his score is the number of pins he did knock down in that frame. After reading the data, compute the bowler's score. Write out the computed score, the numbers of the frames he made spares, and the number of frames he made strikes.

Input: 7,2,10,0,7,9,1,8,2,10,7,1,6,3,4,6,3,3
10,10,10,10,10,10,10,10,10,10,10,10
8,2,8,2,8,2,8,2,8,2,8,2,8,2,8,2,8,2,8,2,8

Output: Score = 125
Spares = 3
Strikes = 2
Score = 300
Spares = 0
Strikes = 12
Score = 180
Spares = 10
Strikes = 0

34. Write a program that reads in a one-dimensional array of up to 100 elements (use the number 9876.54 to terminate the input). First, write out the array, then search the array for its greatest and least elements. Write out the greatest and least elements along with their positions in the array as described below. If, for example, A(31)= 62047 was the largest and A(62)= -493 was the least, your output should contain these lines:
ELEMENT 31 = 62047 IS LARGEST
ELEMENT 62 = -493 IS SMALLEST

35. Write a program that inputs sets of 4 numbers each. The program is to compute the maximum of the 4 numbers and print it with an

appropriate message. Further, it is to find the maximum of all the numbers read and print it. (The program is to recognize all zeros as the last data set). None of the numbers will be negative.

Input: 12,42,3,15
64,23,122,7
1345,543,2341,8766
0,0,0,0

Output: The largest item in set 1 is 42
The largest item in set 2 is 122
The largest item in set 3 is 8766
The largest in the data was 8766

36. Write a program that prints a neat table with appropriate headings for all the prime numbers less than 500. At the end the number of prime numbers found should be printed out with a message.

Output: Primes = 2
3
5
7
11
.
.
.
499

Number of primes = XX (where XX is the actual number of primes)

37. Write a program to input a positive integer then print - 'the number is perfect' or 'the number is not perfect'. (A number is perfect if it is equal to the sum of its divisors excluding itself - Ex. 6 = 1 + 2 + 3)

Input: 64

Output: The number 64 is not perfect.

38. Write a program to tabulate the x- and y-coordinates for an equation of the form y = f(x). The information to be provided is the initial value of x, the final value of x, and the incremental step change in x. The

incremental step change in x is the value successively added to the initial value of x until the final value for x is obtained or first exceeded. The formula to be used is:

$$y = x^4 - 10x^2 + x + 2$$

The initial, final, and incremental change of x will be read from an input line.

Input: INITIAL VALUE ? -5
FINAL VALUE ? 5
INCREMENT ? 1

Output:

X	Y
-5	372
-4	94
-3	-10
-2	-24
-1	-8
0	2
1	-6
2	-20
3	-4
4	102
5	382

39. Write a program to compute miles per gallon per car, total number of cars, total miles driven, total gallons used, and the average miles/gallon for all the miles driven. The input shall be the car number, miles driven, and gallons used. Terminate the input when a zero is read for the car number.

Input: 1, 200, 5, 2, 1200, 55, 3, 150, 10, 4, 440, 20, 0

Output:

CAR NUMBER	MILES	GALLONS	MPG
1	200	5	40
2	1200	55	21.81818
3	150	10	15
4	440	20	22
4	1990	90	22.11111

40. Write a program to compute y, when

$y = ax^2 + bx + c$; if $x<a$

$y = ax + b$; if $x = a$

$y = ax^3 + bx^2 + c$; if $x > a$

Input: a=4, b=-6, c=12, x=2

Output:

a	b	c	x	y
4	-6	12	2	16

41. The power company supplies electricity to a small business. They charge 10 cents per KWH (kilowatt hour) for the first 800 KWHs and 8 cents per KWH thereafter. Write a program that allows the operator to input the KWH used for selected months. The input consists of the month number (1-12) followed by the KWH for that month. The end of the input is flagged by entering month 0. Print out a table giving the month number, the KWHs, and the cost for all the months for which data have been entered. The output must be in order by the month number.

Input: 4, 824, 5, 750, 3, 1236, 1, 1313, 0

Output:

MONTH	KWH	COST
1	1313	121.04
3	1236	114.88
4	824	81.92
5	750	75.00

42. Write a program to input identification numbers and names, and then print out in alphabetical order the names and then from low to high print the identification numbers.

Use an identification number of -1 to terminate the input of data.

Input: 123,THOMAS,432,DALE,728,PAT,069,BUD
666,KATHY,001,BRAD,985,JOSEPH,076,JAN, -1

Output: BRAD
BUD
DALE
JAN
JOSEPH
KATHY
PAT
THOMAS
1
69
76
123
432
666
728
985

43. Write a program that determines people's ages in years when given the current month and year and each person's birth month and year. The report format is as shown below:

Input: CURRENT DATE (month and year): 6,1980
NAME: JAMES
BIRTH DATE (month, year): 5,1959

Output: JAMES IS 21 YEARS OLD.

44. Write a program that reads a list of positive numbers and finds the largest and how many times it occurred. The input will be terminated with a 0.

Input: 42,19,35,41,42,19,42,13,0

Output: The largest number is 42 and it occurs 3 times.

45. Write a program to print a student's grade report and calculate a student's grade point average, which is defined to be the total quality points divided by the total credits. The input data should contain letter grades, which are to be converted to numeric grades for calculations.

Terminate the input of records when a grade of Z is read.

Grade A = 4; Grade B = 3; Grade C = 2; Grade D = 1; and Grade F = 0. The quality points for a course are the number of credits times the grade value.

Input:

CS 150,4,A
MAT 176,3,C
ENG 207,3,A
ART 100,2,B
YYY,0,Z

Output:

COURSE	CREDITS	GRADE	QUALITY POINTS
CS 150	4	A	16
MAT 176	3	C	6
ENG 207	3	A	12
ART 100	2	B	6
TOTALS	12		40
GPA = 3.333333			

46. Print the prime factorization of any positive integer greater than 1. For example, if 35 is input, the output should be 35 = 5*7; if 41 is input, the output should be 41 IS PRIME; if 90 is input, the output should be 90 = 2*3*3*5. The program must be able to handle any input up to 5 digits long in less than 5 seconds.

Input:

35
41
90

Output:

35 = 5 * 7
41 is prime.
90 = 2 * 3 * 3 * 5

47. Using the following figures:

Item	Datson Pickup	Ford Pickup
Initial Cost	$6500.00	$5775.00
Miles per gallon	30	X

Assume that the cost of gas is $1.25 a gallon during the first month of operation, $1.26 during the second, and that the cost will continue to increase by 1 cent every month. Assume that the pickup will be driven 1500 miles a month. The only input is X, the miles per gallon for the Ford. Write a program which will tell how far the pickup would have traveled, and how many months would have elapsed at the end of the month in which the total cost of buying and operating the Ford would become greater than or equal to that of the Datson. If the input is 30 or more, print an appropriate message.

Input: 20

Output: MILES = 33000
MONTHS = 22

48. Suppose you expect to retire at age 65 and expect to live to age 90. During the intervening 25 years you would like to withdraw $25,000 each year from your bank account to live on. Furthermore, as soon as you withdraw the last $25,000 from your account at age 90, you want your bank account to be zero. Assuming a fixed rate of interest, how much must you deposit (per year) from age 25 to 65 in order to do this?

Input: Interest Rate = 10.00

Output:

```
Year    Interest    Transaction    Balance
------  ----------  ----------------  -----------
```

49. The Hermite polynomials are a group of polynomials that are solutions to the quantum mechanical oscillator problem. The first three of these are:

$H_0(X) = 1$
$H_1(X) = 2*X$
$H_2(X) = 4*X*X-2$

These polynomials have the useful property that any one of them can be obtained from the two polynomials of next lower order through the relationship

$H_n(X) = 2*X*H_{n-1}(X) - 2*(n-1)*H_{n-2}(X)$

As an example, for n = 2

$H_2(X) = 2*X*H_1(X) - 2*(1) * H_0(X)$

and substitution of $H_1(X)$ and $H_2(X)$ from above shows this to be correct.

Devise a program that will calculate $H_n(X)$ for any n and X starting with $H_0(X)$ and $H_1(X)$ as known polynomials in X. You can assume n to be less than or equal to 10.

Input: 2,2
4,5

Output: $H_n(X) = 14$
$H_n(X) = 8812$

50. Legend has it that the inventor of chess was brought before the king and told to name his own reward. The inventor replied, "Sire, I ask but for one grain of wheat for the first square of my chessboard, two grains for the second square, four grains for the third, eight for the fourth, and so on for all 64 squares." The king thought this was reasonable enough. But when his science advisor told him how much grain would be needed to satisfy the inventor's request, the enraged king had the inventor beheaded. Write a program to determine how many grains of wheat the inventor requested. (The answer will not be correct to the last grain, but only to the number of significant figures your computer can handle.)

51. In legal and business matters (particularly loans), it is often necessary to determine when a prescribed time period will be up. To determine

this terminal date, it is necessary to know the BEGINNING DATE and the TIME PERIOD and to note that (a) January, March, May, July, August, October, and December all have 31 days, (b) April, June, September, and November have 30 days, and (c) February has 29 days when i) the year is an integer multiple of 4, but not of 100, or ii) the year is an integer multiple of 400. (Thus 1972 as a leap year by the criterion (i), and the year 2000 will be a leap year by criterion (ii). Otherwise assume February has 28 days.

Assume that the input data will be in the form

6,30,1972,10

which would be interpreted as meaning that the beginning date is June 30, 1972, and that the time period involved is 10 days.
Your output should be in the form
FOR A BEGINNING DATE OF JUNE 30, 1972, AND A TIME PERIOD OF 10 DAYS, THE TERMINAL DATE IS JULY 10, 1972.
A flowchart as your first step comes highly recommended. The number of days will always be less than or equal to 360.

52. Write a BASIC program that will allow a person to play a game of tic-tac-toe against the computer. Write the program in such a manner that the computer can be either the first or the second player. If the computer is to be the first player, let the first move be generated randomly. Write out the complete status of the game after each move. Have the computer acknowledge a win by either party when it occurs.

53. Write a program that will find one root of the following to within .0001 accuracy.

$$x^5 + 3*x^3 - 4*x^2 + 2*x - 9 = 0$$

54. The Legendre polynomials can be calculated by means of the formulas

P(0) = 1
P(1) = x
...
P(n)=((2*n-1)/n)*x*P(n-1)-((n-1)/n)*P(n-2)
where n = 2,3,4, ... and x is any number between -1 and +1.

Write a program that will generate a table of P vs. n for n running from 1 to 10 for any specified value of x.

Input: x=.5

Output: n=1 P=.5
n=2 P=-.125

55. Calculate the total distance traveled by a bouncing ball. Assuming a ball is dropped from a distance of H above the floor and recoils one-half the height of the previous bounce for each bounce thereafter, find the total distance the ball has travelled after N bounces. Consider a bounce to have been completed each time the ball hits the ground.

Input: H? 100
N? 3

Output: Distance = 250

56. Suppose N$ represents a multi-letter word. Examine each of the letters and print them in alphabetical order. The word will be at most 10 characters in length.

Input: COMPUTERS

Output: CEMOPRSTU

57. Write a program to read in the names and grades of students in a class, and then print this information with the students' names in alphabetical order. The end of the list is indicated by the dummy name END (with a score of 0). Names will be no more than 9 characters long. The grades should be output in a column. There will be no more than 20 students.

Input: BILL,90
JANE,88
SUZANNE,98
TOM,68
KATHY,84
JAMES,75
AMY,93
JOHN,100
KIM,86

KENT,90
JIM,79
MONICA,96
JAN,89
PAT,93
RANDY,60
JOSEPH,88
MEG,73
WILL,87
ANDREA,97
BETH,77
END,0

Output:

```
AMY       93
ANDREA    97
BETH      77
BILL      90
JAMES     75
JAN       89
JANE      88
JIM       79
JOHN     100
JOSEPH    88
KATHY     84
KENT      90
KIM       86
MEG       73
MONICA    96
PAT       93
RANDY     60
SUZANNE   98
TOM       68
WILL      87
```

58. A magic square is an array with N rows and N columns where each location contains an integer in the range 1...N. Each item in the range can only be used once.

Write a program to read in an alleged magic square and determine whether it really is magic by checking whether or not all rows, columns, and diagonals have the same sum. Your program should input the number of rows in the magic square, along with each element of the square. You can assume the square will have 6 or fewer rows.

Input: Number of rows? 4
ELEMENTS OF ROW 1 ? 1,2,3,4
ELEMENTS OF ROW 2 ? 5,6,7,8
ELEMENTS OF ROW 3 ? 9,10,11,12
ELEMENTS OF ROW 4 ? 13,14,15,16

Output: Not a Magic Square

Input: Number of rows ? 4
ELEMENTS IN ROW 1 ? 16,2,3,13
ELEMENTS IN ROW 2 ? 5,11,10,8
ELEMENTS IN ROW 3 ? 9,7,6,12
ELEMENTS IN ROW 4 ? 4,14,15,1

Output: This is a magic square!

59. Write a program to read a list of numbers and find their average. The program will then print each number accompanied by one of the words, BELOW, AVERAGE, or ABOVE, depending on whether the value in question was less than, equal to, or greater than the average. The data should terminate with a negative number.

Input: 12,54,239,344,76,935,0,144,633,89,103,-1

Output:

12 BELOW
54 BELOW
239 AVERAGE
344 ABOVE
76 BELOW
935 ABOVE
0 BELOW
144 BELOW
633 ABOVE
89 BELOW
103 BELOW

60. Given a list of students with grade point averages (GPA), write a program to read the student names and GPA (one student per line) then print two lists:

    (1) student's name and GPA in alphabetical order by name
    (2) student's name and GPA in order from high GPA to low GPA

Use a student name of JESSIE to trip or terminate your program. Maximum number of names and grades will be 30.

Input:

```
MARK,3.90
JANET,2.00
SARAH,3.88
BILLY,2.48
TONY,3.04
TAMARA,3.33
BRENT,4.00
JESSIE,0.00
```

Output:

```
BILLY    2.48
BRENT    4.00
JANET    2.00
MARK     3.90
SARAH    3.88
TAMARA   3.33
TONY     3.04
BRENT    4.00
MARK     3.90
SARAH    3.88
TAMARA   3.33
TONY     3.04
BILLY    2.48
JANET    2.00
```

61. A tall tower is on the other side of a wall. Given the height of the tower, the height of the wall, the height of the person's eyes off the ground, and the distance between the wall and the tower. Find how far the person must be from the wall to see the tower. All distances will be in feet.

Example

Input: Tower: 45
Wall: 20
Person: 6

Distance between Wall and Tower: 20

Output: Distance the person must be from the wall to see the tower is 11.2 feet

62. The table shown below may be used for computing tax due for a person whose income is from $4500 to $5000, and who has no more than 6 exemptions. Write a program, which tells the user how much tax he or she will owe. If the user enters an income or number of exemptions outside the range covered by the table, print a message directing the user to the IRS. The income/exemptions table will be an input. The person's income and number of exemptions should be read with an INPUT statement. The income will be an integer amount.

TAX TABLE

Income	Number of Exemptions / Tax Due					
	1	2	3	4	5	6
4500-4549	565	430	326	218	116	18
4550-4599	565	430	326	218	116	25
4600-4649	581	444	342	224	130	32
4650-4699	589	451	350	241	137	39
4700-4749	597	459	358	249	144	46
4750-4799	606	463	366	256	151	53
4800-4849	614	474	374	264	159	60
4850-4899	622	482	382	271	166	67
4900-4949	630	490	390	279	174	74
4950-4999	638	497	398	286	181	81

Input: Income = 4570
Number of exemptions = 4

Output: Tax Due = 218

63. Given a list of equivalent words, translate a sentence from the first set of words into the second set of words. Input will consist of 2 words per line (ending with End Input) and a sentence to translate. Words that are not in the list should be left alone. Whereas, every other word should be replaced by its equivalent. All words in the first list will be single words, but they may be replaced by double words. The list will not contain more than 50 sets of words, and one space will separate words.

Input: dog rat
are might be
cat pig
End Input
Sentence: The dog and the cat are lost.

Output: The rat and the pig might be lost.

64. Write a program, which accepts a body of text, one line at a time, and determines which words appear in the (entire) text, and the number of times each word appears. You may assume that not more than 300 unique words will appear in the text. If your program finds more, have it give an error message and quit. Otherwise your program should quit when it gets the line END OF DATA. Once your program has accepted its last line, have it print each different word it found, the number of occurrences of each word, the total number of different words, and the total number of characters in the text.

Input: TOMORROW AND TOMORROW AND TOMORROW
CREEPS IN THIS PETTY PACE FROM DAY TO DAY,
TO THE LAST SYLLABLE OF RECORDED TIME,
AND ALL OUR YESTERYEARS
HAVE LIGHTED FOOLS THE WAY TO DUSTY DEATH.
OUT, OUT BRIEF CANDLE!
LIFE IS BUT A WALKING SHADOW,
A POOR PLAYER THAT STRUTS AND FRETS
HIS HOUR UPON THE STAGE

AND THEN IS HEARD NO MORE.
TIS A TALE TOLD BY AN IDIOT
FULL OF SOUND AND FURY
SIGNIFYING NOTHING.
END OF DATA

Output:

TOMORROW	3
AND	6
CREEPS	1
IN	1
THIS	1
PETTY	1
PACE	1
FROM	1
DAY	2
TO	3
THE	3
LAST	1
SYLLABLE	1
OF	2
RECORDED	1
TIME	1
ALL	1
OUR	1
YEARS	1
HAVE	1
LIGHTED	1
FOOLS	1
WAY	1
DUSTY	1
DEATH	1
OUT	2
BRIEF	1
CANDLE	1
LIFE	1
IS	2
BUT	1

A	3
WALKING	1
SHADOW	1
POOR	1
PLAYER	1
THAT	1
STRUTS	1
FRETS	1
HIS	1
HOUR	1
UPON	1
STAGE	1
THEN	1
HEARD	1
NO	1
MORE	1
TIS	1
TALE	1
TOLD	1
BY	1
AN	1
IDIOT	1
FULL	1
SOUND	1
FURY	1
SIGNIFYING	1
NOTHING	1

Number of unique words = 58
Number of characters = 382

65. Given a set of points that make a polygon, find the perimeter. Assume the points will be given in order (i.e. as one walked around the outside, the points would be given in the order passed). Remember to connect the first and last points. Input will be ended with the point (-1,-1), and there will be between 3 and 50 points.

Example:

Input:	2,10
	8,10
	8,5
	2,5
	-1,-1
Output:	The perimeter is 22.

66. Write a program, which figures out how long it will take to mow a rectangular lawn with a rectangular house on it. Your program should ask for the dimensions of the lawn and the house, the width of your mower's cut in inches, your walking speed in MPH, and the fraction of the total time you spend resting or drinking lemonade (i.e. .25 if you rest a quarter of the total time it takes you to mow the yard).

Input:	Length of House	60 (Feet)
	Width of House	35 (Feet)
	Length of Lawn	150 (Feet)
	Width of Lawn	150 (Feet)
	Width of Mower Cut	18 (Inches)
	Walking Speed	1.5 (Miles per Hour)
	Fraction of Time Rested	.25 (1 Quarter of the Time)
Output:	Time Needed to Mow Lawn is 2.3 Hours	

67. Write a program which solves this problem when you enter the appropriate numbers:

    Generous electric's 60-Watt, 820-lumen, "long life" light bulbs cost 1.39 for 2 and last 1500 hours each on the average. General Electric's 60-watt 855-lumen "regular" light bulbs cost 2.13 for 4, and last about 1000 hours each. Assuming it costs you nothing to change a bulb when it goes out, which type of bulb gives you the most lumens*hours for the dollar? Which one gives you the most hours per dollar?
    Your program should input all pertinent information that might look something like this:

    60,820,1.39,2,1500
    60,855,2.13,4,1000

Output: Most lumens*hours per dollar = long life
Most hours per dollar = long life

68. Perform a bubble sort on the given array to arrange the numbers in descending order. Show the order of the numbers after each exchange. Count the number of comparisons and the number of exchanges required to sort the array.

    50, 85, 80, 70, 60, 82

69. Write a program to determine whether or not the three values of a set could represent the lengths of the sides of a triangle. If the three values could make a triangle, calculate its area and print a message like:

    WHEN AB=3.00 AND BC=4.00 AND CA=5.00 THE AREA OF TRIANGLE ABC IS 6.00

    If a, b, c are three side lengths, then the area is the square root of s(s-a) (s-b) (s-c), where s is half the perimeter. The formula is due to Hero, an ancient mathematician.

    If the three values in a set could not represent the sides of a triangle, print a message like:

    23.37, 9.51, AND 9.37 COULD NOT POSSIBLY BE THE SIDES OF A TRIANGLE

    Note that a property of Hero's formula states that if s(s-a) (s-b) (s-c) is negative then a, b, and c cannot make a triangle.

70. Design a program, which asks the user for a year, and then tells whether that year was or will be a leap year. Although this won't be a lengthy program, it will require a careful plan to express the necessary selection in a clear, correct manner. Here are the rules for leap years: If a year is evenly divisible by 4, then it's a leap year unless it's divisible by 100. If it's evenly divisible by 100 it's not a leap year unless it's divisible by 400, in which case it is a leap year.

    Input: 1634

    Output: Not a leap year

71. Write a program to calculate the month and the day of the year, given a number that represents the day of the year and a number that represents

the year. Example: if daynum = 35 and year = 1977, then month = 2 and day = 4.

72. The Good News Ice Cream Company sells 500,000 quarts of ice cream a year. The stores pay 85¢ a quart for each of Good News' 12 natural flavors. Raw materials cost 30¢ a quart.
Good News' research department reports that a new process has been developed that will cut the cost of raw materials by 1/3 to 20¢ a quart. However, the new process has the side effect of making ice cream a little foamy and slightly less smooth. The marketing department estimates that sales will be hurt by these changes. When pressed for figures, they say sales could drop by as little as 10% or by as much as 50% - They cannot tell.
Assume that Good News still charges 85 cents a quart, and that the conversion of the plant to handle the new process is paid for with a 10-year loan, with payments of $32,000 a year. Write a program which, given the percentage loss of sales that the user enters, show the loss or gain that would result each year for the first 10 years if a switch to the new ingredients is made.
Input: Percent drop in sales? 25

Output: Loss per year for first 10 years = $63250

73. If you get 23 people together and ask them all their birthdays, the odds are a little better than fifty-fifty that two of them will have the same birthday.

Hard to believe? Pick a person. That eliminates one birthday, and the odds that the next person you pick will have a different birthday are about 365/366 (This includes February 29 birthdays - the leap year people). That eliminates 2 birthdays. The third person will have yet another birthday with a likelihood of about 364/366. For the fourth person the odds are 363/366, and so on.
In the end, the odds that at least two people have the same birthday are the inverse of the likelihood that they all have different birthdays.
Likelihood of n people all having different birthdays = 1- (365/366) * (364/366) * ... * (367-n/366)

Write a program, which asks how many people are at the party and computes the odds that at least two people have the same birthday. Also use your program to find out how many people it takes to make the odds 90% or better.

Input: Number of people = 4

Output: Odds of at least 2 people having same Birthday = 1.6%
Number of people needed to make odds greater than 90% = xx

74. If a principal of $1 is invested at 8% compounded annually, the actual interest is $0.08, the same as the rate. However, if the rate quoted were 8% compounded semiannually, the actual interest earned at the end of the year would be $0.0816 or 8.16%. In this case the stated rate of 8% is called the nominal rate. The corresponding rate of 8.16% is called the effective rate. Devise a formula to determine the effective rate, using the symbols - R as the effective rate, J as the nominal Rate, and M as the number of conversions per year, then write a program, using your formula, to compute the effective rate in percent equivalent to a given nominal rate and a given number of conversions.

Input:

Nominal Rate in %	Number of Conversions
10.55	6
11.65	12
12.75	2
15.65	4
17.85	3

Output:

Nominal Rate in %	Number of Conversions	Effective Rate in %
10.55	6	11.0246
11.65	12	12.2923
12.75	2	13.1564
15.65	4	16.5926
17.85	3	18.9331

75. For every number x greater than 1 there corresponds a number n such that:

    $2^{(n-1)} <= x < 2^n$

    (2^n is used to denote 2 raised to the power of n)

    Write a program, which would:

    1. input a number m
    2. input a number x
    3. determine the value of n such that $2^{(n-1)}<=x<2^n$
    4. output x and n
    5. determine if m numbers {x(i),i=1,m} have been processed
    6. if m numbers have not been processed, return to step 2.

76. An annuity or installment plan is a series of payments made at equal intervals of time. Examples of annuities are pensions and premiums on life insurance. More often than not, the interest conversion period is unequal to the payment interval. Devise a formula to determines the eventual cash value annuity of R dollars paid per year in P installments for N years at an interest rate of J percent converted M times a year:

    Where S = Eventual cash value
    R = Payment per year
    P = Number of installments per year
    N = Duration of annuity in years
    J = Nominal interest rate
    M = Conversions per year

    Write a program and use your formula to determine the eventual cash value of an annuity.

Input:	Payments Per year	$2000
	Installments per year	12
	Time in years	20
	Interest rate in %	13
	Conversions per year	2

Output: Eventual Cash Value = 180330.4

77. Write a program that can count in any base B (Where B<=10). The base should be obtained from an input statement, and the program should count to the decimal equivalent 50.

Input: Base 3

Output:

```
   0
   1
   2
  10
  11
  12
  20
  21
  22
 100
   .
   .
   .
1212
```

78. Write a program to generate the first N rows of Pascal's triangle. Each entry in a given row of the triangle is generated by adding the two adjacent entries in the immediately preceding row. For example the third entry in row 4 is the sum of the second and third entries in row three. The first six rows of Pascal's triangle are as follows:

```
          1
        1   1
      1   2   1
    1   3   3   1
  1   4   6   4   1
1   5  10  10   5   1
```

To eliminate the complexity of spacing start each row in column 1. The number of rows will be input and less than 11.

Input: Number of rows to print = 4

Output:

```
1
1 1
1 2 1
1 3 3 1
```

79. Write a program to count the numbers of words and sentences that are in a paragraph.

80. Write a program to input strings of characters which represent Roman numerals, and convert them to equivalent integers. M = 1000, D = 500, C = 100, L = 50, X = 10, V = 5, I = 1; if the Roman digit has a lower integer value than the digit on its right, subtract its value from the right value. No uncommon Roman numerals will be used; that is, 98 will be represented by XCVIII, not ILIL.

Input: INPUT ROMAN NUMERAL: IX

Output: THE NUMBER IS: 9

81. In Pig Latin a word such as PASCAL is converted to ASCALPAY. For this programming exercise, the translation of English to Pig Latin calls for taking the first character of the word and moving it to the end of the word followed by an appended AY. If a word begins with a vowel, then the vowel remains in its beginning position and the string WAY is appended to the end of the word. For example, ADA becomes ADAWAY.

Write a program that displays the Pig Latin translation for a string of English words. Also display the number of words that begin with a vowel, the total number of words in the string and the percentage of words that begin with a vowel. Do not include punctuation. Assume that the string is to have a maximum of 60 characters and is to be read from input. The output should be printed with one converted word per line.

Input: THIS IS NOT DIFFICULT

Output:

```
HISTAY
ISWAY
OTNAY
IFFICULTDAY
Number of words beginning with a vowel = 1
Total number of words = 4
Percentage of words beginning with a vowel = 25.00
```

82. Write a program that reads a series of numbers in base 2 (binary) and converts them to base 10 (decimal).

83. Write a program to find the greatest common divisor between two numbers using the Euclidean algorithm. The Euclidean algorithm is a method of finding the greatest common divisor of two positive integers by repeatedly replacing the largest number with the difference (largest minus smallest) between the numbers. When both the values are equal, the common value is the greatest common divisor.
Input: 18,24

Output: The greatest common divisor of 18 and 24 is 6

84. Craps Simulation: A front line bet in a game of craps works as follows:
First roll of dice:
You win what you bet if on the first toss you roll 7 or 11 (a natural).
You lose what you bet if on the first toss you roll a 2, 3, or 12 (a Crap).
If you roll a 4, 5, 6, 8, 9, or 10 on the first toss then this number becomes your point for subsequent rolls.
Subsequent rolls of dice:
To win you must roll your point again before you roll a 7.
If you roll a 7 while trying to get your point, then you lose.
If neither your point nor 7 is rolled, then roll again.
Write a program to simulate a game of craps using a random function to simulate the roll of each die, and print the results of each roll.

Output:

Die #1	Die #2	Total	Result
2	6	8	Roll again
3	6	9	Roll again
1	1	2	Roll again
5	2	7	You Lose

Note that your output need not necessarily be the same as that shown above. However, it should closely resemble the given format.

85. Given binary vectors v and w, how close are they? The measure of closeness is the "Simple Matching Coefficient", or SMC, defined as:

$$SMC(v,w)=\{a(0,0) + a(1,1)\}/N$$

where N is the number of entries in the two vectors, a(0,0) is the number of 0-0 matches and a(1,1) is the number of 1-1 matches. For example,

v=(1 0 0 1 0 1 0 1)
w=(0 1 0 1 1 0 0 0)

for which a(0,0) = 2, a(1,1) = 1, N = 8 and SMC(v,w) = 0.375.

The input will be the length of the vectors, followed by the two vectors. Your program should compute the SMC of the two vectors, and print that value as your answer.

Input: 8
10010110
00100101

Output: .375

Note that input need not be restricted to vectors with eight entries. Hence, your program should accept vectors with 1-12 entries each.

86. A physics student conducts an experiment to measure the relationship of two variables, which we shall call X and Y. He made 10 measurements, for various values of X, and recorded the corresponding Y values. The 10 pairs of measurements (X,Y) were then plotted on a graph. The physics student discovered that the points lie approximately on a straight line. Thus, the student conjectures that X and Y are approximately related by the formula

$$Y = a + bX$$

What are the values of a and b that give the best approximation of this relationship? The solution is given by the statistical technique called "Method of Least Squares". The formulas are:

a = (SY*SX2 - SX*SXY)/(N*SX2 - SX2*SX2)
b = (N*SXY - SX*SY)/(N*SX2 - SX2*SX2)

where

N	=	Number of (X,Y) pairs
SX	=	X1 + X2 + X3 + ... + XN
SX2	=	X1*X1 + X2*X2 + X3*X3 + ... + XN*XN
SY	=	Y1 + Y2 + Y3 + ... + YN
SXY	=	X1*Y1 + X2*Y2 + X3*Y3 + ... + XN*YN

Write a program that reads a set of up to 50 (X,Y) measurements from data (terminate with X=-1 and Y=-1) and computes the numbers a and b that give the best line according to the above formulas.

Input:

X Value	Y Value
-------	-------
1.0	3.25
2.0	4.1
3.0	4.0
4.0	4.75
5.0	5.0
6.0	5.5
7.0	5.5
8.0	6.0
9.0	7.0
10.0	6.5
-1.	-1.

Output: a = 3.08
b = .38

87. Suppose that someone made the following claim: "When you flip a coin and it comes up heads twice in a row, the chances are that it will come up heads the next time."

You can test this hypothesis with a computer simulation, as follows. Input a string of 50 tosses. Count the number of times the coin comes up heads twice in a row. Each time it does, count the number of times the following toss is heads, and print the percentage of times this toss is heads. Note: In the count of doubles, do not count the instance where the 49th and 50th tosses are heads since the 51st toss is not known.

INPUT 50 COIN TOSSES:
HHTHTTTHTHHTHTTHTHHHTTHTHHHTHTTTH
HTHHTTTHTHHHHHHTT

Output: the third toss will be heads approximately 46.15385% of the time.

88. Write a program that accepts 2 positive integers less than 10000, the first less than the second. Then it prints one line for each number K between those two given numbers (exclusive of the two). Each line contains 12 numbers. The first number in a line is the K for that line. Each number after the first is the "Ziel" of the one before. The "Ziel" of a number from 0000 to 9999 is obtained by reversing the four digits of the given number (after filling in leading zeros for numbers below 1000) and subtracting the smaller from the larger.

Input: 124,127

Output: 7641 6174 1452 1089 8712 6534 2178 6534 2178
6534 2178 6534 4723 1449 7992 4995 990 8991
6993 2997 4995 990 8991 6993

89. Write a program to input a phrase and tell how many 1- character words there were, how many 2-character words, and so on. Define a word to consist of no spacing characters bounded by spacing. Define spacing to be blanks, the end of a line, and the beginning of a line. If the longest word in your phrase is 8 letters long then you should terminate your output with "Number of 8 letter words=N." If the longest word in your phrase is 10 letters long your output should terminate with "Number of 10 letter words=N", etc. You can assume that commas will not be found in the text.

Input: To be or not to be that is the question.

Output: number of 1 letter words = 0
number of 2 letter words = 6
number of 3 letter words = 2
number of 4 letter words = 1

number of 5 letter words = 0
number of 6 letter words = 0
number of 7 letter words = 0
number of 8 letter words = 0
number of 9 letter words = 1

90. Write a liar program as follows: Tell the user you have picked an integer from 1 to 10 inclusive, and the user is to guess it in as few guesses as possible. Give the user nine guesses and say they are all wrong. Then print a reply telling the correct answer (any number that was not guessed).

Input/Output:

```
Your Guess = 3
     Wrong! Try Again.
Your Guess = 6
     Wrong! Try Again.
Your Guess = 5
     Wrong! Try Again.
Your Guess = 4
     Wrong! Try Again.
Your Guess = 10
     Wrong! Try Again.
Your Guess = 9
     Wrong! Try Again.
Your Guess = 1
     Wrong! Try Again.
Your Guess = 2
     Wrong! Try Again.
Your Guess = 8
     Wrong! Try Again.
Sorry. The number I picked was 7
```

91. Calculate all the possible ways that a given number of dollar bills can be converted into nickels, dimes, quarters, and half-dollars. For example, one way to divide one dollar uses three quarters, one dime and three nickels. Another way uses a half-dollar, a quarter, two dimes, and a nickel. The output of your program should be a chart in the

following (or similar) format. The order in which the possibilities are listed is arbitrary, but each line should be numbered.

Input: 1

Output:

	Half-Dollars	Quarters	Dimes	Nickles
1.	2	0	0	0
2.	1	0	5	0

(etc.)

92. Write a game in which the computer tries to guess the number 1-100 inclusive that you are thinking of. Have the computer guess it within seven turns. Help the computer by telling it whether its guesses are too high or two low. (Don't cheat if you want your program to work)

Input: Input number to guess: 45

Output:

I Guess 50 Lower
I Guess 25 Higher
I Guess 37 Higher
I Guess 43 Higher
I Guess 47 Lower
I Guess 45 Correct

93. Write a program to do fractional arithmetic. Have the user enter a fraction, an operation (/ or *), and another fraction. Report the result as a proper fraction reduced to its lowest terms. The operation to be performed should be read from an input statement. Also note that spaces may be placed anywhere within the input. For example, 1/15 / 1/3 could be input as 1/15 / 1/3

Input: 7/21 / 5/3
Output: 1/5

Input: 4/3 * 4/2
Output: 2 & 2/3

Input: 8/4 * 9/3
Output: 6

94. Construct a program to perform simple arithmetic with Roman numerals. The program should be able to handle addition, subtraction, multiplication, and integer division of two Roman numerals; the answer should be printed as a Roman numeral. Assume that the input will consist of Roman numeral, an operator, and another Roman numeral - in that order - all on the same line with no spaces separating them. Do not process a subtraction that would result in a negative number. However, do print an appropriate response if this is the case. Recall that in Roman numerals M=1000, D=500, C=100, L=50, X=10, V=5, and I=1. Generally speaking, the higher valued numerals are listed first as in MMDCCCLXXVI, the Roman numeral representation of 2876. However, there are some exceptions. The numbers 4,9,40,90,400 and 900 are represented by IV,IX,XL,XC,CD and CM, respectively. Four of the same numeral (except M) is not used consecutively. Example: the number IV is one less than five (4) and the number CD is one hundred less than five hundred (400). Assume that each number in the input as well as the number to be output will have a decimal equivalent less than or equal to 5000.

Input: XII/IV
Output: III

Input: CXX - CC
Output: Result is less than zero.

95. There is a property of integers which states that the product P of 4 consecutive integers will always be one less than a perfect square. Write a program, which will input a number N, compute the product of this number and the next 3 consecutive integers, and print this product and the corresponding perfect square.

Input: 10

Output: Product = 17160
Perfect Square = 131

96. Four dice are rolled. Accept the four numbers, which appear on the top faces of the dice and decide whether 0, 2, 3, or 4 of the dice show the same value, or whether two dice show one value and two dice show another value.

Input: Numbers rolled = 2,1,3,2
Output: Two show the value 2

Input: Numbers rolled = 4,5,5,4
Output: Two show the value 4
Two show the value 5

Input: Numbers rolled = 2,3,6,5
Output: No two show the same value

97. Determine if a given point (X1,Y1) lies within, on, or outside a circle with center (X2,Y2) and radius R. Your program should accept all needed information from input statements.

Input: X coordinate for center of circle = 10
Y coordinate for center of circle = 10
Radius of circle = 5
X coordinate of point = 14
Y coordinate of point = 12

Output: This point is inside the circle.

98. The number 153 has an interesting property. It equals the sum of the cubes of its digits, that is, $153 = 1^3 + 5^3 + 3^3$. There are no two digit or four digit whole numbers with this property and only four three-digit numbers (including 153). Write a program to find these four whole numbers. A check on the program is that the first integer found should be 153. Do not list the digits separately in the output--that is, the output should be 153, not 1 5 3.

Your output shall be the four numbers, printed one per line, followed by the sum of the four numbers.

99. There are times when an ILLEGAL cancellation produces correct results. For example, 16/64 (cancel the sixes) = 1/4. Cases like this have been humorously called "mathematical mistakes". Assuming that the numerator is less than the denominator, write a program to find all 4 "mistakes" with two-digit numerators and denominators where

this illegal cancellation (cancelling diagonally) gives a correct result. Your program must find and output mistakes; it's not sufficient to just output mistakes.

Output: 16 / 64 = 1 / 4

100. Write a program to input a number X, then print the rational numbers greater than or equal to X but less than 1. Note that these rational numbers are of the form A/B where A and B are integers from 1 to 10 inclusive. Print the rationals from largest to smallest - 4 per line, making sure that they are reduced to their lowest terms and that no duplication occurs in the output.

Input: X = .73

Output:
```
9/10 8/9 7/8 6/7
5/6 4/5 7/9 3/4
```

101. A "palindrome prime" is a prime number that is also a prime when its digits are reversed 11, 13, and 17 are such primes. Write a program to find all the 2-digit palindrome primes.

Output:
```
11
13
17
.
.
.
97
```

102. Three sailors, shipwrecked with a monkey on a desert island, have gathered a pile of coconuts that are to be divided early the next morning. During the night one sailor arises, divides the pile into three equal parts, and finds one coconut left over, which he gives to the monkey. He then hides his share. Later during the night, each of the other two sailors arises separately and repeats the performance of the first sailor. In the morning all three sailors arise, divide the pile into three equal shares, and find one left over, which they give to the monkey. Write a program to compute and output the smallest integer that could represent the number of coconuts in the original pile.

103. Roots of numbers can be computed by making an initial guess, then obtaining a better estimate by using the guess. This process is continued until sufficient accuracy is obtained. In the case of square roots, the procedure can be represented as:
E(0) = X/2
E(n) = ½(E(n-1)+X/E(n-1))

Where X = number whose square root is needed
E(0) = initial estimate for square root of X
E(n-1) = estimate after n-1 attempts
E(n) = estimate after n attempts

Use this method to compute the square root of any positive number. Print the iteration number and the approximation. Continue this process until the absolute value of difference between E(n) and E(n-1) is less than .0001.

Input: Number = 12

Output:

Iteration #	Approximation
1	4.0000
2	3.5000
3	3.46428571
4	3.46410162
5	3.46410162

104. In 1900 the world's population was approximately 1.65 billion people. The number of births per year had equaled approximately 2.6 percent of the population at the beginning of a particular year. The death rate in 1900 was approximately 1.4 percent of the population at the beginning of the year. The death rate has been increasing at an annual rate of .01 percent (1.4% in 1900, 1.41% in 1901, 1.42% in 1902, etc.) because the food supply has not been increasing fast enough, natural resources are being depleted, and pollution is increasing. Assume that the death rate never decreases and that every increase of 100,000,000 people causes the death rate to jump by .01% due to crowding. Assuming these trends continue, print a table showing the population figures from 1900 to 2100 (in increments of 20 years).

Output:	Year	Population (Billions)
	1900	1.65
	1920	2.049693
	1940	2.428718
	.	.
	.	.

105. Write a program that could be used to write a check for a small business. Your program should input the date (in MM/DD/YYYY format), the amount of the check (in XXXX.XX format), and the payee of the check. Your program output should be in the following form. (Although your output need not be exactly as follows, it should be a very close imitation).

```
                                                        #328
Heavenly Bank
4120 Ashby Avenue
Emeryville, CA 94601                March 8, 1977
                          Amount $ 4975.89

Pay to the order of: OSBORNE & ASSOCIATES

Four Thousand Nine Hundred Seventy-Five Dollars and 89 Cents

Miracle Corporation
1111 Country Road
Countryville, CA 94132                ______________________
```

Input: Date: 03/08/1977
Amount: 4975.89
Payee: Osborne & Associates

106. A common multiple of three numbers, A, B, and C is an integer exactly divisible by all of them. The least common multiple (LCM) is the smallest such multiple. For example, the LCM of 2, 3, and 6 is 6. Write a program to find the LCM of three integers.

Input: 4,5,15

Output: LCM = 60

107. When a customer of Jim's Drug Store makes a purchase, he or she gets a card with three different numbers on it ranging between 1 and 1000. Jim then draws a number from a bowl containing numbers between 1 and 1000. If any of the customer's numbers matches the one drawn, the customer gets $50. Write a program to issue 50 customer cards, each with three random numbers, and to make 10 draws from the bowl. Determine the dollar amount lost by Jim so he can estimate how much this scheme will cost him.

Output:	Card	Number drawn	Amount Lost
	234,769,001	736	0.00
	100,047,878	554	0.00
	238,654,900	654	50.00
	.	.	.
	.	.	.
	666,724,390	409	0.00

Total Amount Lost = XXX.XX

108. Write a program that will input a sequence of positive integers and output a list of distinct input integers, and for each of these, the number of times each integer occurs among the input integers. For example, if the input values are 4, 3, 6, 4, 6, 5, 6, 4, 3, and 9, then the report should show that the number 3 occurred twice, the number 4 occurred three times, the number 5 occurred once, the 6 occurred three times, and the number 9 occurred once. The input will be terminated with a -1.

109. Write a program to calculate the date following a given date. You will have to take into account leap years.

Input: 01/19/2012

Output: 01/20/2012

110. Write a program that plays the game of HANGMAN. Input the word to be guessed and the number of incorrect guesses that should be allowed before printing an appropriate losing message. The program should then ask for a letter, print the phrase with the appropriate letters revealed or, if no occurrences of the letter were found, print a message informing the player that the letter was not found. Terminate the program when the phrase is solved or when the maximum number of incorrect guesses is exceeded. Be sure to print an appropriate termination message. All input should be in caps.

Input: MARY HAD A LITTLE LAMB,6

Input/Output:
ENTER A LETTER? A
PHRASE SO FAR: _A__ _A_A______ _A__
ENTER A LETTER? E
PHRASE SO FAR: _A__ _A_A_____E_A__
ENTER A LETTER? I
PHRASE SO FAR: _A__ _A_A_I___E_A__
ENTER A LETTER O
PHRASE SO FAR: _A__ _A_A_I___E_A__
NO OCCURENCES OF O WERE FOUND.
YOU HAVE 5 INCORRECT GUESSES LEFT.
ENTER A LETTER? U
PHRASE SO FAR: _A__ _A_A_I___E_A__
NO OCCURENCES OF U WERE FOUND.
YOU HAVE 4 INCORRECT GUESSES LEFT.
ETC.

111. Two positive integers are said to be relatively prime if there exists no integer greater than 1 that divides into both evenly. Write a program to accept as input two positive integers, and tells whether each one is prime, and whether they are relatively prime.

Input: Enter two positive integers: 121,7

Output: 121 is not prime
7 is prime
121 and 7 are relatively prime

112. The expression for computing C(n,r), the number of combinations of n items taken r at a time, is:

$$C(n,r) = n! / (r!(n-r)!)$$

X! is defined to be (1 * 2 * 3 * ...* X) for X>0, and 1 for X=0. Write a program that will input n and r and output C(n,r). Assume that 0<n<=20 and 0<r<n.

Input: ENTER n? 15
ENTER r? 7

Output: C(n,r) = 6435

113. A throw of a die can produce any number from a two (Snake-eyes) to a twelve (Box-cars). Write a program to determine all possible outcomes (1st digit 1-6, 2nd digit 1-6) for two dice and to produce the table below. Your program must calculate and output the table below. Also output the sum of each column.

Roll Value	Number of ways of getting this roll	Probability of getting this roll	Probability of a roll greater than or equal to this one
2	1	.028	1.000
3	2	.056	.972
.	.	.	.
.	.	.	.
.	.	.	.
11	2	.056	.083
12	1	.028	.028
XX	XX	X.XXX	X.XXX

114. Write an arithmetic expression translator that compiles fully-parenthesized arithmetic expressions involving the operators *,/,+, and -. For example, given the input string:

"((A+(B*C))-(D/E))"

the compiler would print out:
Z=(B*C)
Y=(A+Z)
X=(D/E)
W=(Y-X)

Assume only the letters A through F can be used as variable names. Hint: Find the first right parenthesis; remove it and the four characters preceding it and replace with the next unused letter at the end of the alphabet. Print out the assignment statement used. For example, the following is a summary of the sequence of steps required to process the expression. The asterisk points to the first right parenthesis at each step.

Expression Status	Print
((A+(B*C)-(D/E))	Z=(B*C)
*	
((A+Z)-(D/E)	Y=(A+Z)
*	
((Y-(D/E))	X=(D/E)
*	
(Y-X)	W=(Y-X)
*	

115. For n ships you are given the location of the ship designated by its x and y coordinates, the speed t, and a code indicating whether or not a doctor is aboard. One of the ships xs, ys with speed ts, is in need of a doctor. Write a program to find the ship with a doctor aboard which is closest in time. Produce as output the coordinates of its present location. Assuming that both ships sail directly toward each other, produce as output the coordinates of the point at which they will meet.

116. Write a program that reads in a tic-tac-toe board and determines the best move for player X. Use the following strategy. Consider all squares that are empty and evaluate potential moves into them. If the move fills the third square in a row, column, or diagonal that already has two

X's, add 50 to the score; if it fills the third square in a row, column, or diagonal with two O's, add 25 to the score; for each row, column, or diagonal containing this move that will have 2 X's and one blank, add 10 to the score; add 8 for each row, column, or diagonal through this move that will have one O, one X, and one blank; add 4 for each row, column, or diagonal that will have one X and the rest blanks. Select the move that scores the highest. If two or more squares tie for the best move, have the computer randomly move into one of those squares. The possible moves for the board below are numbered. Their scores are shown to the right of the board (Move 5 is selected). Assume that the initial input is read from input, row by row, with all empty squares being represented by 1's. Your output will be your move. You do not have to display the board.

```
 1 | O | X          1: 10+8=18
___|___|___         2: 10+8=18
 2 | X | 3          3: 10+10=20
___|___|___         4: 8
 O | 4 | 5          5: 10+10+8=28
   |   |
```

Input: 1,O,X,1,X,1,O,1,1

Output: My move is move number 5

117. Each card of a poker deck can be represented by a pair of integers: the first integer representing the suit (1-4) and the second integer representing the value of the card. For example, 4, 10 would be the 10 of spades, 3, 11 the jack of hearts, 2, 12 the queen of diamonds, 1, 13 the king of clubs, 4, 14 the ace of spades. Read in five integer pairs representing a poker hand and evaluate the poker hand. Your program should be able to evaluate whether the hand is a flush (all one suit), a straight (five consecutive cards not all of the same suit), a straight flush (five consecutive cards of the same suit), 4 of a kind, a full house (three of one kind, 2 of another), 3 of a kind, 2 pair, 1 pair, or Ace high, King high, etc.

Input: Enter cards: 3,6
1,9
2,10
2,7
2,8

Output: Straight

118. The game of Life, invented by John H. Conway, is supposed to model the genetic laws of birth, survival, and death. We will play it on a board consisting of 10 squares in the horizontal and vertical directions (for a total of 100 squares). Each square can be empty or can contain an X indicating the presence of an organism. Each square (except the border squares) has eight neighbors. The small square of asterisks on the board below, represents the neighbors of the organism in row 3, column 3.

```
   1 | 2 | 3 | 4 | 5
1 ___|___|___|___| ___

     |   |   |   |
2 ___|_*_|_*_|_*_| ___

     |   |   |   |
3 ___|_*_|_X_|_*_| ___

     |   |   |   |
4    | * | * | * |
```

The next generation of organisms is determined according to the following criteria:

1. BIRTH: An organism will be born in each empty location that has exactly three neighbors.
2. DEATH: An organism with four or more organisms as neighbors will die from overcrowding. An organism with fewer than two neighbors will die from loneliness.
3. URVIVAL: An organism with two or three neighbors will survive to the next generation.

Write a program to read in an initial configuration of organisms. Print the original game array, calculate the next generation of organisms in a new array, copy the new array into the original game array and repeat the game for as many generations as you wish. {Hint: Assume that the borders of the game array are infertile regions where organisms can neither survive nor be born; you will not have to process the border squares.} Also note that the underscore should be printed for an empty cell and an X should be printed for a cell containing an organism.

Input:

0, 0, 0, 0, 0, 0, 0, 0, 0, 0
0, 0, 0, X, 0, X, 0, 0, 0, 0
0, 0, 0, 0, X, 0, 0, 0, 0, 0
0, 0, 0, 0, X, 0, 0, 0, 0, 0
0, 0, 0, X, 0, X, 0, 0, 0, 0
0, 0, 0, 0, 0, 0, 0, 0, 0, 0
0, 0, 0, 0, 0, 0, 0, 0, 0, 0
0, 0, 0, 0, 0, 0, 0, 0, 0, 0
0, 0, 0, 0, 0, 0, 0, 0, 0, 0
0, 0, 0, 0, 0, 0, 0, 0, 0, 0

How Many Generations? 3

Output: Generation 1

____
___X_X____
____X_____
____X_____
___X_X____
____
____
____
____
____

Generation 2

____
____X_____
___XXX____
___XXX____

____X_____

____

____

____

____

____

Generation 3

____

___XXX___

____

____

___XXX___

____

____

____

____

____

119. Given a list of integers, find the longest consecutive run of increasing values in the list.
Print the run. The list is given as input. The end of the list is marked with a 0, which is not part of the list.
Input: 54,17,45,84,63,70,13,39,0

Output: 17
45
84

If there are two or more runs with the longest length, print out all of them.

120. You are given 9 lines of character data, all of the same length. Such as:
Input: XXXBBBBCCFFFFDQQH
WDDDTRAGGCCCCCDFE
KKLBBBBBBCCCCCEET
WWBBBBBBBCCCCCVBB
UUUBBBBBBCCCCCLLB
UUUBBBBBBUOOKKKKB

IILLLLLMMMVVBBBEE
ZZLLLLLGGGEEEEMEG
ZWLLLLLITTYYYKKLS

Find the letter, which makes up the biggest BLOCK of characters. A BLOCK is defined as a RECTANGULAR group composed of one character. The size of a BLOCK is the number of characters in it. To be a BLOCK, the group must be at least 2 characters wide and 2 characters long. A BLOCK must not touch other occurrences of the same character.
For the above example, there is a block of C's of size 20, a block of L's of size 15, and a block of U's of size 6. The B's do not form a block because the shape is not rectangular (and we do not allow part of such a group to be called a block).

Output: Block C is the biggest with 20 elements
Note: If there is a tie for the biggest block, print an appropriate reply.

121. In working with two-dimensional patterns, we might be interested in the feature called an EDGE. An EDGE is anyplace where an area with one quality meets an area with a different quality.
For example, suppose strings of patterns are read from INPUT, such as:

AAAAAABBB
AAAAABBBB
AAABBBBBB
ABBBBBBBB
BBBBCCCBB
BBCCCCBBB
BBCCCBBBB

The edges could be represented by this printed diagram:

------X--
-----X---
---XX----
-XX------
X---XXXX-

--XX--X--
--X--X---

Other sample input/output pairs are:

HHHHHLLLL	------------X---	PPPPPPPPP	---------
HHHHHHHLL	-------------XXX-	PPPPCPPPP	----XX---
HHHHHHHHH	----------------XX	PPPCCCPPP	---X-XX--
OOOOOOOOO	XXXXXXXXX	PPPCCCPPP	---X--X--
OOOOOOOOO	---------------------	PPPCCCPPP	---X--X--
OOOOOHHHH	------------XXXX	PPPPPPPPP	---XXX---
OOOOOHHHH	---------------X---	PPPPPPPPP	------------

Write a program to READ such input, and produce the edge diagram composed of -'s and X's. There will always be 7 lines of input, and each line will be 9 characters long.
(Note that our diagrams arbitrarily place the X's just below and to the right of the actual edges, which would occur between lines.)

122. Write a program that will determine the cost of a book based on the following information: The base cost of the book is $0.75 plus $0.02 per page if the book is a paperback. If the number of pages is greater than 400, a cloth binding will be used, increasing the base price by $1.50. Also, if the number of pages is greater than 700, stronger binding is used, raising the cost by another $1.00. The maximum that can be bound is 1000 pages, which means that books over 1000 pages will be published in volumes of equal length, each subject to the above restrictions. Finally, if the number of pages is greater than 1500, the charge is reduced to $0.0175 per page. The number of pages should be the only input required.
Input: Number of pages = 1800

Output: Cost = $38.00

123. El Junko - Rent-A-Car would like you to write a program to handle its billing procedures.
For each bill you should include the following:
    a. The total number of hours the car was kept

b. The daily rate (24 hours) for the particular car
c. The miles driven
d. The mileage charge in cents per mile for that car
e. A value of 1 if the customer took out insurance at $3.00 per day, 0 if not

The bill is computed by using the above information plus the following:

1. The minimum charge is one day's rate.
2. The hourly rate is 1/8 the daily rate, but an hourly charge should not exceed the daily rate. Thus a 30-hour period would be charged for 1 day plus 6 hours.
3. If the car is held for 5 days or more, a 10% discount is applied to the daily rental rate and the hourly charge.
4. A 4% sales tax should be added to the total bill.

Input: Hours car was kept = 145
Daily Rate = 19.98
Miles Driven 300
Mileage charge (cents per mile) = 25
Insurance = 0

Output: $192.55

124. Write a program to compute the monthly service charge on a bank checking account. The charge is 10 cents each for the first 10 checks, 5 cents each for the next 10 checks, and 3 cents each for each check after the 20th check. A one-time surcharge of $1 is added if the minimum balance falls below $200. If the minimum balance is $1000 or greater, all checks are charged at the rate of 2 cents each. There is no charge for deposits. The inputs consist of the initial balance followed by one line for each deposit or withdrawal by check. Deposits are preceded with a D and withdrawals with a W. The end of the input is indicated by a Q,0 entry.

Input: 1200.00
W,10.00
W,15.23

D,50.00
W,84.63
Q,0

Output: Service charge = $ .06

125. Write a program to input a line of English text and print a list of all the words that occur in the line. The words appear on the list in the same order that they appear in the line, and each word appears on the list the same number of times it appears in the line. The text may be punctuated with periods, commas, question marks, colons, and semicolons; the punctuation marks do not appear on the list.

126. In a complete Gregorian cycle of 400 years there are 400 x 12 = 4800 thirteenths of the month. Since 7 does not divide 4800 evenly, it follows that the thirteenth of the month is more likely to fall on some days of the week than others.

 Write a program to compute the relative frequencies with which the thirteenth of the month falls on each weekday. (Note: Triskaidekaphobics will not be comforted by your results.)

127. A credit card company bases its evaluation of card applicants on four factors: the applicant's age, how long the applicant has lived at his or her current address, the annual income of the applicant, and how long the applicant has been working at the same job. For each factor points are added to a total as follows:

Factor	**Value**	**Points Added**
Age	20 and under	-10
	21-30	0
	31-50	20
	Over 50	25
At Current Address	Less than 1 year	-5
	1-3 years	5
	4-8 years	12
	9 or more years	20

Annual income	$15,000 or less	0
	$15,001-$25,000	12
	$25,001-$40,000	24
	over $40,000	30
At same job	Less than 2 years	-4
	2-4 years	8
	more than 4 years	15

On the basis of the point total the following action is taken.

Points	Action
-19 to 20	No Card Issued
21 to 35	Card Issued With $500 Limit
36 to 60	Card Issued With $2000 Limit
61 to 90	Card Issued With $5000 Limit

Write a program that accepts an applicant's number, age, and years at current address, annual income, and years at the same job. Then the program should evaluate the applicant's credit worthiness and display the applicant's number plus a phrase describing the action taken by the company. The following sample information should be read from data.

Terminate the input when an applicant number of 0 is encountered

Input:

Applicant number	Age	Current address	Annual income	Same job
1234	55	10	$42000	15
2345	18	0	$10000	1
3456	35	2	$32000	4
4567	22	5	$21000	1
5678	50	1	$25000	2
6789	31	4	$40000	5
0000				

Output:

Applicant Number	Action
1234	Card issued with $5000 limit
2345	No card issued
3456	Card issued with $2000 limit
4567	No card issued
5678	Card issued with $2000 limit
6789	Card issued with $5000 limit

128. A theater sells tickets for $5.00 and averages 100 tickets sold for each performance. At this rate the theater's cost per patron is $2.00. The theater manager estimates that for each $.25 reduction in ticket price the number of tickets sold will increase by 30 and the theater's cost per patron will increase by $.10.

     Write a program to calculate and display a table listing the ticket price, the number of tickets sold, the gross revenue (ticket price multiplied by the number of tickets sold), the theater's total cost (cost per patron times number of tickets sold), and the net profit (revenue minus total cost) for each ticket price ranging from $5.00 to $3.00. As the ticket price decreases from $5.00 to $3.00, the profit will steadily increase to a maximum and then start to decrease. Use this fact to display the phrase
     'MAXIMUM' point in the table that corresponds to the greatest profit.

     Output:

Ticket Price	Number of Tickets sold	Gross Revenue	Theater's Total cost	Net Profit	
5.00	100	500.00	200.00	300.00	
4.75	130	617.50	273.00	344.50	
.	.	.	.	.	
.	.	.	.	.	MAXIMUM
.	.	.	.	.	
3.00	340	1020.00	952.00	68.00	

129. Assume that rabbits reproduce at the rate of 20% per month until overpopulation occurs, at which time they begin dying at the

rate of 15% per month. Rabbits continue to die at this rate until their population is reduced by one third, at which time they begin reproducing again. Write a program to simulate the rabbit population for N months. Accept from input the number of rabbits present in month 1, the overpopulation threshold, and the number of months to run the simulation. Your output should consist of the number of the month followed by the population. Round the population to the nearest rabbit at the end of each month.

Input: Number of months = 12
initial number of rabbits = 1000
overpopulation threshold = 2000

Output: Month 1 = 1000
Month 2 = 1200
Month 3 = 1440
Month 4 = 1728
Month 5 = 2074
Month 6 = 1763
Month 7 = 1499
Month 8 = 1274
Month 9 = 1529
Month 10 = 1835
Month 11 = 2202
Month 12 = 1872

130. Write a program to determine the frequency of each vowel in some English language text. The input will consist of sentences running over a number of lines. The end of the text is indicated by the special symbol '*'. The output of the program should be the input text and the count for each of the characters a, e, i, o, and u.

Input: this is fun*

Output: this is fun
Number of a's: 0
Number of........

131. Write a program to solve quadratic equations of the form:
$ax^2 + bx + c = 0$ using the quadratic formula:
$x_{1,2} = (-b +- \text{sqrt}(b^2 - 4ac))/(2a)$
Be sure to check for:
a) Complex roots ($b^2 - 4ac < 0$)
b) Double roots ($b^2 - 4ac = 0$)
c) Non-quadratic equations ($a = 0$).
The input will be the three corresponding coefficients.

132. Given k distinct characters, write a program to print all possible strings of length k that contain each character exactly once.
Input: input K: 3
Input 3 distinct characters: ABC

Output: ABC
ACB
BAC
BCA
CAB
CBA

133. Write a program to find all integer solutions to the equation
$Ax + By - Cz = D$
for values of x, y, and z in the range 0 to 50. Input A,B,C,D as single digit integers.
Input: A,B,C,D: 3,2,7,5

Output: --- --- ---

134. Given an array of numbers, find the average of the numbers, and then find the number in the array that is closest to the average. You can assume this closet number is unique. Use 9999 to indicate the end of the list; the 9999 will not be considered a member of the array.
Input: 35
44
42
29
9999

Output: The average is 37.5
The number closest is 42

135. In many mathematical problems it is necessary to determine whether a given sequence of numbers is monotonic increasing, monotonic decreasing, or neither. The sequence is monotonic increasing if given a sequence x(1), x(2), ... x(n)), x(i) < x(i+1) for all i, 1 to n-1. Similarly, the sequence is monotonic decreasing if x(i) > x(i+1) for all i, 1 to n – 1. Write a program that, for a given sequence of input integers, finds and prints the longest monotonic increasing sequence and the longest monotonic decreasing sequence and prints them both. Assume that the input sequence will not contain more than 200 integers. Numbers will be entered one per line and the input will be terminated by a - 1 or 20 numbers, whichever comes first. Print a proper message if either is not found.

Input: 45,34,78,100,115,14,12,56,34,99,76,54,23,-1

Output: Longest increasing sequence: 34 78 100 115
Longest decreasing sequence: 99 76 54 23

Input: 1,2,3,4,5,6,-1

Output: Longest increasing sequence: 1 2 3 4 5 6
There is no decreasing sequence.

136. The XYZ Company makes widgets, and it employs salespeople to sell these widgets. The salespeople are paid by the hour, but they also qualify for a bonus equal to 10% of that part of their total sales which exceeds 70% of the average sales of all salespeople. For example, if all salespeople sell an average of $2000 worth of widgets each and salesclerk A sells $1800 worth of widgets, then salesclerk A gets a bonus of $40.

Write a program to compute the bonuses for those salespeople who qualify. Input: The salesclerks' ID numbers (as integers) and the amount (in dollars) that each has sold.

137. An inner product (or dot product) is the sum of the products of the corresponding elements of 2 one-dimensional arrays. For instance, the inner product of 2

A(1) * B(1) + A(2) * B(2)

Write a program that computes the inner product of 2 arrays of any size up to 10.

Input: input size of arrays?4
input A 1? 3
input A 2? 7
input A 3? 4
input A 4? 2
input B 1? 2
input B 1? 2
input B 2? 3
input B 3? 1

Output: Inner product of A and B is: 34

138. Hidden in a normal line of text will be some integers. Write a program that filters the text, finds the numbers, prints them out, and also prints their sum.

EXAMPLE:

Input: This 1s a234 te5t.

Output: Numbers: 1, 234, 5
Total: 240

139. Write a program to output the factorials for the integers 1 through N, N<=10. N factorial is represented as N! and is calculated as N*(N-1)*(N-2)*...*1.
For example, 6 factorial = 6! = 6*5*4*3*2*1
and 4 factorial = 4! = 4*3*2*1.

Also output the sum of all factorials found.

140. Write a program to input a set of numbers, then find and output the mean, median and mode of the set of numbers. Trip the input with the number 0.0.

141. A palindrome is a word, phrase, or sentence that reads the same from left to right. Two simple examples are the words: PEEP and RADAR. Blanks are ignored in considering palindromes.

Write a program that will input a string of characters, then find all palindromes in the string. The string will be a maximum of 40 characters in length - all upper case with no punctuation.

Input: MADAM IM ADAM ARE YOU RADAR.

Output: MADAM IM ADAM
RADAR

142. An n by n matrix is symmetric if, for each r (1<= r <= n) and each s (1<= s <= n), the element a (r, s) is the same as the element a (s, r). Write a program to input an n by n matrix, and determine whether or not it is symmetric.

143. Given a pair of numbers which represent the numerator and denominator of a fraction, write a program to reduce each fraction to its lowest terms.

Input: 100
28

Output: 3 4/7

Input: 200
25

Output: 8

144. Write a program that asks for the coefficients of two linear equations in x and y, and then determines and displays whether the straight lines defined by these equations are parallel, intersecting, or coincident.

Input: 1, 2, and 3
2, 5, and 7

Output: Lines intersect

Input: 2, 5, and 1
4, 10, and 2
Output: Lines are coincidental

145. A perfect number is one for which the sum of the divisors is equal to number, for example, 6 = 1 + 2 + 3. Write a program to find and output all perfect numbers between 1 and 10,000.

146. Write a program to output an n x m array of asterisks; the variable n and m are positive integers to be read.

147. Write a program to output a multiplication table. The input will determine the size of the table. If the input was 12 then the output will be:

```
MULTIPLICATION TABLE
 1  2  3  4  ...  12
 2  4  6  8  ...  24
 3  6  9 12  ...  36
 .  .  .  .        .
 .  .  .  .        .
 .  .  .  .        .
12 24 36 48  ...  144
```

148. Write a program to score the "paper-rock-scissors" game. Each of two users types in 'P', 'R', or 'S', and the program announces the winner as well as the basis for determining the winner: "paper covers rock", "rock breaks scissors", "scissors cut paper", or "nobody wins". In/out can be in either upper or lower case and be sure to check for valid input.

Input: r
s
Output: Player one wins.
Rock breaks scissors.

Input: p
p
Output: Nobody wins.

149. Write a program that will determine the additional state tax owed by an employee. The state charges a 4% tax on net income. Net income is determined by subtracting a $500 allowance for each dependent from gross income. Your program will read gross income, number of dependents, and tax amount already deducted. It will then compute the actual tax owed and output the difference between tax owed and tax deducted followed by the message "SEND CHECK", "TAX PAID IN FULL", or "REFUND" as appropriate. The difference is always rounded to the nearest dollar to determine the additional tax owed.

Input #1: GROSS INCOME? 5000
OF DEPENDENTS? 2
TAX ALREADY DEDUCTED? 450

Output #1: 290 REFUND

Input #2: GROSS INCOME? 20020
OF DEPENDENTS? 4
TAX ALREADY DEDUCTED? 500

Output #2: 221 SEND CHECK

Input #3: GROSS INCOME? 1200.98
OF DEPENDENTS? 4
TAX ALREADY DEDUCTED? 0

Output #3: 0 TAXES PAID IN FULL

150. Write a program that accepts a character string and prints the character string with all blanks deleted, along with an integer that indicates how many blanks existed in the input string. The string will be at most 60 characters in length and should end with a period. There will be no other periods in the character string.

Input: I love to write computer programs.

Output: Ilovetowritecomputerprograms.
5

151. The New Telephone Company has the following rate structure for long-distance calls:
    1. Any call started after 6:00 PM (1800 hours) gets a 50% discount.
    2. Any call started after 8:00 AM (0800 hours) is charged full price.
    3. All calls are subject to a 4% federal tax.
    4. The regular rate for a call is $0.40 per minute.
    5. Any call longer than 60 minutes receives a 15% discount on its cost (after any other discount is taken but before tax is added).

    Write a program that processes a call by reading the start time for the call based on a 24-hour clock and the length of each call. The gross cost (before any discounts or tax) should be output followed by the net cost (after discounts are deducted and tax is added).

152. Let n be a positive integer consisting of up to 10 digits, d(10), d(9), ..., d(1). Write a program to list in one column each of the digits in the number. The rightmost digit d(1) should be listed at the top of the column.

153. An integer n is divisible by 9 if the sum of its digits is divisible by 9. Write a program to determine whether or not a given number is divisible by 9. Your output should also consist of the sum of the digits of the number.

    Input: 23

    Output: The sum of digits for 23 is 5
    23 is not divisible by 9

154. The interest paid on a savings account is compounded daily. This means that if you start with STARTBAL dollars in the bank, then at the end of N days you will have

    $$\text{STARTBAL}^* (1 + \text{rate} / 365)^N$$

    dollars, where rate is the annual interest rate (0.10 if the rate is 10%). Write a program that processes a set of data records, each of which contains values for STARTBAL, rate, and N and computes the final account balance.

155. Write a program that will scan a sentence and replace all multiple

occurrences of a blank with a single occurrence of a blank. The sentence will be on one line, and will be at most 60 characters in length.

156. Input an integer numbers, and determine the following information about it:
    a. Is it a multiple of 7, 11, or 13?
    b. Is the sum of the digits odd or even?
    c. What is the square root value (if positive)?
    d. Is it a prime number?

    Some sample input data might be: 104 3773 13 121 77 30751

157. Write a program that reads in a positive real number and finds and prints the number of digits to the left and right of the decimal point. Test the program with the following data:

    4703.62 0.01 0.475764 10.1240000

158. Write a program that finds the largest value, the smallest value, and the sum of the input data. Terminate input with a negative value and do not include this value in calculations. Output these results.

    Input: 50
    70
    83
    18
    94
    65
    -17

    Output: Largest Value: 94
    Smallest Value: 18
    Sum: 380

159. Write a program to input a positive integers and print all divisors, except for 1 and the number itself. If the number has no divisors, print a message indicating that it is prime.

160. Write a program to input 10 data items into each of 2 arrays X and Y. Compare each of the elements of X to the corresponding element of Y.

In the corresponding element of a third array Z, store:

+1 if X is larger than Y
0 if X is equal to Y
-1 if X is less than Y Then print a three-column table

displaying the contents of the arrays X, Y, and Z, followed by a count of the number of elements of X that exceed Y, and a count of the number of elements of X that are less than Y.

Input: 1,2 4,3 5,5 7,6 8,9 10,10 11,12 14,13 15,15 17,16

Output:

ARRAY X	ARRAY Y	ARRAY Z
1	2	-1
4	3	1
5	5	0
7	6	1
8	9	-1
10	10	0
11	12	-1
14	13	1
15	15	0
17	16	1

Number of elements in X greater than Y is: 4
Number of elements in X less than Y is: 3

161. A sentence is to be processed. The sentence consists of a sequence of words, separated by one or more blank spaces. Write a program that will input the sentence and count and output the number of words with one letter, two letters, etc., up to ten letters. The input will be typed in one line ending with a carriage return (hitting <ENTER>), be in uppercase, have no punctuation, and be less than or equal to 60 characters.

Input: THIS IS MY INPUT

Output:

NUMBER OF WORDS OF 1 LETTER: 0
NUMBER OF WORDS OF 2 LETTERS: 2
- -
NUMBER OF WORDS OF 10 LETTERS: 0

162. Write a program to input a character string of arbitrary length. For the string input, your program should do the following:
    a. Print the length of the string.
    b. Count and output the number of occurrences of four letter words. We define a four-letter word as a series of four non-blank characters separated by blanks and punctuation characters.
    c. Replace each four letter word with a string of four asterisks and print the new string.

    The input will terminate with an * and return. Do not print the * on output or count it in the length of the string.

    Input: This is the requested four letter word string*

    Output: The length is: 45
    The number of four letter words is: 3
    **** is the requested **** letter **** string

163. Write a program to manipulate a pair of square matrices. You should add, subtract, and multiply the matrices (maximum size 10 x 10).

164. Write a program that inputs a sentence of English text and reports the number of words in the text and the average word length. You can assume that the sentence will be one line of input and at most 60 characters in length. Words are separated by blanks and normal punctuation characters.

165. Write a program that provides the following information in response to a user input of the month and day of the current year: The day of the week on which this date occurs, and the number of this day, assuming January 1 to be day 1. The program needs a program constant that indicates the day of the week on which January 1 falls for the current year.

    The output should look as follows:

    03/06/2012 falls on Tuesday and is day 66.

166. Write a program that computes the accumulated balance on a fixed

deposit at the end of each interest period. The program should receive as input from the user the amount of the deposit, the annual interest rate, the number of compounding periods per year, and the number of years for which the balance is to be computed. The program should deliver as output a table showing the accumulated value and the accumulated interest at the end of each compounding period.

167. A number of computing applications use stacks. A stack can be visualized as a vertical structure in which new data elements are placed on top of the stack pushing the elements already there further downward. Elements can be removed from the stack only at the top. Write a program that simulates a stack by using an array with 10 numbers. The program should allow for entry and placement of a new element on the stack, removing the top element on the stack, and issuing the appropriate error messages if an attempt is made to place a data element on top of a full stack or to remove a data element from an empty stack. Use a P with an element to denote an element to be placed onto the stack and an R to denote that the last element is to be removed from the stack. An element of -1 signifies end of input and the -1 is not to be placed onto the stack. When -1 is encountered, output the items that remain on the stack in order from the top (most recent) down. P and R will be uppercase only.

Input:

```
P,5
P,3
R,0
P,2
P,-1
```

Output:

```
2
5
```

Input:

```
P,73
R,0
R,0
```

Output: Error: stack is empty.

168. Write a program that identifies the modal value in an array x of integers. (The modal value is the most frequently occurring data value.) The program should also report a count of the number of its occurrences. If two or more different values occur "most frequently" the program should detect this and indicate that the modal value is not unique.

169. Write a program that requests two fractions from the user. The program will then find the sum, difference, product, and quotient of the fractions. The answers will be presented with proper output and be presented as the most simplified fraction.

170. Write a program to generate a table of statute miles, nautical miles, and kilometers. The statute miles should begin at 25 miles and end at 500 miles, and be in increments of 25. Include the headings as shown in the sample.

Output:

Statute Miles	Nautical Miles	Kilometers
25	21.70893	40.23804
50	43.41785	80.47608
.	.	.
.	.	.
.	.	.
500	434.1785	804.7608

Recall that 1 nautical mile = 1 statute mile/1.1516 and that 1 kilometer = 1 nautical mile*1.853525.

171. An approximation of the transcendental number (e = 2.71828...) can be found by summing the expression

$$1 + \frac{x^1}{1!} + \frac{x^2}{2!} + \frac{x^3}{3!} + ... \frac{x^N}{N!}$$

Where N! = 1 * 2 * 3 * ... * N

Write a program to input x and N and then form the sum to approximate e^x.

Input: x = 1
N = 2

Output: e to the power of 1 is approximately 2.5

172. Write a program to find all integer solutions to the equation $a^2 + b^2 = c^2$, where $a < b$ and $c < 50$. For given values of a and b, simply test whether the sum of their squares is a perfect square and print a, b, and c if so.

173. In this problem, you are asked to determine if two words come from the same base alphabet (letters only). If one word is a re-arrangement of the other, the two words are called "anagrams", like "rose" and "sore". This problem asks you to determine if two words use the same letters, but do not necessarily use equal numbers of them. For example, "curse" and "rescue" come from the same alphabet, but "cure" does not, since its base alphabet does not contain the "s" that both "curse" and "rescue" use.

Your program is to REPEATEDLY read pairs of words from a file. The pairs are presented one word per line and are left justified in the first twenty positions of the line (any remaining positions are filled with blanks). Your program should output to a file both words and a message indicating that they use the same letters or different ones. A pair of words, "LAST" and "PAIR" will indicate the end of the data. The pair of words is not to be processed.

174. The circumference of a circle C is given by C=2(pi)R, where R is the radius of the circle. The value of pi can be calculated to many places of accuracy by calculating C and then dividing by 2R.

To find C inscribe polygons within a circle and find the perimeter of the polygon to approximate the value of C.

Start with a polygon of 6 sides (hexagon) and continuously double the number of sides, thus better approximating C. Consider the circle to have radius of one.

Output N, the number of sides and pi sub N for N=6 to 6144. Label output. DO NOT USE TRIGONOMETRIC FUNCTIONS.

175. Write a program that finds the series of consecutive positive integers

whose sum is exactly 1000. If there is more than one such series, find all of them. The program must complete in no more than 5 seconds.

Output: Series that sums to 1000:
28 29 30 31 32 33 34 35 36 37 38 39 40
41 42 43 44 45 46 47 48 49 50 51 52

176. Write a program that finds the specified six-digit number (What six-digit number can be split into two parts of three digits each, such that when the two numbers are added and the sum squared, you get the original number?). In C, your program should execute in less than 3 seconds; in Pascal, it should run in 5 seconds or less; in BASIC, it should take 1 minute or less.

177. Write a program that finds a four-digit number that is the sum of the fourth power of its digits. In C or Pascal, your program should execute in less than 1 second; in BASIC, it should take less than 35 seconds.

178. Write a program that finds two five-digit numbers that between them use the digits 0 through 9 once, such that the first number divided by the second is equal to 9.
That is:

$$\frac{abcde}{fghij} = 9$$

where each letter represents a different digit. Output all solutions.

179. A deque or double ended queue, is an access method in which insertions and deletions may be made at either end. Write a program that places numbers on a deque with all negative numbers placed on one end and all positive numbers on the other. "Seed" the deque with the number zero, which will always separate the positive and negative numbers. Input a set of numbers, and print out the final deque from negative to positive.

180. A Latin square of order n is an n x n matrix whose elements are chosen from integers 1 to n in such a way that each integer occurs exactly once in each column and once in each row. As an example, the following matrix is a Latin square.

$$A = \begin{pmatrix} 1 & 2 & 3 & 4 \\ 2 & 3 & 4 & 1 \\ 3 & 4 & 1 & 2 \\ 4 & 1 & 2 & 3 \end{pmatrix}$$

Latin squares have a long history of use in mathematical problems, such as magic squares and scheduling problems.

Two Latin squares A and B of order n are said to be orthogonal if the n squared ordered pairs (A_{ij}, B_{ij}), 1 <= i <= n, 1 <= j <= n, are distinct.

Write a program to determine the orthogonal Latin squares, if any, to the square A given above. You must consider all 4 x 4 Latin squares which could be formed with the elements of the A matrix. Your program should output the total number of matrices generated and tested against A excluding testing A against itself. Also, list the matrices which are orthogonal to A in the row/column format as in the case of matrix A above.

181. Write a program to input two lines of characters. Compare the lines for equality. Consider the two lines the same if they differ only in blanks and punctuation.

182. Write a program to print out any number (up to three digits) in words. For example, 297 is written as: two hundred ninety seven.

183. A fictitious dart-board is centered at the origin of a Cartesian coordinate system. The board is divided into 80 regions by 10 concentric circles of radii 1, 2, 3, ... , 10 and eight rays starting at the origin and making the following angles (in degrees) with the positive x-axis: 0, 45, 90, 135, 180, 225, 270, and 315.

The regions on this board are numbered in increasing order from 1 to 80 in counter-clockwise fashion starting with the innermost circle and moving outward.

A dart will bounce off and will be considered a miss if it lands exactly on a ray or if its distance from a boundary circle is less than 0.001. Any dart that lands outside the largest circle will also be considered a miss. A miss will be assigned a score of 81. A hit will be assigned a score equal to the number of the region in which the dart lands.

Two players, A and B, will compete in this dart game. Each game consists of exactly 3 shots from each player. The player with the lowest cumulative score after 3 shots is a game winner. A maximum of 10 games will be played. The match winner is the first player to win 6 games.

Your program should input a list of shots, each represented by a Cartesian pair of real numbers, x and y. (The numbers are separated by a single space.) Each input line contains A's shot followed by player B's shot. You will be given exactly enough shots to determine the match winner. The program should output the match winner's name (A or B), how many games that the player won, and his total score (total is score defined as the sum of all game scores for that player).

184. Write a program that creates a circular list. Populate the list with alphabetic characters. Write a function that, when given a character on the list, prints out all the characters from that point on the list forward until the character just preceding it is printed.

185. An anagram of a word is another word containing the same letters but rearranged in a different order (e.g., "stops" and "tops" are both anagrams of "pots".) To correctly solve this problem you must be able to identify anagrams and count the number of unique sets of anagrams of different lengths. For instance, the anagrams "stop", "pots", and "tops" form one set of anagrams of length four. A different set of anagrams of length four might contain the words "star", "arts", and "rats".

The data will consist of a list of words. Each word begins in the first column of a new input line. All words contain no digits, punctuation, or special characters. No word contains more than ten characters. The end-of-input condition is specified as an "*" on the last input line. There will not be more than 30 words in the input list. A proper solution to the problem will contain the following information:

Total number of words in the data input list. Number of different sets of anagrams of length x (x=2, 3, 4, ..., 10).

Input: stop
axaxax
ante
tennis
top
arts
tops
xaxaxa
star
pot
*

Output: Length of input List: 10

Anagram Set Number	Number of Sets
10	0
9	0
8	0
7	0
6	1
5	0
4	2
3	1
2	0

186. This problem deals with Magic Squares that aren't quite magic. Recall that a magic square is a two-dimensional array of number such that the sum of each of the elements in each row and in each column are the same. (In some magic squares, the diagonals also sum to the same value as the rows and columns. For this problem, our magic squares do not necessarily share this property.) For example, this 3 x 3 array:

2 9 4
6 1 8
7 5 3

is magic, since each row and column sums to 15. Note: All values input and output are positive integers.

For this problem, you are to read a 5 x 5 array of integers. The array is encoded in 5 input lines, one line per row (hence, each line contains 5 integers, separated by commas).

The square you read is "not quite magic". That is, the sums do not all equal the same number. Three elements of each square have been modified. One element had the number 1 added to it, another had the number 2 added to it, and a third had the number 4 added to it. Your problem is to find these incorrect elements.

Your output should have four lines for each square. The first line is the magic square value: the correct sum of any row or column. The next three lines contain the row and column number of each of the three incorrect entries in order (off by 1 entry, off by 2 entries, then off by 4 entries).

Input:
```
4,4,4,4,4
5,5,3,5,4
5,3,5,4,4
8,4,4,4,4
4,4,4,4,4
```

Output:
```
20
3 4
2 1
4 1
```

187. A black and white picture can be modeled by a rectangular grid of pixels (picture elements), each of which is either on (a one) or off (a zero). For example, below is a 10 x 10 grid of the letter 'A'.

```
0111111110
0110000110
0110000110
0110000110
0111111110
0111111110
0110000110
0110000110
```

0110000110
0110000110

A picture need not occupy the entire space on a grid. In-fact, you may have a number of objects on the grid as in the five by five grid below:

00110
01001
01000
00010
10000

This image has four objects in it. "What!" you say, "How is that possible?" This brings up an interesting point. How you determine what points belong to an object is dependent on how you define two points as being connected. If eight-connectedness had been used then any pixel which was touching a pixel would be considered to be part of the same object, if it were a one.

So, given the following:

```
***
***
***     , stars denote points which would be adjacent.
```

This would be simple to check for. There is another kind of connectedness called six-connectedness. That is what was used on the first binary image and that is what you are to use in the program you are asked to write for this problem. In six-connectedness, you would use the following as your criteria:

```
* *
* 1 *
* *
```

Write a program which will read image data, and produce as output a list of the number of objects in each image input.

Each image is 10 characters across. No image has more than10 lines. Each image is separated by a blank line.

Input file:	**Output:**
0000110000	IMAGE 1: 3 OBJECTS
0000100000	
0001010011	
0000100000	
0011001100	IMAGE 2: 3 OBJECTS
0011101100	
0001110001	
0000001001	
0000000001	IMAGE 3: 1 OBJECT
0000000010	
0000000100	
0000001000	
0010010000	IMAGE 4: 10 OBJECTS
0001001000	
0000100100	
0000010010	
0000001001	

188. A bubble sort can be made somewhat more efficient if we realize that, after the first complete iteration of the loop, the largest value is at the end of the array. Similarly, after the second complete iteration the second largest value will be the next to last element, etc. Therefore, in each successive pass, through the loop, it is not necessary to check the last most element(s). Write a program that will sort an array and write out the sorted array and how many passes it took to do it using this method as well as the usual bubble sort.

189. Serial communications is one of the more popular means of digital data transfer. Your mission, should you choose to accept it is to write a program which simulates a serial communications controller.

    A text character is represented by a number of bits (7 or 8) which form a character code (as if you didn't know). The bits in this character code are sent over a communications line one bit at a time, starting with the least significant bit and ending with the most significant bit. In addition to the character code bits, synchronizing, and error-checking information is also sent. In summary the data stream format looks like:

| 0 | 0 | Parity | Data0 | Data1|........................| DataN | 0 |

The first two 0's represent the "start bit"; this indicates to the serial communications controller that a character is coming down the line. The next bit is the "parity" bit. The parity bit can represent either "even" or "odd" parity. Even parity means that the sum of the data 1 bits and the parity bit, inclusive, is an even number. Likewise, odd parity means that the data and parity bits have an odd number of 1's. In other words, for even parity, if the number of 1's in the data bits are odd then the parity bit will be a 1 (to make the sum of 1's an even number); the parity bit would be 0 if there was an even number of 1's in the data bits. The next 7/8 bits comprise the data bits. These bits make up the character code, where Data0 is the least significant bit and DataN the represents the most significant bit. The final 0 is the "stop" bit, this indicates to the controller the end of character transmission.

When a communications line does not have data being sent over it, it normally has a "1" level on it. That is, the controller will receive 1's until the two 0's (comprising the start bits) are encountered. The controller then interprets the following bits in the scheme described above.

A number of errors can occur in transmission, we will be concerned with two: parity and framing errors. Parity errors occur when, for a given parity (odd or even), the bits do not sum to a respective odd or even number. A framing error occurs when the stop bit encountered is not a 0 as it should be.

Your program will input the configuration value on one line, the next line will contain a data transmission of no more than 100 bits. The configuration value consists of a letter followed by a number. The letter represents the parity type ("E" for even, "O" for odd), then number represents the number of data bits (7 or 8). For example, "E7" means an even parity, 7 data bit transmission. Your program should input a number of such line pairs until "*" is input for the configuration value, at which time your program should terminate. The data transmission consists of a series of "1"'s and "0"'s.

Your program should read this transmission and output the corresponding ASCII characters (you will receive only alphabetic). If you encounter a parity error then your program should output <PE>, for a framing error, output a <FE>. Each transmission should be output on one line, followed by a blank line between transmissions.

Input:
E7
11111001011000100010100101000110100010001101000101111110000
100001000110010010001001010100001100101011111
O8
0001010001000000100101000000100001000001111001000000100101
0000101110111111001110010100
O7
11101110011111111000010111011001100000010001111
E7
1111110001000001000001000010000111000010001001001
*

Output:
FREEBITS
ER<PE>OR<FE>S
<PE><FE>A<FE>
ABC<FE>

190. Assume that data is available about the citizens of a (very) small town in the following format:

Nine digit integer social security number, integer age, sex code (1=female, 2=male). It is desired to know the percentage of females over twenty-one years of age. The last data entry has a social security number of zero.

191. Write a program that will read text from a file and reformat the text for display. The text is to be centered in the display area. It should be

surrounded by a border constructed from a character specified in the input data. For each data set, the test should be displayed as follows:

1. For each data set, the output is to begin on a new page and should be centered in a display area 80 columns wide. Output for each data set will reside on a single page.
2. The line length for displayed text will be specified in the input data and will be within the limits of 1 - 78 characters.
3. The text should be formatted to the specified line length and should be printed in the display area completely surrounded by a border as specified by the input data.

It can be assumed that for each data set, the text contains no words that are longer than the selected line length, and once formatted, can be printed on a single line printer page. The delimiters for words in the text are spaces, end-of-line, beginning-of-line, and end-of-file. Each formatted line of text is to contain the maximum possible number of words that create a line less than or equal to the selected line length.

INPUT SPECIFICATION

Multiple data sets are contained in and arranged as follows:

Record #	Value
1	Line length for displayed text (1-78)
2	Character to be used for the border
3	The number of text lines following (1-50)
4 --+	
. :	
. +-	The text to be formatted and printed.
. :	(contains no adjacent blanks)
n --+)	

OUTPUT SPECIFICATION

For each data set, your program should write to a file the formatted text centered with an 80-column line. The first line written to the file is to be a border line create from the user-selected character, followed by the remaining lines of formatted text (beginning and ending with the border character), and ending with another border line at the end of the text. Each data set should begin at the top of a new page.

Example:

A Sample Data Set:
19
#
6

This is some sample text that has been formatted by this program for display. The specified line length was 19 characters with the text to be surrounded by a border consisting of '#'.

Sample Formatted Text (to be centered in 80 columns):

```
#####################
#This is some sample #
#text that has been  #
#formatted by this   #
#program for         #
#display. The        #
#specified line      #
#length was 19       #
#characters with the #
#text to be          #
#surrounded by a     #
#border consisting   #
#of '#'.             #
#####################
```

192. Given a string to locate within another string, find all permutations of the search string in the destination string. Assume input will be in all caps and at most 60 characters in length. The output should be the location of string and location for each string permutation found.

Example:

Input: Source: RAT
Destination: RATZINATRORRAT

Output:

Location	Permutation
1	RAT
7	ATR
12	RAT

193. A peasant was trying to solve the problem of placing the integers from one to sixteen into a four by four matrix, such that if the products of the numbers of each row and the products of the numbers in each column were computed, and then those eight products were added together, the sum would be as large as possible. The peasant had drawn his matrix in the sand with a stick, and had placed the sixteen numbers in the matrix. The old wizard was riding by on his dragon, and saw the matrix drawn by the peasant. The wizard remarked, "Your matrix is good, but the largest sum can be achieved by rearranging these four numbers." He dismounted and rubbed out four of the numbers in the matrix. However, before he could replace the numbers in the matrix, he gasped and fell dead of old wizard's syndrome.

    Write a program that will reconstruct the matrix that the wizard was about to complete. The input will come from a file and will consist of a single line containing sixteen integers, each right justified in a three column field. These values represent the matrix at the time of the wizard's death. The first four values are the first row, the next four the second row, etc. Four of the input values will be zeroes, representing the values that the wizard had erased. The other values will be in the range 1 to 16, and are in the positions chosen by the peasant.

    Your program shall output to a file of the reconstructed matrix as a square, with rows of four values each. This matrix will be followed by the products of the numbers of each row and the products of the numbers from each column.

194. Write a program that reads in two sentences and compares them. Define a word as any string of characters separated on the left and right by at least one blank (except for the beginning and end of the sentence, of course). Test the two sentences to see if one sentence is a subset of the other (i.e., the larger contains all of the words in the smaller sentence plus, optionally, some more).

195. A ten by ten array of characters contains 5 "X"'s, 5 "O"'s, and 90 periods (see examples below). The 5 "X"'s are all connected, either orthogonally or diagonally; similarly for the 5 "O"'s. It is desired to determine whether the pattern of "X"'s matches the pattern of "O"'s, by

which we mean that one pattern can be exactly superimposed on the other. Only translations and rotations are allowed; reflections are not allowed.

There will be exactly four data sets in a file to process. Each data set consists of ten lines of ten characters each (periods, "X"'s, and "O"'s). The letters are uppercase, and there are no intervening blanks. The output for the program shall be written to a file. For each data set, your program should skip a line and then write the data set as ten lines of characters, but with one space between adjacent characters (exactly as shown below). Your program should determine if the two patterns match, and write either "Patterns match" or "Patterns do not match," as appropriate, directly under the array.

Below are examples of output from two data sets, correctly written, with the correct output message below.

```
..........
..........
..........
......X...
......XX..
......X...
..O...X...
OOOO.....
..........
..........
Patterns do not match
..........
.....X....
......X...
.......X..
...OOXX..
...O.O....
..O.......
..........
..........
..........
Patterns match
```

196. Due to a strike by Local 2 of the Amalgamated League Secretaries and Plaster Casters Union, the manager of a nearby bowling alley, Peter Piper's Pin Palace, needs some programming in a hurry to automate the calculation of averages and handicaps for the leagues that bowl there. The parameters in each league's handicapping formula are not available, but some old status sheets for each league have been found and must be used to infer what the parameters might be. Naturally, none of the league secretaries will tell what values his or her league uses. The handicap calculation algorithm is known to be the same for all leagues and goes as follows:
    1. The bowler's (per game) average score, truncated to an integer (between 0 and 300), is subtracted from a parameter called PAR.
    2. If the difference is negative, the handicap is zero. Otherwise, a percentage given by the parameter FCT is taken and the result truncated to an integral value for the handicap.
       Symbolically:
       Handicap = floor (max(0, PAR - average) + FCT/100)

    It is known to be a national policy that the parameters are integer with FCT in the range of 50 to 100 and PAR in the range of 150 to 300. The data file contains a record for each league and contains the following information right justified in each field:

Columns	**Contents**
1-3	League Number
5-6	Number of Average-Handicap Pairs in Record
8-10	Average 1
12-14	Handicap 1
16-18	Average 2 (if present)
20-22	Handicap 2 (if present)
.	.
.	.
64-66	Average B (if present)
68-70	Handicap B (if present)

    You may assume that the N pairs supplied will be in the leftmost position and that all other characters in the line are blanks.

For each record in the file until League Number = 0, the program is to output to a file in a readable format the League Number and all FCT-PAR pairs which could be used to give the Average-Handicap pairs given for that league. If no such pairs exist, print a notice that at least one given handicap is wrong, and print all the FCT-PAR pairs which could be used to give all but one of the Average-Handicap pairs on the league's data record. If no FCT-PAR pairs exist with fewer than two errors in the input data, so indicate.

197. In a pattern tree, leaf nodes contain letters as data and have no children. Interior nodes have either a "+" or a "*" as data and have two children--a left subtree and a right subtree. A "+" means alternation--either the string from the left subtree or the string from the right subtree may be chosen here. A "*" means concatenation-- the string from the left subtree must be concatenated with the string from the right subtree.

For example:

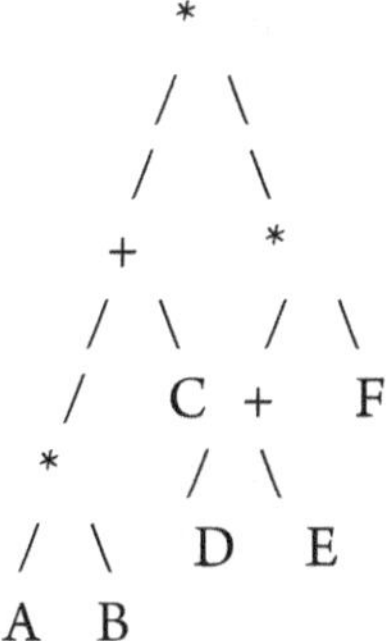

represents the following words:

ABDF
ABEF
CDF
CEF

You are to write a program which reads in binary pattern trees from a file and then outputs to a file all words represented in each pattern tree. Input data will occur in sets, with one set representing a pattern tree. The first record in the set contains the number of nodes in the tree, N, right justified in columns 1-2. The next N records contain the following information about the nodes:

Column	Contents
1-2	number of the node (the root is always node #1; other nodes may have any number, in any order)
4	data at the node (either an alphabetic character or a "+" or a "*")
6-7	number of the left child node (0 = none)
9-10	number of the right child node (0 = none)

All values are right justified in the indicated fields.
For each tree, output to the file all occurrences of all words represented by that tree, one word per line. Continue processing sets of pattern tree data until a trailer record with a negative value for the number of nodes is encountered.

198. Write a program that finds an integer that, when a specific digit is removed, it is reduced to one-ninth of its value, and that, when a second digit is removed, is further reduced to one-ninth of the second value. Your program should output the complete set of numbers. (You can always find a new set by adding a 0 to the end of each member of a given set).

199. Write a program to multiply large integers. The input will be two integers, one per line, each with as many as 20 digits read as characters.

200. Write a program that will accept as input an equation filled with any number of spaces and prints out the results. The program should look for correct syntax and print out an appropriate message. The program should check for division by zero. Use the standard rules of mathematics when evaluating the problem: multiply and divide, and then add and subtract.

    Ex. 5 + 6 - 1 + 4 * 2 = 18

201. Write a program to take a number in base 10 and transform to any base less than or equal to 5 (base 1 omitted). The base 10 number will be of form XX.XX. The input will be of form NUMBER, BASE. Note that some numbers cannot be transformed exactly to another base. Use 13 positions (12 digits and a decimal point) for output. Also print the base 10 conversion of your transformed number. The first line of output will be the transformed number. The base 10 conversion will be on the second line. Use proper titles for each number and terminate the program with a base input of 0.

Input: 2.20,2

Output: 2.2 converted to base 2 is 10.0011001100
The base 10 conversion of that number is 2.199219

202. Input a set of numbers, 4 per line. Find and print the average of the smallest and largest number, for each set. Finally print the average of all numbers. Stop input when all four input values are 1's. Both positive and negative numbers can be used as input. No output should appear until all input has been read. No output should appear for the 1's. Round all output to two places to the right of the decimal.

Input: 2, 4, 9, 5
8.4, 6.75, 5, 19
1, 1, 1, 1

Output: 5.5
12

Average of all: 7.39

203. Write a program that reads a message and prints it with all blanks and vowels deleted. For example, WHO CAN SOLVE THE PROBLEM EASIER becomes WHCNSLVTHPRBLMSR.

204. A perfect number is imbedded in a 3x3 matrix. Write a program to find the perfect number and print the number with its location. All numbers in the matrix will be positive. A perfect number is a number

equal to the sum of its divisors (excluding itself). For example, 6 is a perfect number because 6 = 1 + 2 + 3.

The input will be row by row.

Input:

```
3 7 4
2 5 1
3 6 8
```

Output: The perfect number 6 is found in row 3 and column 2.

205. To test a student's keyboard skills, devise the following program:
    a. Print out an alphabetic character for the student to type, for example:

        Please type in an a

    b. Read the student's response and give the student feedback as follows:

    If the student responded correctly type: Excellent! If you asked for a lowercase letter and the student type the correct letter but in uppercase type: Sorry, correct letter but I wanted lowercase. Same for uppercase. If the student types a totally in-correct letter: Not even close, respond: try typing with your mittens off!!

206. A turtle and a rabbit have agreed to race. The turtle runs at the rate of 2 meters per minute and the rabbit runs at the rate of 20 meters per minute. The turtle plods steadily along, but the rabbit runs one minute and then stops for an 11 minute nap. When he wakes, he runs for another minute, and then stops for another 11 minute nap, etc. Write a program to report the race. Input to the program should be the length of the race (in meters). If necessary, make the user keep giving input until the input length is a multiple of 10 (such as 60, 150, etc.). Output should be a table showing, for each 10-meter interval, the time required for the turtle to reach that point and the time required for the rabbit to reach that point. Finally, the program should tell you which animal wins. For example, if the input looks like this:

HOW MANY METERS? 65
NOT A MULTIPLE OF 10. TRY AGAIN.
HOW MANY METERS? 60

then the output should look like this (with correct numbers filled in):

METERS	TIME (IN MINUTES)	
COVERED	TURTLE	RABBIT
10	5	.5
20	10	1
30	.	12.5
40	.	.
50	.	.
60	30	25

RABBIT WINS!

207. Write a program to accept a series of solvable mathematical equations in which two variables are to be used. The program should read in the equations and solve for the appropriate variable.

equation, equation; variable to solve for
Ex. a = 3*b + 5, b = 1 – 5a; b Answer b = -3/2

208.

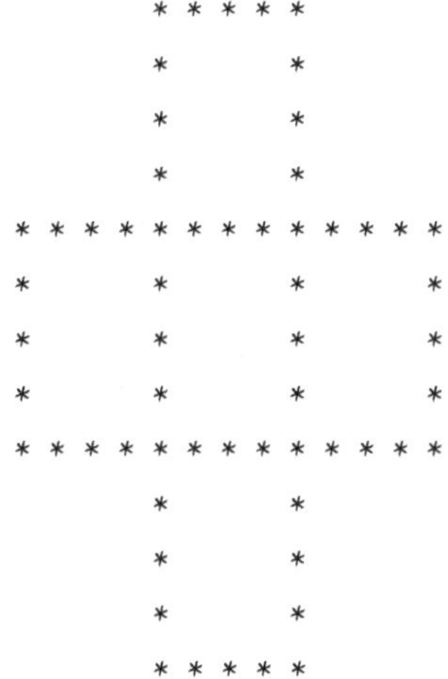

Write a program which prints an arrangement of 5 of the digits 1-9, one digit per box such that no digit appears twice and no two consecutive digits are in horizontally or vertically adjacent squares. The input will be the digit that appears in the top box and the digit that appears in the bottom box. An output is shown below when the input was 7 and 9.

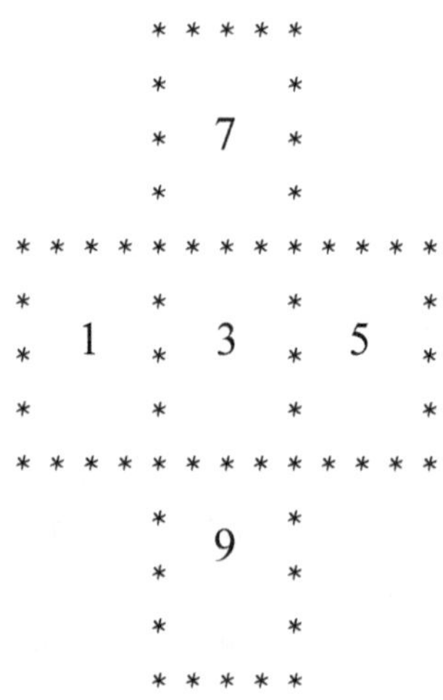

209. Concrete paint can be purchased only in gallon containers, each of which covers 350 square feet. Write a program that determines the minimum number of cans of paint needed to paint a given surface.

210. Roofing is purchased in bundles, each of which covers exactly 21square feet of roof. Write a program that will prompt for a specific roof area and compute the number of bundles to be purchased to cover the roof. The program should also output the number of square feet of roofing left over.

211. The surface area of a city water tank is given by the equation:

$$S = 6.28 * R * (R+H)$$

where R is its radius and H is its height. Write a program that calculates the gallons of paint and man-hours required to paint such a tank. A gallon of paint covers 270 square feet and it takes an average of 3 man-hours to pre-clean and apply a gallon of paint. Express the results to the nearest tenth of a unit in each quantity. The program should prompt for R and H.

212. Generate a table of values of X and Y from the equation:

$$Y = 3X + .05$$

Let X start at 1 and increase by 1 each time the loop is repeated. Stop the table output when Y becomes greater than 30. The output should be in the following form:

X-Value	Y-Value
1	3.5
2	6.5
.	.

213. Write a program to allow the user to input a specified number of integers then format the output EXACTLY as shown.

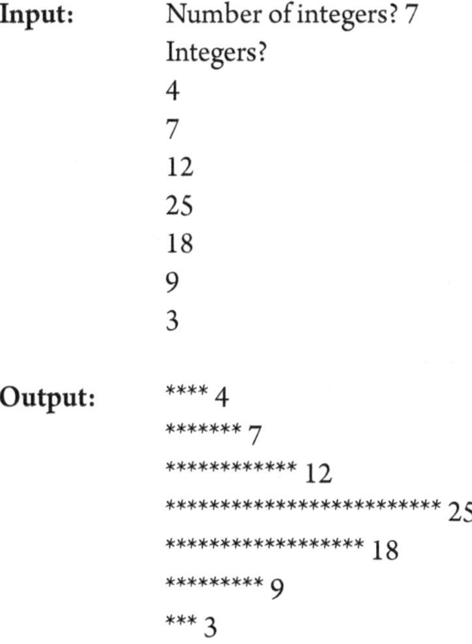

Input:

```
Number of integers? 7
Integers?
4
7
12
25
18
9
3
```

Output:

```
**** 4
******* 7
************ 12
************************* 25
****************** 18
********* 9
*** 3
```

214. Buzz is a party game in which the integers are repeated in sequence, with the provision that any integer that contains the digit 7or that is divisible by 7 be replaced with the word BUZZ. In fact, one BUZZ is to be given for each digit 7 as well as for divisibility by 7. Write a program that prints each integer as well as the appropriate response. The program should allow the user to select the largest integer to be displayed. Display the output in the following format:

Integer	Response
1	1
2	2
.	.
7	BUZZ BUZZ
.	.
14	BUZZ
.	.

215. The number 55 has the interesting property that its square can be divided into two, two digit integers whose sum is 55. That is,

    55 = 3025

    and

    55 = 30 + 25

    Find all the two-digit integers that have this property.

216. Write a program to input identification numbers and name and then print out in alphabetical order a 2 cross referenced list giving the identification number for each name. Use an identification number of -1 to terminate the input of data.

    Input: 123,THOMAS,432,DALE,728,PAT,069,BUD
    666,KATHY,001,BRAD,985,JOSEPH,076,JAN,-1

    Output:

BRAD	1
BUD	69
DALE	432
JAN	76
JOSEPH	985
KATHY	666
PAT	728
THOMAS	123

217. Write a program to input a line of up to 70 characters, then count and output each unique non-blank character found and the number of times found. A period will terminate the input, and is not included in the counting. Only upper case letters will be used. The output should be in the order in which each character first appeared in the input.

Example:
THERE IS A TIME WHEN ALL MEN WILL COME TO THEIR SENSES.
T - 4
H - 3
E - 9
R - 2
I - 4
S - 4
A - 2
M - 3
W - 2
N - 3
L - 4
C - 1
O - 2

COMPUTERS ARE #1.
C - 1
O - 1
M - 1
P - 1
U - 1
T - 1
E - 2
R - 2
S - 1
A - 1
- 1
1 - 1

218. A cryptogram is a coded message found by substituting a code character for each letter of an original message. The substitution is performed uniformly throughout the original message, i.e. all A's might be replaced by S, all B's by P, etc. All punctuation (including blanks between words) remains unchanged. Write a program to input the 26 characters used to code A through Z then read a message of up

to 70 coded characters and print the message decoded. A period will terminate the input.

Example:	JEISLWMROVNCQPTBZXKDFGHAUY
Coded message:	HXODOPM BXTMXJQK OK WFP.
Uncoded message:	WRITING PROGRAMS IS FUN.

219. A generalization of dates program is called a "date canonizer". The program takes dates in numerous forms and places the date into a single "canonical" form. Write a program that will recognize a variety of dates and convert them into the form: month-day-year, for example, 2-19-1961 for February 19, 1961. Some forms of dates your program should accept are:

July 30, 1930
24 June 1963
7-20-1931
March 4th 1963
1962: 7/5

You should make the forms that your program accept as general as possible. Months with long names should allow abbreviations (February, for example, should allow Feb as an acceptable abbreviation.)

220. The results of a true-false exam given to a Computer Science class have been coded for input to a program. The information available for each student consists of a student's identification number and the student's answers to 10 true-false questions.

Sample data:	**Student Identification**	**Answer String**
	0080	FTTFTFTTFT
	0340	FTFTFTTTFF
	0341	FTTFTTTTTT
	0401	TTFFTFFTTT
	0462	TTFTTTFFTF
	0463	TTTTTTTTTT
	0464	FTFFTFFTFT
	0512	TFTFTFTFTF
	0618	TTTFFTTFTF
	0619	FFFFFFFFFF

0687 TFTTFTTFTF
0700 FTFFTTFFFT
0712 FTFTFTFTFT
0837 TFTFTTFTFT

Write a program that first inputs the answer string representing the 10 correct answers, and then the student's id and answers to the 10 test questions. Compute and store the number of correct answers for each student in one array, and store the student ID number in the corresponding element of another array. Determine the best score, BEST. Then print a three-column table displaying the ID number, score, and grade for each student. Print in order by number of correct responses - most correct to least correct. The grade should be determined as follows: If a score is equal to BEST or BEST -1, give an A; if it is BEST-2 or BEST-3, give a C; otherwise give an F. Assume no more than 50 students and input terminates with ID = 9999.

221. Write a program that will input a positive number, then output all primes less than or equal to that number. Also, output the sum of the primes found.

Input: 3

Output: 2
3

SUM=5

222. Many consider that preserving the security of files stored on secondary media such as disk, or other magnetic media an increasing problem. Some files contain sensitive or classified information not intended for general consumption. While this is true with corporate or military secrets, it may even be true for any persons wanting to keep their correspondence private. Hundreds and hundreds of hours have been invested in developing highly sophisticated encryption schemes. In essence, though, they all process an input file to produce an encrypted output file. A very simple encryption scheme for a text file is:

a. If a character is a letter or a digit, replace it with the next character in the sequence, except that Z should be replaced with A, z should be replaced with a, and 9 should be replaced by 0. Thus 1 becomes 2, D becomes E, p becomes q, and so on.

b. Any character other than a letter or a digit should simply be copied. Commas will not be part of the input.

Input: When the zookeeper filed bankruptcy in 1986 the entire community

Output: Xifo uif applffqfs gjmfe cbolsvqudz jo 2097 uif foujsf dpnnvojuz

223. Design and implement a program that determines the first N twin prime pairs. Twin primes are prime numbers that differ by exactly 2.

Input: N=4

Output:

```
3    5
5    7
11   13
29   31
```

224. Suppose that a text file contains information about the grades for students in a particular course. Assume that the first line contains a description of the course (not longer than 50 characters). Assume that the second line contains two numbers. The first of these represents the number of test grades, NumTests, for each student. The second represents the number of students, NumStudents. Following these first two header lines are NumStudents lines, each of which contains NumTests test scores. Assume that there will never be more than MaxStudents (100) students and never more than MaxGrades (10) grades for each student. For example, one such file contains the following information for 17 highly motivated students:

```
CS 4603 ADVANCED ALGORITHMS AND INFORMATION STRUCTURES
3,17
88,79,93
74,86,95
98,97,90
52,64,76
78,84,65
```

97,86,94
76,89,91
99,76,88
88,78,93
23,99,65
77,95,86
93,56,89
98,98,100
100,100,100
89,94,79
79,87,98
100,84,93

Design and implement a program that inputs this data and calculates the average test grade for each of the students. Also calculate the average grade for each of the exams. This information should be reported in a table. For example, a report might look as follows, where each of the averages are rounded to the nearest hundredth:

CS 4603 ADVANCED ALGORITHMS AND INFORMATION STRUCTURES

STUDENT #	EXAM 1	EXAM 2	EXAM 3	AVERAGE
1	88	79	93	86.67
2	74	86	95	85.00
3	98	97	90	95.00
.	.	.	.	.
.	.	.	.	.
.	.	.	.	.
17	100	84	93	92.33
AVERAGES	82.88	85.41	87.94	85.41

225. The prices of stocks are normally given to the nearest eighth of a dollar; for example, 29 7/8 or 89 1/2. Write a program that computes the value of the user's holding of one stock. The program asks for the number of shares held, the whole dollar portion of the price and the fraction portion. The fraction portion is to be input as two integer values, one for the numerator and one for the denominator.

Input: Number of Shares: 10
Whole dollar portion: 136
Fraction price per share: 5/8

Output: Holding value: 1366.25

226. Telephone dials and push-buttons have letters as well as numbers. Hence, some phone numbers spell words. For example 452-4357 is also 452-HELP. Write a program to help people find words for phone numbers. The program should read in the last four digits of a phone number and then output possible letter versions of that number. For example, 4357 can be HELP. It can also be GEJP, as well as other letter combinations. Omit any words that do not contain at least one vowel (AEIOU). There are no letters for 0 and 1. If no words are possible either because a 0 or 1 appears in the number, or because no combinations contain vowels, then print out the message "NO POSSIBLE WORDS".

Letters for each of the numbers are as follows:
2 - A B C
3 - D E F
4 - G H I
5 - J K L
6 - M N O
7 - P R S
8 - T U V
9 - W X Y

Output your words in alphabetical order.
Input: 4357

Output: GEJP
.....
.....
HELP
.....

227. An hourly employee is paid at a rate of $9.73 per hour up to 40 hours worked per week. Any hours over that are paid at the over-time rate of 1.5 times that. From the worker's gross pay, 6% is withheld for social security tax, 14% is withheld for federal income tax, 5% is withheld for state income tax, and $6 per week is withheld for union dues. If the worker has three or more dependents, an additional $10 is withheld to cover the extra cost of health insurance beyond that paid by the employer. Each item is rounded to the nearest cent, with half cents and above rounded up. Write a program that takes as input the number of hours worked in a week and the number of dependents and then outputs the worker's gross pay, each withholding, and the net take home pay for the week. Omit the Health Insurance line if nothing is with-held.

Input: HOURS: 42
DEPENDENTS: 2

Output:

GROSS PAY:	$ 418.39
SOCIAL SECURITY TAX:	$ 25.10
FEDERAL TAX:	$ 58.57
STATE TAX:	$ 20.92
UNION DUES:	$ 6.00
NET PAY:	$ 307.80

Input: HOURS: 46
DEPENDENTS: 4

Output:

GROSS PAY:	$ 476.77
SOCIAL SECURITY TAX:	$ 28.61
FEDERAL TAX:	$ 66.75
STATE TAX:	$ 23.84
UNION DUES:	$ 6.00
HEALTH INSURANCE:	$ 10.00
NET PAY:	$ 341.57

228. Write a program to find and print a list of all numbers less than 300 having the property that the number is equal to the sum of each digit in the number raised to the number of digits in the number. For example,

$$153 = 1^3 + 5^3 + 3^3.$$

229. Write a program that accepts a year written as a four digit Arabic (ordinary) numeral and outputs the year written in Roman numerals. Important Roman numerals are I for 1, V for 5, X for 10, L for 50, C for 100, D for 500, and M for 1000. Recall that some numbers are formed by using a kind of subtraction of one Roman "digit"; for example, IV is 4, produced as V minus I; XL is 40; CM is 900, and so forth. Here are a few more sample years: MCM is 1900, MCML is 1950, MCMLX is 1960, MCMXL is 1940, and MCMLXXXIX is 1989. Assume the year is between 1000 and 3000. The only allowed subtraction combinations are:

    A single I can come before a V or X.
    A single X can come before a L or C.
    A single C can come before a D or M.

    A letter will never appear more than 3 times in succession.
    Input: 1950
    Output: MCML

    Input: 1989
    Output: MCMLXXXIX

230. Given an input string of digits, determine if it contains a repeated string of digits. Output the repeating group. Some examples:
    Input: 625625625
    Output: 625

    Input: 18347183471834
    Output: 18347

    Input: 2865397385
    Output: 2865397385

    Input: 33333333333
    Output: 3

231. Write a program to read in four letters and then output 24 permutations of these letters. Use an array to hold the four letters. Do not cut corners in designing this one; it can be confusing.

Example

Input: A B C D

Output:
A B C D
A B D C
A C B D
A C D B
A D B C
A D C B
B A C D
B A D C
B C A D
B C D A
B D A C
B D C A
C A B D
C A D B
C B A D
C B D A
C D A B
C D B A
D A B C
D A C B
D B A C
D B C A
D C A B
D C B A

232. Write a program acquiring a character text of 500 characters from the input stream. The input stream text is followed by a number of different words (each contains a maximum of 10 characters). The word list is terminated by a null string constant. For each word, determine how often it appears in the text supplied and print the resulting count with each of the words.

233. Write a program that will add, subtract, multiply, and divide fractions. Input will consist of a single line representing a fraction arithmetic problem as follows:

integer/integer operation integer/integer

For example, a line of input might be
2/3 + 1/2

Your program should give output for each of the following:
a) Check for division by zero.
b) Check for proper operation symbols.
c) Print the problem in its original form.
d) Print the answer.
e) Print all fractions in horizontal form.

Your answer need not be in lowest terms.
Input: 2/3 + 1/2
Output: 2/3 + 1/2 = 7/6

Input: 4/0 * 1/3
Output: Error: Division by zero.

Input: 5/2 # 1/7
Output: Error: Improper Operation Symbol

234. Write a program to translate Morse Code into English-language characters.
The table of Morse Code to be used is:

A .-	F ..-.	K -.-	O ---	S ...	W .--
B -...	G --.	L .-..	P .--.	T -	X -..-
C -.-.	H	M --	Q --.-	U ..-	Y -.--
D -..	I ..	N -.	R .-.	V ...-	Z --..
E .	J .---				

The Morse text is written as a character string (max 200 char) in the input stream. A single blank character separates the code of individual letters. Two blanks separate words.

Input: -.... .. ...
.. ...
-- -.--
-.-. .... . -.-.-.-

Output: THIS IS MY CHECK.

235. The force of gravity is different for each of the nine planets in our solar system. Write an interactive program that allows you to enter your (Earth) weight and your choice of planet to which you would like your weight converted. Output should be your weight on the desired planet together with the planet name. The relative forces of gravity are as follows:

Earth	1.00
Jupiter	2.65
Mars	0.39
Mercury	0.38
Neptune	1.23
Pluto	0.05
Saturn	1.17
Uranus	1.05
Venus	0.78

Input: Planet: Pluto
Weight on Earth: 100
Output: Your weight on PLUTO is 5 pounds

236. Write a program to compute the average of all legal examination scores. A legal score is one in the range 0 to 150 Inclusive. Your program should input scores until a score of -1 occurs and then produce as output:
a. The average of all legal scores.
b. The number of legal scores.
c. The number of illegal scores.
If no scores are legal, report an average of zero. Note that -1 is not included in the count of illegal scores.

Input: 100
200
50
-1

Output: Average = 75
Legal = 2
Illegal = 1

237. Parkside's Triangle is generated from two positive integers, one for the size and one for the seed. For example,

```
Size 6, Seed 1        Size 5, Seed 3
1 2 4 7 2 7            3 4 6 9 4
  3 5 8 3 8              5 7 1 5
    6 9 4 9                8 2 6
      1 5 1                  3 7
        6 2                    8
          3
```

The size gives the number of columns. Seed specifies the starting value for column 1. Column N contains N values. The successive values are obtained by adding 1 to the previous value. When 9 is reached, the next value becomes 1. Write a program that gets pairs of positive integers from input and produces Parkside's Triangle for each pair. The check for bad data should include checking for seeds between 1 and 9 inclusive. You can assume the size to be less than 16.

Input: Size: 6
Seed: 1

Output:

```
1 2 4 7 2 7
  3 5 8 3 8
    6 9 4 9
      1 5 1
        6 2
          3
```

238. There are some programs whose only task is error recovery. Write a spelling checker that reads in a table of words from input ending in the word "0000" to signify the end of the dictionary. Then, text is entered to the program, and each word in the text is looked up in the dictionary. If a word cannot be found, the program informs the user that the word is misspelled. He or she is then offered the opportunity to accept the word as is or to manually correct the spelling. As each word is examined, if it is found in the dictionary, it is written to a corrected text, and the final corrected text is printed.

239. Four track stars enter the mile race at the Penn Relays. Write a program that will read in the race time in minutes and seconds for a runner and compute and print the speed in feet per second and in meters per second. (Hint: There are 5,280 feet in one mile and 3,282 feet in one kilometer.)

Input: Race Time: 3 minutes 52.83 seconds

Output: Speed in Feet per second: 22.68
Speed in Meters per second: 6.91

240. When shopping for a new house, you must consider several factors. In this problem, the initial cost of the house, the estimated annual fuel costs, and the annual tax rate are available. Write a program that will determine the total cost after a five-year period for each set of data below. Your program output should give the "best buy." Input will be terminated by the input of 0,0,0.

Initial House Cost	Annual Fuel Cost	Tax Rate
$67,000	$2,300	0.025
$62,000	$2,500	0.025
$75,000	$1,850	0.020

To calculate the house cost, add the initial cost to the fuel cost for five years, then add the taxes for five years. Taxes for one year are computed by multiplying the tax rate by the initial cost.

Input: Initial house cost, annual fuel cost, and tax rate?
67000, 2300,.025
Initial house cost, annual fuel cost, and tax rate?
62000,2500,.025

Initial house cost, annual fuel cost, and tax rate ?
75000,1850,.02
Initial house cost, annual fuel cost, and tax rate ?
0,0,0

Output: The best buy is the house with a cost of $62000, a fuel cost of $2500, and a tax rate of .025.

241. The New Telephone Company has the following rate structure for long-distance calls:
    1. Any call started after 6:00 pm (1800 hours) but before 8:00 am (0800 hours) is discounted 50 percent.
    2. Any call started after 8:00 am (0800 hours) but before 6:00 pm (1800 hours) is charged full price.
    3. All calls are subject to a 4-percent Federal tax.
    4. The regular rate for a call is $0.40 per minute.
    5. Any call longer than 60 minutes receives a 15 percent discount (after any other discount is subtracted and before tax is added).

    Write a program that reads the start time for a call based on twenty-four-hour clock and the length of the call. The gross cost (before any discounts or tax) should be printed followed by the net cost (after discounts are deducted and tax is added).

    Input: Start time? 1550
    Time of call (minutes)? 32

    Output: Gross cost: $12.80
    Net cost: $14.08

242. Write a program that inputs a positive real number and finds and prints the number of digits to the left of the decimal point.

    Input: 4703.62
    Output: Number of digits left of decimal: 4

    Input: 123456789.4567
    Output: Number of digits left of decimal: 9

243. Write a program that generates the Morse code for a sentence that ends with a period and contains no characters besides letters and blanks. Input the sentence and display its Morse equivalent word by word, each word on a separate line and each letter separated by a space. The Morse code is as follows:

A .-, B -..., C -.-., D -.., E ., F ..-., G --., H ...., I .., J .---,
K -.-, L .-.., M --, N -., O ---, P .--., Q --.-, R .-., S ..., T -,
U ..-, V ...-, W .--, X -..-, Y -.--, Z --..

You can assume the input will be at most 70 characters in length, ending with a period. Also output the number of dashes and the number of dots used. Punctuation will be ignored in output. Input will all be in upper case.

Input: THIS IS MY CHECK.

Output:

```
-.... .. ...
.. ...
-- -.--
-.-. .... . -.-. -.-
12 DASHES
25 DOTS
```

244. Write a program that inputs the five cards representing a poker hand into an array. Evaluate the poker hand to determine if the hand is a flush (all one suit), a straight (five consecutive cards), a straight flush (five consecutive cards of one suit), four of a kind, a full house (three of one kind, two of another), three of a kind, two pairs, or one pair.

Input:

C,3
D,4
H,10
S,8
C,5

Output: Nothing

Input: H,3
H,6
H,5
H,2
H,4

Output: A straight flush

245. You are given the X and Y coordinates of the upper left hand corner, and the lower right hand corner of each of a group of rectangles (the end of the list is flagged by four 0's). Determine whether the group is "nested." They are nested if they fit inside each other in a series (in any order). For example:

```
* * * * * * * * * * * *   * * * * * * * * * * * * * * * * * * * * *     * * * * * * * * * * * * * *
*                     *   *                                       *     *                         *
*   * * * * * * * *   *   *   * * * * *             * * * * *     *     *                 * * * * *
* *
*   *             *   *   *   *       *               *     *     *     *                 *       *
*
*   *   * * * *   *   *   *   * * * * *             * * * * *     *     *                 * * * * *
* *
*   *   *     *   *   *   *                                       *     *                         *
*   *   * * * *   *   *   * * * * * * * * * * * * * * * * * * * * *     * * * * * * * * * * * * * *
*   *             *   *                   Not nested                                    Not nested
*   * * * * * * * *   *
*                     *
* * * * * * * * * * * *
      Nested
```

EXAMPLE

Upper Left (X,Y),Lower Right (X,Y)

Input: 30,70,70,20
40,50,60,40
20,80,80,10
0,0,0,0

Output: Nested

Input: 20,80,80,10
30,70,50,20
60,40,70,30
0,0,0,0

Output: Not Nested

Input: 30,70,50,20
40,40,70,30
0,0,0,0
Output: Not Nested

246. Given an integer with a value between 0 and 255, convert it to a string of 8 bits with the high order bit first and then going down to the low order bit.
EXAMPLE
Input: Number: 30

Output: Bits: 00011110

247. Given an input decimal fraction between 0 and 1, output the number as a rational fraction in lowest terms. The number will have no more than 4 digits to the right of the decimal point, and will not be 0 or 1.
EXAMPLES
Input: .375
Output: 3/8

Input: .20
Output: 1/5

Input: .387
Output: 387/1000

Input: .774
Output: 387/500

248. Write a program to input a string of characters, at most 70 in length, containing numbers separated by a comma. You can assume that the first blank will terminate the string. The numbers can be any of the standard modes, integer or real (scientific or non-scientific) and can be either positive or negative. If the sign is missing, the number will be assumed to be positive. Your program will get each number from the

string and print one per line in the order found and will also print the sum of all numbers found. You can assume that the characteristic will be at most two digits and will be preceded by a sign.

Input: 156,18.43,-10,.145E+03

Output:
156
18.43
-10
145
SUM IS 309.43

249. Write a program to help a person reconcile his check book each month. Input to this program consists of a series of one or more lines of data with each line indicating a transaction according to the letter code in column 1:

B = beginning balance
C = check paid by bank
D = deposit to account
E = end of input
S = service charge

Lines beginning with B, D, and S have an amount, expressed in dollars and cents, appearing on the same line. Lines beginning with a C have a check number, and an amount given in dollars and cents. For output, print a neatly arranged statement indicating the beginning balance first, the total of all deposits made second, the total of all checks paid third, the total of all service charges fourth, and the ending balance fifth. The ending balance is computed by adding deposits to, and subtracting checks, and service charges from the beginning balance. Following this summary list each check paid, by number and amount, in increasing check number order. Place an asterisk after check number for which the preceding check number is missing. Assume there will not be more than 100 checks paid each month.

Input:

B		100.00
D		50.25
C	100	12.50
C	103	100.00
C	102	7.98
D		75.00
C	106	2.50
S	5.00	
E		

Output:

Beginning Balance	$ 100.00
Deposits	125.25
Checks	122.98
Service Charge	5.00
Ending Balance	$ 97.27

Checks Paid:

100	12.50
102*	7.98
103	100.00
106*	2.50

250. When the intrepid Texarkana Clone first sees towering Mount Mongo it is a mere 100 yards high. "I can easily reach the treasures that lie at the summit," he says to no one in particular, and he immediately begins to climb. The ascent is difficult, and he is without his ropes and pitons; but even so, the mighty Clone is able to climb 10 yards before nightfall.

While our hero snoozes, however, the mysterious mount grows 100 yards higher, leaving him farther from the top than he was when he began. Fortunately the growth of the mountain does not take place only at its peak; the entire mountain side stretches, bearing Clone up with it. Since the whole mountain doubles in height, so does the height of Clone's camp, and he wakes to find himself 20 yards up a 200 yard mountain.

The next day Clone climbs another 10 yards, putting him 30 yards up. But once again the mountain swells 100 yards overnight and carries Clone part of the way with it. This puts him 45 yards up a 300 yard mountain. While brewing his morning cup of mountain-grown coffee, Clone admits to himself that the climb will be more difficult than he had expected. Every day he climbs another 10 yards, and every night the mountain grows another 100 yards. How many days does it take Clone to reach the summit? How tall is the mountain when Clone reaches the summit?

Write a program which computes the answers to the two questions posed. Express your answer to the second question rounded to the nearest mile. (There are 1760 yards per mile.)

251. Write a program that will input a positive number, then output whether or not the number is perfect. A number is perfect if it is equal to the sum of its divisors, excluding itself.

Input: 4
Output: 4 is not perfect.

Input: 6
Output: 6 is perfect.
(Note: 6 is perfect since its divisors are 1, 2, 3, and 6, and 1+2+3=6)

252. Develop a program that reads text and translates it into Braille. The Braille alphabet is a system of writing for the blind; it uses patterns of raised dots in a 3 by 2 array to represent letters and digits:

a	b	c	d	e	f	g	h	i	j	k	l	m
.o	.o	..	..	.o	..	..	.o	o.	o.	.o	.o	..
oo	.o	oo	o.	o.	.o	..	..	.o	..	oo	.o	oo
oo	oo	oo	oo	oo	oo	oo	oo	oo	oo	.o	.o	.o

n	o	p	q	r	s	t	u	v	w	x	y	z
..	.o	..	..	.o	o.	o.	.o	.o	o.	..	..	.o
o.	o.	.o	..	..	.o	..	oo	.o	..	oo	o.	o.
.o	.o	.o	.o	.o	.o	.o	..	..	o.	..	..	..

```
Capital Digit
  oo    o.
  oo    o.
  o.    ..
```

(The symbol "." indicates a raised dot on the page; "o" indicates that the paper is smooth.)

The pattern capital means that the letter following is an upper-case letter. The pattern digit is an indication that the letter following should be interpreted as a digit: "a" through "i" should be interpreted as the digits 1 through 9, respectively, and "j" should be interpreted as the digit 0. Your program should write three lines of output for each line of input, using an "x" to represent a "." and a blank to represent a "o". Characters other than letters and digits should be ignored. Leave one space between adjacent letters and two spaces between adjacent words. Write a blank line between successive lines of Braille. Words should not be split onto two lines; assume an 80 character line length. Keep accepting lines of input, and outputting their corresponding Braille lines, until a line starting with "***" is input.

Input: This is a sample line of input.
***

Output:

```
    x x  x  x  x x  x  x x xx x x   x  x xx x  x   xx
  xx xxx x  x x     x        x   x x x  x  x  x  x
x x       x     x     x    x  x      x    x      x

 x xx xx x   x
x   x x     xx
  x  x  xx x
```

253. This problem requires you to write a program to determine individual and team winners in a competition. Each line of data contains an individual's name (columns 1-20), the team name he or she is associated with (columns 22-31), and the time this individual took in

the competition (in the form minutes:seconds.tenths in columns 33-39). A team is composed of four individuals; a team time is the sum of the four individuals' times. It is possible that a team may not have four members present at the competition. If there are fewer than four members then these individuals may compete for individual prizes but not for team prizes. If there are more than four members of a team present then only the first four members' times encountered in the input data are used to determine the team score. Your program should determine the first, second, and third place finishers for individual and team times. Lowest time is the winner. Output should follow the format listed in the sample below. There will be at most 20 teams in a competition; it is possible that fewer than three teams and/or individuals will compete. You may assume that there will not be any ties. Input is terminated by a line containing "END" for the individual's name, "NONE" for the team name, and 0:00.0 for the time.

Input:

```
John Doe        Engineers   1:02.5
Mary Smith      Sycamores   0:59.8
Craig Hill      Sycamores   1:01.2
Jeff Jones      Engineers   1:00.2
Jerry Grimes    Sycamores   1:01.4
Holly Bright    Sycamores   0:58.9
Greg Bell       Engineers   0:57.2
Frank Walsh     Engineers   0:59.3
END             NONE        0:00.0
```

Output:

```
INDIVIDUAL WINNERS:
1. Greg Bell       Engineers   0:57.2
2. Holly Bright    Sycamores   0:58.9
3. Frank Walsh     Engineers   0:59.3

TEAM WINNERS:
1. Engineers       3:59.2
2. Sycamores       4:01.3
```

254. A popular computer simulation problem is that of population growth and decline for predators and their prey, for example, foxes and rabbits. The fox population increases as it feeds on its food supply, rabbits,

creating a corresponding decrease in their number. If there are too many foxes, there may not be enough rabbits to go around, and the fox population will begin to decline. Write a program to simulate the daily population of foxes and rabbits. The daily changes in the fox-rabbit populations are given by the following equations:

$$f(n+1) = (1 - d(f) + p * i(f) * r(n)) * f(n)$$
$$r(n+1) = (1 + i(r) - p * f(n)) * r(n)$$

where f(n) is the number of foxes that exist on day n, r(n) the number of rabbits on day n, p is the probability that a fox will catch and eat a rabbit, d(f) is the rate of decrease in foxes if there are no rabbits available, i(r) is the rate of increase in rabbits if they are not eaten, and i(f) is the rate of increase in fox population corresponding to one rabbit being eaten.

Print the rabbit and fox population over a five-year period (1500 days). Print the values every 50 days, but be sure to update the population daily. Start with the following values:

$f(0) = 500$	$r(0) = 5000$	$d(f) = .005$
$p = .0001$	$i(f) = .01$	$i(r) = .01$

255. Write a program to simulate the operation of a furnace in a home under control of a thermostat. When the inside temperature drops 4 degrees below the current thermostat setting, t, the furnace goes on. It shuts off when the temperature is 5 degrees greater than t.

You may assume that the temperature in the house drops at a rate proportional to the difference between the inside temperature t(i) and the outside temperature t(o), if the furnace is shut off. That is, let:

$$t(d) = k(t(i) - t(o))$$

represent the temperature drop in degrees per hour. Let k = .05. If the furnace is on, the temperature increases at a rate given by:

$$t(inc) = max(6-t(d),0)$$

Print out the temperature in the house over different 24-hour periods, and the total amount of time the furnace is running for the various values t, t(o), and the initial values of t(i).

256. A forestry management team is studying the infestation of the Pine Bark beetle in the Rocky Mountains. They made a count of the number of infected trees found in a square unit of land at various altitudes and summarized their findings as shown below.

Altitude (ft.)	Number of infected trees
5000	310
5300	285
5700	202
6000	160
6500	110
7000	52
7500	8

They have theorized that the number of infected trees, t, is related to altitude, a, by the linear equation

$$t = b + m * a$$

where b and m are constants. The team would like you to write a program that will compute b and m so that the above equation best fits the experimental data in certain sense.

One way to do this is the method of least squares, which determines the values of b and m that minimize the sum of the squares of the deviations from the observed data. This can be done by solving the following system of linear equations for b and m:

A = sum of all a's
A2 = sum of all a*a's
AT = sum of all a*t's
T = sum of all t's
A*b + A2*m = AT
n*b + A*m = T

where n is the number of observed pairs of a and t.

257. Write a program that will print all prime palindromes between two given numbers. Recall that a palindrome is a number that is read the same forward and backward, and a prime has no divisors other than one and itself.

258. Write a program to simulate the game "Life" (the one invented by John Conway: Scientific American, October 1970, p.120). The game generates interesting patterns that are produced by a colony of "living organisms." Use a 30-by-30 character array that is initialized to blanks; organisms are placed in the array as the form of asterisks, or some other character. The organisms give birth to others, survive to the next generation, or die according to the following rules. Note that a neighbor is an organism on an adjacent—including the diagonal—element (each organism has at most eight neighbors).
   a. BIRTH: each empty position with exactly three organisms as neighbors gives rise to a birth in the next generation.
   b. DEATH: organisms with fewer than two neighbors die from isolation; those with four or more die from overcrowding. They are replaced by a blank space in the next generation.
   c. SURVIVAL: organisms with exactly two or three neighbors survive to the next generation.

For example:

```
1st generation    2nd generation    3rd generation
      *                ***                *
     ***               * *               * *
      *                ***              *   *
                                         * *
                                          *
```

Read in the row and column positions of a set of organisms. Print out 10 successive generations of the array to the screen but stop sooner if the array is empty (the population has died out). Use two arrays, each of the next generation of the other. In order to handle the borders in an elegant way; include a border of array elements around the array that is initialized to blanks and treated as an infertile region in which no organisms can grow. Each of the rules apply only to the current generation, and the births are not used to calculate the deaths.

259. One system used in cryptology was developed by Sir Francis Beaufort, and is referred to (not surprisingly) as the "Beaufort method." The system makes use of a key word and uses a Beaufort table, a two-dimensional array, (shown in the following).

ABCDEFGHIJKLMNOPQRSTUVWXYZA
BCDEFGHIJKLMNOPQRSTUVWXYZAB
CDEFGHIJKLMNOPQRSTUVWXYZABC
DEFGHIJKLMNOPQRSTUVWXYZABCD
EFGHIJKLMNOPQRSTUVWXYZABCDE
FGHIJKLMNOPQRSTUVWXYZABCDEF
GHIJKLMNOPQRSTUVWXYZABCDEFG
HIJKLMNOPQRSTUVWXYZABCDEFGH
IJKLMNOPQRSTUVWXYZABCDEFGHI
JKLMNOPQRSTUVWXYZABCDEFGHIJ
KLMNOPQRSTUVWXYZABCDEFGHIJK
LMNOPQRSTUVWXYZABCDEFGHIJKL
MNOPQRSTUVWXYZABCDEFGHIJKLM
NOPQRSTUVWXYZABCDEFGHIJKLMN
OPQRSTUVWXYZABCDEFGHIJKLMNO
PQRSTUVWXYZABCDEFGHIJKLMNOP
QRSTUVWXYZABCDEFGHIJKLMNOPQ
RSTUVWXYZABCDEFGHIJKLMNOPQR
STUVWXYZABCDEFGHIJKLMNOPQRS
TUVWXYZABCDEFGHIJKLMNOPQRST
UVWXYZABCDEFGHIJKLMNOPQRSTU
VWXYZABCDEFGHIJKLMNOPQRSTUV
WXYZABCDEFGHIJKLMNOPQRSTUVW
XYZABCDEFGHIJKLMNOPQRSTUVWX
YZABCDEFGHIJKLMNOPQRSTUVWXY
ZABCDEFGHIJKLMNOPQRSTUVWXYZ

In this table, the twenty-six letters of the alphabet are repeated in a pattern. The Beaufort method can best be illustrated by example. It uses a key word system together with the Beaufort table. Suppose it is desired to encrypt the word "PROGRAMMING" using the key word "HELP." To encode, start with the key letter H (at the top border) and trace downward to the test letter P, turn left and emerge at the border letter I, which is the encoded value of P using the key letter H. The results for the entire process are as follows:

key	HELP	HELP	HEL
text	PROG	RAMM	ING
encoded	INDR	KWBX	BJV

To decode (unscramble) a message, locate the key letter (in this case H) on the top border, the encoded text letter (here it is I on the left border), and find the letter at which the two lines intersect (here it is P).

Design and implement a program to encode and decode text using the Beaufort method described above.

260. You are taking a trip to Europe and are concerned about handling all those currencies, and wish to use your computer to convert the sums. Write a program that reads a value in French francs, British pounds, German marks, Italian lira, or American dollars of the user's choice and converts to another currency of the user's choice. The exchange rate is as follows:

7.2 French francs	=	1 dollar
0.64 British pounds	=	1 dollar
2.4 German marks	=	1 dollar
1439 Italian lira	=	1 dollar

Develop a code to allow the user to enter the types of currency to be converted. The output should include the amount, the type of currency entered, and the amount and the type of currency wanted.

261. The Olympics Judging Committee needs a program to calculate scores for the diving competition. The program must read a diver's name and seven scores in the range 0.0 through 10.0. The highest and lowest scores are thrown out; then the total and average of the remaining five scores are calculated. The diver's name, average, and total scores should be output. Use the following data:

Apollo Creed	7.5	5.5	6.5	6.0	5.7	6.1	8.0
Yani Petrok	3.1	4.6	3.8	5.0	4.9	4.5	3.9

Pedro Valecia	5.7	6.1	6.9	5.9	6.8	4.9	6.4
Igor Trovanski	8.0	8.2	7.0	9.1	7.5	8.3	9.2
Thomas Kerry	6.5	6.6	6.5	4.8	5.7	6.8	6.0
Gino Balducci	9.1	8.5	9.9	8.1	8.8	7.6	7.9

262. Write a program that will allow a rabbit owner to determine the number of rabbits that will be born over a given period of time. Starting with a single male and female, assume that each female rabbit will reproduce every four months and that the litters will have an average of eight rabbits. Also assume that half of the baby rabbits are female. The program should allow the user to enter a given number of months and then output the number of rabbits there will be by the end of that time period.

263. Write a program that accepts two integers indicating the maximum subscripts for a two-dimensional array. Initialize the array to blanks with an outer boundary of asterisks (*). Then read a list, one pair at a time, of coordinates indicating where a question mark (?) should be placed in the array. Check to make sure the coordinates are within the maximum boundaries of the array, printing an error message if not. The end of the coordinate list will be signaled by the sentinel value of '-1 -1.' Use prompts to enter the necessary data. The program should run as follows:
Enter the array boundaries

    10 6
    Enter a set of coordinates
    2 3
    Enter a set of coordinates
    2 4
    Enter a set of coordinates
    3 2
    Enter a set of coordinates
    3 5
    Enter a set of coordinates
    4 5
    Enter a set of coordinates
    5 4

```
Enter a set of coordinates
6 3
Enter a set of coordinates
7 3
Enter a set of coordinates
8 3
Enter a set of coordinates
9 3
Enter a set of coordinates
-1 -1
* * * * * *
*   ? ?   *
* ?     ? *
*       ? *
*     ?   *
*   ?     *
*   ?     *
*         *
*   ?     *
* * * * * *
```

264. The university postal service needs program that will keep track of the postage bill for each department, as well as the revenue earned each day by the postal service. The service charges three rates: 0.25 an ounce for first-class mail, 0.18 an ounce for second-class mail, and 0.10 an ounce for third-class mail. A menu should prompt the user to enter the name of the department and the number of pounds of mail in each class for that department. If the user enters an invalid response, he or she should be prompted to re-enter the value. Use the following data to test your program:

Department	First Class	Second Class	Third Class
Computer Science	5.6	15.7	0
Psychology	10.3	25.1	10.6
Popular Culture	0	60.1	70.1
Registrar	5.2	30.2	25.3
Bursar	20	50.5	0

The output should first list each department, the amounts (in pounds), of first-class mail, second-class mail, and third-class mail sent by that department and the amount the department owes the university postal service. Next the total pounds of first-class, second-class, and third-class mail processed and the total amount of revenue earned should be printed.

265. Given a character (A-Z or a-z) and one point, and the slope of a line, draw a straight line through the point with specified slope. Assume a vertical range of 1-20 and a horizontal range of 1-35 for the coordinates.
Example

Character: W
point: 3,3
slope: -1

Output: (Numbering around border is not required.)

```
W
 W
  W
   W
    W
     W
```

266. The board of directors at Steiner's Electronics is looking for a new location to build another factory. Thus far, the board has narrowed down the new site to two possible locations. Now the board wants to use two criteria to choose one of them. One criterion is the transportation costs of shipping the goods to retailers. The cost of shipping to a given city (per unit) is shown below.

	To Boston	To Cleveland	To Tampa	To Denver
Site 1	\$0.50	\$2.25	\$3.50	\$4.00
Site 2	\$5.00	\$4.25	\$0.50	\$2.25

The other criterion is a point rating questionnaire that employees filled out for each site. Make up your own data for each site to test your program.

Category	Blue Collar	Site #X Manager	Executive
Community atmosphere			
Recreation in community			
Parks			
Educational facilities			

The employees gave each site a rating between 0 and 100 for each of the above categories. Write a program that will compute the total transportation cost from each site for a thousand units to each destination. Then add the points for each site to get a total. The output should be similar to this:

Rating of Factory Locations

Transportation costs	$xxxx.xx	$xxxx.xx
Point Ratings:		
Community Atmosphere	xxx	xxx
Recreation	xxx	xxx
Parks	xxx	xxx
Educational Facilities	xxx	xxx
Total Points	xxxx	xxxx

Decision: Site x

If one site rates higher on both categories, then that site is chosen. However, if one site rates higher than the other site in only one criterion, some rules must be used. If transportation costs differ by $200 or more, then the less expensive site should be chosen. If transportation costs differ by less than $200, then the site with the largest number of points should be chosen.

267. Write a program to perform the following selection process.
FIND A DATE — If a person wants a date, we use his (or her) personal interests and activities to reduce the large number of potential

candidates that are kept on record. For the selection process, we shall make use of the following criteria:

A) The sex of the person looking for a date.
   Female = 1   Male = 0

B) The activities of a person in these fields
   1) Theatre, Movies, Opera   2) Sports, Dancing   3) Politics, Social events

   The existence of an interest is signaled by a 1 and no interest is a 0. Numbers appear in the input stream in the same order as appear above.

C) The minimum and maximum ages of the acceptable person(s) selected. Last value in input stream specifies age. You can use 1 to signal the end or an additional field may be used.

This data must all be available for each of the persons on record and for the person looking for a date. The following rules are used for electing a possible date. The person selected:

A) Must have a different sex.

B) Must have at least one common interest in the 1st set of B.

C) Must have at least one common interest in either 2nd or 3rd set of B.

D) Age of partner must be >= minimum and <= maximum specified.

SAMPLE DATA

19256,0,1101110,27,38
10021,1,1000101,26,   * No maximum age *
12671,0,1111111,29,
26192,0,0011010,35,
21003,1,1011111,23,
29001,0,1001110,33,
32310,0,0100011,26,
04568,1,0111001,28,
10026,1,1101011,31,
31198,0,1101110,43,
11921,0,0100100,37,1 - TRIP VALUE or may add an additional field

```
ID    S    B  AGE          with 1 for age.
NO.   E       M M
      X       I A
              N X
```

Input: 21731,1,1100101,25,35
Output: Selected partner(s) for 21731:
ID NO. SEX AGE OF PARTNER

268. Given a string consisting of A's, B's, and C's, use the following rules to create a new string of the same length. The character in position 1 of the new string will be determined by the characters in positions 1 and 2 of the old string. Likewise, the character in the last position will be determined by the characters in the next-to-last and last positions of the old string. The characters in every other position n of the new string will be determined by the characters in locations n-1, n, and n+1 of the old string. If all 3 positions in the old string contain the same letter, then put an A in position n in the new string. If 2 alike characters are represented in the 3 positions, then put a B. If all 3 characters differ, then put a C. Once you've accomplished this, treat this new string as the old string and repeat the process. Assume strings of less than 70 characters and no more than 20 repetitions.

Example

Input: String: AABBCA
Number of repetitions: 3

Output: AABBCA
ABBBCB
BBABBB
ABBBAA

269. One common problem in computer science is evaluating user entered functions. Write a program to evaluate the functions SIN, COS, and TAN. Input will be one of the following: SIN(number), COS(number), or TAN(number). Assume the input will be in all caps with no imbedded spaces. Also assume the number will be in degrees.

Example

Input: sin(30)
Output: sin(30) = .5

Input: tan(0)
Output: tan(0) = 0

270. Given a list of parents and children, your job is to find the grandparent of the list and the number of children, grandchildren, great-grandchildren, etc., the person has. The data will be one parent and one child per line and will terminate with "End Input". There will not be more than 50 people or 10 generations. If the family tree looked like this:

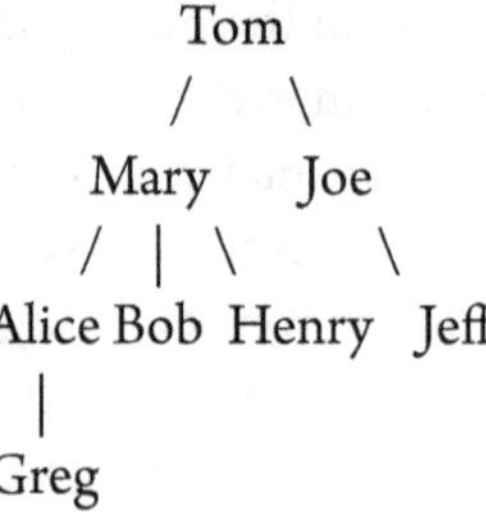

Then the input might look like this:

Tom Mary
Alice Greg
Joe Jeff
Mary Henry
Mary Bob
Mary Alice
Tom Joe
End Input

The output should look like this:

Grandparent of this tree is Tom.
There are: 2 children
4 grandchildren
1 great-grandchild

271. If you asked people at random for their birth month (the month in which they were born), how many people would you expect to ask until someone shared your birth month? For example, if you were born in January and you asked people at random for their birth month, you might get the following response:

MAR JUN APR DEC FEB NOV JAN

In this EXPERIMENT it took seven months chosen randomly until someone shared your birth month. Set up a random experiment that COUNTS how many people were asked until someone shared your birth month. Repeat this experiment 100 times and report the average count for all 100 experiments.

272. We're holding a road race on a 10 mile stretch of road. The racers start at one end, race down the 10 miles, turn around, race back 10 miles, turn around, etc. Given the distance of the particular race and the speed of a particular racer, your job is to show the racer's position RELATIVE TO THE STARTING LINE every 10 minutes. Be sure that if the finish time does not fall on an even 10 minute mark you still show the finish time and position. Give times and distances to the nearest minute and 0.01mile as shown in the example. Decimal places and colons should be aligned.

Input: Length of race (in miles)? 65
Speed of racer in (mph)? 40

Output:

Time	**Position**
:10	6.67
:20	6.67
:30	0.00
:40	6.67
:50	6.67
1:00	0.00
1:10	6.67
1:20	6.67
1:30	0.00
1:38	5.00

273. Write a program to input 25 numbers and output even numbers in one column and odd numbers in a second column. Label the output column headings as shown in the sample.

Input:
```
15
22
12
13
...
```

Output:
```
Even    Odd
22      15
12      13
...     ...
```

274. In physics, the 3 formulas relating acceleration, velocity, distance traveled, and time are: v = a*t, d = a*t*t/2, and v*v = 2*a*d where a is acceleration, v is velocity, d is distance traveled, and t is time. The input will consist of 2 of the 4 quantities for a given object, and the output will consist of the values for all 4 quantities. Assume that all units are proper without conversion. Also assume no values will be zero. A line of input shall consist of the variable name in lower case, then a space, then finally the numeric value of the variable.

Example

Input:
```
a  2
v  4
```

Output:
```
a = 2
v = 4
d = 4
t = 2:00
```

Output for time should be in hours:minutes format (rounded to the nearest minute). All others should be decimal.

275. Write a program that does addition of large numbers. The input will be two numbers on one line in character mode separated by a comma. The input line will be at most 60 characters in length. You are to add

the two numbers contained in the strings. Your output should place the longer number on top, the smaller number aligned correctly with a plus sign placed before it, followed by a line and the solution. In other words, the output should look just like a normal arithmetic problem. If both numbers have the same number of digits, either may be placed on top.

Input: 23789214513,1844765132

Output:

```
 23789214513
+1844765132
------------
 25633979645
```

Hint: Don't try to use normal integer addition. Since these integers (in most cases) will be larger than MAXINT, such an attack would be futile.

276. The Fibonacci series begins with 1, 1 and each succeeding element is the sum of the previous 2 { a(n) = a(n-1) + a(n-2) }. There are similar series that use the same principle except these series add up the previous 3, 4, 5, etc. numbers. You will be given the number of previous numbers to add and the number of numbers in the series to print. Assume the second number will be longer than the first. Start the series with ones.

Example

Input: number of previous: 4
number of numbers: 9

Output: 1,1,1,1,4,7,13,25,49

277. Count in any base up to hex (16). If the base is higher than 10, then use A, B, C, etc. The input will be the base and the number to stop the count (in base 10).

Example

Input: Base: 13
Stopping number: 30

Output: 1,2,3,4,5,6,7,8,9,A,B,C,10,11,12,13,14,15,16,17,18,19,
1A,1B,1C,20,21,22,23,24

278. Given a cube located entirely within a sphere or a sphere located entirely within a cube, your job is to find the volume of the area between the inside object and the outside object.

Example

Input: Length of side of cube: 2
Length of radius of sphere: 3

Output: Volume between 2 objects is 105.097

Input: Length of side of cube: 4
Length of radius of sphere: 2

Output: Volume between 2 objects is 30.489

279. Write a program that will input an integer N greater than or equal to 2 and less than or equal to 10. This program then will output a square whose side is of length N. Be sure that the square fits entirely on the screen. Place the area of the square in its center. Use 2 print positions for one unit; also use ' - ' for the horizontal sides and "I" for the vertical sides. Use a ' + ' for the four vertices of the square. The vertices count as a print position for both a horizontal and a vertical side.

Input: 5

Output:

```
+--------+
I        I
I        I
I        I
I   25   I
I        I
I        I
I        I
I        I
+--------+
```

280. Write a program that will take as input two numbers, a and b, and then output the solution to the equation $ax + b = 0$. Call this solution c.

The program will next find solutions to the quadratic equation:

$$a x^2 + b x + c = 0.$$

You can assume that a and b will be selected such that the quadratic equation has real solutions. Output the solutions to the quadratic as real numbers.

Input: 2,6

Output: Solution to a x + b = 0 is -3
Solutions to quadratic are 0.436492 and 3.436492

281. Write a program that will create the letter V of any even size less than or equal to 20.

Input: 6

Output:

```
*        *
 *      *
  *    *
   *  *
    **
     *
```

282. The number 1001 is a super palindrome because both it and its square, 1002001, are palindromes (a number that is the same when read forward and backward). Write a program that will find all super palindromes between two numbers a and b. You may assume that a and b are between 10 and 32,000. Print out the number and its square.

Input: 100,2000

Output:

number	square
101	10201
111	12321
121	14641
202	40804
212	44944
1001	1002001
1111	1234321

283. Write a program that lists all triplets (groups of size 3) that can be selected from a group of size N (less than or equal to 26). Use a letter of the alphabet to identify each person. Print three letters to represent each triplet and compute the total number of triplets that can be formed from a group of size N.

Note: ABC and CAB are considered to be the same triplet.

Input: Group size? 7

Output:

```
ABC ABD ABE ABF ABG ACD ACE
ACF ACG ADE ADF ADG AEF AEG
AFG BCD BCE BCF BCG BDE BDF
BDG BEF BEG BFG CDE CDF CDG
CEF CEG CFG DEF DEG DFG EFG
```

Total number of triplets: 35

284. Write a program to input a set of 25 numbers. Find and output the median and all numbers greater than the median. You need not list the numbers greater than the median in the order they were entered. In this problem, the median is the entry that would appear in the middle of a sorted list of the entries.

Input:

```
1
3
25
4
2
7
6
5
8
9
10
23
21
```

22
24
19
20
11
15
12
13
14
16
18
17

Output: The median is: 13
Entries higher than 13:
14
15
16
17
18
19
20
21
22
23
24
25

285. Write a program to input 25 numbers, then output the average of the numbers followed by all the numbers greater than the average.

Input: 25
33
20
10
...

Output: The average is: 22
Numbers greater than the average are:
25
33
. . .

286. It's a Saturday night and you're sitting at home with nothing to do, so you decide to call the 24-hour Live Psychic Party Line (nobody says anything, they just read each other's minds over the phone). The line costs $3.99 for the first minutes, $1.99 each additional minute. Minutes are counted from the first second (61 seconds would count as two minutes). Write a program to compute the minutes and total amount you owe them, having been given the time in seconds that you were on. Your output should show exactly two places to the right of the decimal.

    Example

    Input: Number of seconds: 119

    Output: Number of minutes : 2
    Charge: $5.98

287. Given a single-line English sentence, go through it finding and removing all occurrences of "A", "AN", "AND", and "THE" (case doesn't matter); and all punctuation. Print the new sentence, and the number of words in it.

    Example

    Input: Get the sword. Go North, and lance the Brain Tumor.

    Output: Get sword Go North lance Brain Tumor
    Number of words : 7

288. The Knight in chess is a special piece. The only moves it can make are in an "L" shape. That is, it can go either two spaces forward in a given direction (no diagonals are allowed) and one space to either side, or one space forward and two spaces to the side. For example, a knight could go two spaces to the left and forward one. Going one space forward and two spaces left would put you at the same place. The

"joint" of the L has to be at right angles with the first direction (i.e., you cannot go left two and right one, for example).

Write a program that determines whether or not a move to the knight is legal. Input the starting coordinates (on an 8x8 chessboard) and the destination. Then tell whether or not the move is legal. Be sure to check to make sure that the move doesn't put the piece off the board. The corners of the board are at coordinates (1,1), (8,1), (8,8), and (1,8).

Example

Input: Starting X,Y? 2,8
Ending X,Y? 3,6
Output: (2,8) to (3,6) is legal.

Input: Starting X,Y? 6,4
Ending X,Y? 4,4
Output: (6,4) to (4,4) is illegal.

Input: Starting X,Y? 2,4
Ending X,Y? 0,5
Output: (2,4) to (0,5) is illegal.

289. Input two dates, in this century, in MMDDYY format and calculate the number of days between them. The program should be able to tell which date is earlier and always report the difference as a positive number. Do not take into account leap-years. Remember: January, March, May, June, July, August, October, and December have 31 days. April, September, and November have 30 days. February has 28 days.

Example

Input: Date 1? 040172
Date 2? 040372
Output: From 4/1/1972 to 4/3/1972 is 2 days.

Example

Input: Date 1? 010185
Date 2? 122583
Output: From 12/25/1983 to 1/1/1985 is 372 days.

290. Input a series of numbers terminated by 0. Compare each number to the one after it and get the difference. Continue doing this, and compute the average absolute difference and print this out. There will be at least two input numbers before the terminating 0 (Do not include the terminating 0 in your calculations).

Example

Input:
```
? 100
? 101.5
? 105
? 103
? 98
? 115
? 118.5
? 0
```

Output: Average absolute difference: 5.416667

291. You've been hired by a major TV network to write an automatic bleeper for their TV shows. It will review the scripts, compare them to a database of forbidden words, and replace these words with <BLEEP>.

The following four words are "forbidden" words: politics, idiot, semprini and bull. Enter single sentences and then search and replace each occurrence of a forbidden word with "<BLEEP>". Print out the new sentence.

No sentence will be over 3 lines long, and all sentences will end with a period. Note that the output lines must begin only after all the input lines have been entered.

Example

Input: Smith, the village idiot, has finally admitted that the economy is in, in his words, deep semprini.

Output: Smith, the village <BLEEP>, has finally admitted that the economy is in, in his words, deep <BLEEP>.

Example

Input: The idiots put the
Politics Bull Session notice
on the wrong bulletin board.

Output: The idiots put the
<BLEEP> <BLEEP> Session notice
on the wrong bulletin board.

292. Suppose you have a house of length L and width W (see diagram). The roof on your house slopes up to the middle and reaches height H. Given those values, and given the width of each square roofing tile, compute how many tiles you would need to cover the roof completely. The tiles do not overlap. Any part of a tile that extends over the edge is broken off, and cannot be used elsewhere. For example, it would take four 2-foot square tiles to cover a 3x3 foot area (or even a 2.01 x 2.01 foot area).

Don't forget to take into account the slope of the roof and the fact that tiles may have to be broken at the peak.

Example

Input: Input house Length, Width? 10,8
Input roof Height? 3
Input tile Width? 1

Output: You will need 100 tiles.

Example

Input: Input house Length, Width? 10,8
Input roof Height? 3
Input tile Width? 3

Output: You will need 16 tiles.

```
     _______________________________
    //___/___/___/___/___/___/____/        | \
   /_/___/___/___/___/___/___/____/        |  \
  /__/___/___/___/___/___/___/____/        |H  \
 /___/___/___/___/___/___/___/____/________|_____\
|              L                  |        W      |
|                                 |               |
|                                 |               |
|                                 |               |
|                                 |               |
|                                 |               |
|_________________________________|_______________|
```

293. Input three points in (X, Y) format, then tell whether or not the three points lie on a straight line.

Example

Input:	Point 1? 0,0
	Point 2? 2,1
	Point 3? 4,2
Output:	Yes

Example

Input:	Point 1? 2,3
	Point 2? 4,5
	Point 3? 5,6
Output:	Yes

Example

Input:	Point 1? 1,4
	Point 2? 2,3
	Point 3? 5,1
Output:	No

Example

Input:	Point 1? 3,5
	Point 2? 3,5
	Point 3? 3,5
Output:	Yes

294. Given a number of students (no more than 25), the number of questions on a quiz, and the number of correct responses by each student, figure out the percentage score (rounded to the nearest %) correct for each student. After calculating the rounded percentage scores for each student, add to these scores the difference between 100 and the maximum of the original rounded scores.

Example

Input: Number of students? 5
Number of questions? 20
Enter # of correct questions per each student :
? 19
? 17
? 8
? 16
? 14

Output: Final grades:
100%
90%
45%
85%
75%

Example

Input: Number of students? 5
Number of questions? 6
Enter # of correct questions for each student:
? 1
? 2
? 5
? 4
? 3

Output: Final grades:
34%
50%
100%
84%
67%

295. Input a line of text. Rearrange the words in alphabetical order, and display the new sentence. All characters other than the alphabet are to be considered punctuation and are to be removed. Any punctuation or blank will separate words. Print the words using the same case as the input. (There will be no digit characters or apostrophes in the input).

Example

Input: Sentence to sort?
Other than that, Mrs. Lincoln, how did you like the play?

Output: did how like Lincoln Mrs. Other play than that the you

296. Input a list of numbers (allow up to 100), using -1 to terminate. Some numbers may appear more than once in the list. The program should find only the first occurrences, of unique numbers, in the list. Print out a list of all of the unique numbers in the order in which they first appear. Also, print out the sum of the unique numbers.

Example

Input:

```
Enter the numbers(-1 to end):
? 1
? 4
? 3
? 4
? 5
? 7
? 5
? 5
? 3
? 1
? -1
```

Output:

```
1
4
3
5
7
Total : 20
```

297. Input two integers of maximum length 60 digits, and add them together. Be sure to carry, if necessary. The answer should have no leading zeros.

Example

Input: 1st #?11111111111111111111110
2nd #?22222222222222222222223

Output: 33333333333333333333333

Example

Input: 1st #?99998
2nd #?25

Output: 100023

298. Given a regular polygon with N sides, calculate the size of the interior angle in degrees. N will be greater or equal to 3.

Example

Input: Number of sides : 3

Output: Interior angles are 60 degrees each.

299. One of the basic routines in graphics is learning how to draw a line. At first glance it seems quite easy. However, it can get quite complicated, as the routine has to be able to handle every possible condition. Otherwise, the line could be misplaced, inverted, or the program could simply crash.

Bearing that in mind, write a program that inputs coordinates in (X,Y) format between1-80 (X) and 1-23 (Y). Then, draw a line on the text screen between these points using the asterisk "*" as your marker. The upper left corner of the output is X=1, Y=1. X is measured across the screen to the right; Y is measured down.

Unless the line is horizontal, put one and only one "*" in each row. If the line is horizontal, however, put a "*" in each column.

The input coordinates will be integers, and will be in the specified range (1-80) and (1-23). The two points will not be at the same place.

Example

Input: Enter first point (X,Y)? 10,5
Enter second point (X,Y)? 1,1

Output:

```
*
 *
  *
   *
    *
```

Example

Input: Enter first point (X,Y)? 9,7
Enter second point (X,Y)? 21,5

Output:

```
    *
  *
*
```

Example

Input: Enter first point (X,Y)? 5,2
Enter second point (X,Y)? 12,2

Output: ********

300. Given a two-dimensional array, or matrix, find the row and the column with largest sum. Each array input line will consist of one digit numbers separated by single spaces. The height and width will be in the range 1-10. Output the row and column numbers, and the sums.

Example

Input:

```
Array size (Height,Width)? 5,4
1 3 5 7
0 8 6 4
1 0 2 9
8 4 7 5
3 8 7 3
```

Output: Row with largest sum: 4 Sum: 24
Column with largest sum: 4 Sum 28

301. Write a program to generate Mad-Libs. Have the user enter a line of text. If a certain word is to be entered later by the user, he types a slash ("/") and the type of word. Then, when the text has been entered, the screen clears and the computer prompts for any words that are needed. It then shows the text with the new words in place.

Example

Input: Sentence?
The quick, /color fox jumped over the lazy /animal.
Input a color? fuscha
Input a animal? dodo

Output: The quick, fuscha fox jumped over the lazy dodo.

302. Write a program that, given a starting point and a series of instructions follows the instructions to the ending point. The coordinates will be in X,Y format. The instructions will all be given on one line, and be in the form {Direction}{Distance}. You will have to parse the instructions and move accordingly. Note that on directions such as NE or SW, that you should move the given number of steps each way (i.e., north one and east one for NE1).

Example

Input: ENTER STARTING POINT
?
5,5
ENTER DIRECTIONS
?
N15NE1S2SW3

Output: ENDING POINT: 3,6

303. Write a program that takes a written-out number and converts it to a normal number. Hyphens and fractional notations will not be used. Numbers will not go beyond 32,000.

Example

Input: One hundred twenty three point four five

Output: 123.45

304. There is a trick in building magic squares (squares where all the numbers in the rows, columns, and diagonals add up to the same number) called the Hindu Single-Step. It works only on squares containing an odd number of rows and columns; and goes like this:

A 3x3 square (for example) always starts with 1 in the top middle, so:

x 1 x
x x x
x x x

Then one moves up one and right one, "scrolling over" if necessary:

x 1 x
3 x x
x x 2

If the block to the up-right is already occupied then just go one down and continue as normal:

x 1 5
3 4 x
x x 2

Continue in this manner until all of the squares are filled:

9 1 5
3 4 8
6 7 2

In this case, each row and column adds to: 15.

Write a program that takes as input an odd number, then makes a magic square of that dimension and outputs the square.

Example

Input: Enter size of square: 3

Output:

9 1 5
3 4 8
6 7 2

305. Bit Mapping

Bit mapping is an efficient storage technique in which a lot of information can be stored in a single byte. Say we have a byte with the bits labeled thusly:

ABCDEFGH

A = Does the person have a checking account?

B = Does the person have a savings account?

C = Does the person have a loan?

D&E = Title: 0 0: Mr.

0 1: Mrs.

1 0: Ms.

1 1: Dr.

FG&H Number of dependents (up to 7): in base 2

Number	base 2
: 0	0 0 0
:1	0 0 1
: 2	0 1 0
: 3	0 1 1
: 4	1 0 0
: 5	1 0 1
: 6	1 1 0
: 7	1 1 1

For A-C, 1 = Yes and 0 = No. Therefore, a doctor with a savings and checking account and no loans with two kids would be 11011010, or 218 in decimal.

Using the system above, write a program that inputs data about the client and prints the appropriate decimal value.

For the first three questions, the answers will be Y, y, N, or n. For the fourth, the answer will be Mr., Mrs., Ms., or Dr. only. For the last questions, the answers will be numbers in the range 0-7.

Example

Input:	Does the person have a checking account? Y Does the person have a savings account? y Does the person have a loan? N Title of address (of Mr., Mrs., Ms., or Dr.)? Dr. Number of dependents? 2
Output:	Code : 218

306. Multi-base Calculator

Create a calculator program that can perform addition in any base up to and including 10. It will input the base to work in, and the equation itself. Be sure to check the number to make certain that they are legal (that is, none of the digits may exceed or equal the base). For example, you don't want any 2's or 3's cropping up in a binary number). Then line as shown in the examples, with one space on each side of the plus, but no other spaces. Each of the numbers to be added will be positive, and no more than 20 digits long.

Example

Input: 5,1221 + 3333
Output: 10104

Example

Input: 2,1 + 111111111111111
Output: 1000000000000000

Example

Input: 7,326 + 28
Output: Illegal digits in input

307. Mountain Climbing

Suppose you're climbing Mount Bois, N feet tall. Suppose that, on a given day, you work your way X feet up the slope, and that every night melting snow and such sends you Y feet back down the slopes. Assume

X > Y. Assuming the mountain slopes uniformly at a 45-degree angle, how many days will it take you to get to the top?

Answer with a whole number of days: if you arrive anytime during the first day, answer 1 day; anytime during the second day, 2 days, etc.

Example

Input: Height of mountain: 30599
Feet climbed each day: 2000
Feet down each night: 200

Output: Number of days to reach top: 24

308. Perpetual Calendar
Write a program that, given a date in MM/DD/YYYY format, gives a full calendar for that month. Assume that 01/01/0001 (Jan 1, 1 A.D.) was a Monday, and that the current calendar system has been in effect since then with no changes. Print out the calendar as below, with the requested date highlighted by asterisks.

Remember the rules of leap years: a year is a leap year if it is divisible by four, but NOT if it's also divisible by 100, UNLESS it's also divisible by 400.

The input will be in the form MM/DD/YYYY, where MM, DD, and YYYY are decimal digits. If the date is illegal (such as 13/02/1994 or 02/30/1992), print an error message.

Month	Days
Jan.	31
Feb.	28 (29 if it's a leap year)
Mar.	31
Apr.	30
May	31
Jun.	30
Jul.	31
Aug.	31
Sep.	30
Oct.	31

Nov.	30
Dec.	31

Example

Input: input Date : 07/16/1992

Output:

S	M	T	W	T	F	S
			1	2	3	4
5	6	7	8	9	10	11
12	13	14	15	*16*	17	18
19	20	21	22	23	24	25
26	27	28	29	30	31	

309. Palindromes

Write a program that will input an integer, up to four digits in length, then create a panlindrome number from the input. A palindrome is a word or phrase that reads the same forward and backward. Examples are ATOYOTA and 12321. Any number 2 digits or more in length can be converted to a palindrome by reversing its digits and adding to the original number. This process is repeated and a palindrome will be generated.

310. Changing Length

Write a program that will calculate the new length of an object as it moves. Use the following formula.

New length = Original length*square root (1-B2), where B2 is the square of the fraction (percentage divided by 100) of the speed of light at which the object is moving. The speed will be input as a percentage of the speed of light.

Input: Original Length of Object? 10
Percent of the speed of light? 89

Output: New length = 4.559606

311. Two-Dimensional Array Sorting

Write a program that inputs 3 lines of 3 values each. Sort and output them in increasing order in a 3x3 array as shown in the examples.

The numbers in each column should be aligned. No number will be more than 2 digits long.

Example

Input:	?	7	4	1
	?	8	5	2
	?	9	6	3
Output:	1	2	3	
	4	5	6	
	7	8	9	

Input:	?	7	14	12
	?	18	9	6
	?	5	3	16
Output:	3	5	6	
	7	9	12	
	14	16	18	

312. Fibonacci Numbers

Write a program that will output F(n), the nth number in the Fibonacci sequence. The Fibonacci sequence is the set of numbers: 1, 1, 2, 3, 5, 8, 13, 21, 34, 55, etc. Where F(n) = F(n-1) + F(n-2) from F(3) on up. Take F(1) and F(2) to be 1.

Input: N? 6

Output: F(6) = 8

313. Change Machine

You have been commissioned to write the software for The Great Be-All and End-All of change machines. It can handle checks up to $32,000 and has infinite quantities of reserves. It gives change in coins ($.01, .05, .10, .25, .50) and bills ($1, 2, 5, 10, 20, 50, 100, 500). Your job is to input the amount tendered and then work out, using the denominations above, the MINIMUM bills and coins needed to provide change. (Be sure you understand the directions. The last guy they hired for this misread them and on the first test run regrettably drowned in about 3 million pennies). Do not include lines starting with zeros, like 0 $50 Bills.

Example

Input: Amount to be changed? 1234.56

Output:
2 $500 Bills
2 $100 Bills
1 $20 Bills
1 $10 Bills
2 $2 Bills
1 Half-Dollars
1 Nickels
1 Pennies

314. Data Compression

A simple algorithm for data compression is as follows: suppose you have the string "AAAABCCDDDDDDD". You want to store it in a somewhat smaller form as it seems to be quite wasteful to store 7 D's in a row. Instead, you do the following: for each unique letter, count the number of times in a row it occurs, and write that letter preceded by the number of occurrences. For example, in the string above, you get first four letter "A"'s in a row. So the first two characters in your new string would be "4A". Then you would do "1B", "2C", and so on. Note that in the case of one letter being by itself (in this case, B), what once took one letter ("B") is now taking two ("1B") to record. This is one case in which "compression" actually makes the string longer. That's why this is best suited to data lists that have a lot of repetition in them.

Write a program to input a string, compress it, and print out the compressed string, along with the lengths of the regular and compressed strings, and savings.

Example

Input: ? AAAABCCDDDDDDDDDDDD

Output:
4A1B2C12D
Original string length: 19
Compressed string length: 9
Savings: 10

315. Olympic Scorer
Write a program to score Olympic Competitions. Use the following procedures to Score the competitions.
A. Seven judges assign a score between 0.0 and 10.0 inclusive.
B. Both the high and low scores are dropped.
C. Then average the remaining scores.

Input: Judge(1)? 10
Judge(2)? 5.9
Judge(3)? 7.2
Judge(4)? 8.9
Judge(5)? 9.9
Judge(6)? 6.9
Judge(7)? 8.1

Output: Score: 8.2

316. Date Converter
Write a program that will input the date in numeric format and output it in text form. You may assume that all years are in the Twentieth Century. The year will always be given as two digits.
Input: Date? 12/10/92
Output: December 10, 1992

Input: Date? 2/5/03
Output: February 5, 1903

Input: Date? 4/12/01
Output: April 12, 1901

317. Divisible by 3?
There's a good shortcut to finding out whether or not a large number is divisible by 3. Just add the individual digits together—if the new number is divisible by 3, then so is the original number. For example, take the number 345. It adds up to 3+4+5=12. 12 is divisible by 3. If you need further proof, try the number 12, 1+2=3.

Write a program that inputs an integer and uses the above algorithm to determine whether or not the number is evenly divisible by 3. In each case, sum the digits of the input number and print out the sum. If the sum is more than one digit long, repeat the process until a one-digit result is obtained. If the result is 3, 6, or 9, the original number was divisible by 3.

Example

Input: Enter the number to check? 918

Output: Sum of digits = 18
Sum of digits = 9
918 is divisible by 3.

Input: Enter the number to check? 7313

Output: Sum of digits = 14
Sum of digits = 5
7313 is not divisible by 3.

318. Sort by 2nd digit

Write a program that inputs a group of integers of at least two digits and then sort them in ascending order by the second digit from the left. If the second digits are the same then the order of the two numbers is not important. A zero terminates the input list. Print out the new list.

Example

Input:
? 84
? 3089
? 19
? 45
? 775
? 8663
? 0

Output:
3089
84
45
8663
775
19

319. String Comparison

Write a program that inputs two sentences and compares selected segments of them to see if they are the same. You will be given the start and end of the area in the first sentence and the start of the area in the second sentence (assume the lengths are the same and each is less than 60 characters).

Example

Input: ? This is the first sentence to check.
? This, however, is the second sentence to check.
Input area to check in 1st & second sentences? 18,36,29

Output: String segments are the same.

320. Weight Conversion

Write a program that will input the weight of someone on earth and output the weight on the other eight planets in the solar system. Use the following tables for making the conversions. Earth: 1.00; Jupiter: 2.65; Mars: 0.39; Mercury: 0.38; Neptune: 1.23; Pluto: 0.05; Saturn: 1.17; Uranus: 1.05; Venus: 0.78

Example

Input: Weight? 100

Output: Jupiter: 265
Mars: 39
Mercury: 38
Neptune: 123
Pluto: 5
Saturn: 117
Uranus: 105
Venus: 78

321. Rotating the Array

Input an array of 3 lines of 3 values each. Then, rotate the entire array 90 degrees clockwise and print out the new array. Each item in the array will be a one digit number in the range 0-9, with one blank between each number, and no leading or trailing blanks.

Example

Input: ? 1 2 3
? 4 5 6
? 7 8 9

Output: 7 4 1
8 5 2
9 6 3

322. Combining Fractions

Write a program to input a fractional expression in the form of x/y (+ or -) a/b and combine the fractions, making sure to reduce where possible. Print out the result. There will be no blanks in the input expression. Blanks are allowed in the output expression, but not required.

Example

Input: ? 1/2+3/4
Output: 1/2 + 3/4 = 5/4

Input: ? 1/3+1/6
Output: 1/3 + 1/6 = 1/2

Input: ? 1/6-1/3
Output: 1/6 - 1/3 = -1 / 6

323. Bouncing Ball

Write a program that will input specified information on the bounciness of a ball and the number of bounces, then output the total number of feet traveled. Input the height the ball was dropped from, the height it bounced to on the first bounce, and the number of bounces. All distances will be feet. The ball rises to the same fraction of the height of the previous bounce each time.

Input: Height when dropped? 10
Height bounced to? 6
Number of bounces? 2

Output: The number of feet travelled is 25.6 ft.

324. Letter Count

Write a program that will input up to 4 lines of text and output the number of times each letter is used in that text. Do not output zero counts. The last input line is signaled by a period at the end.

Input: Transy is a wonderful school to attend, if you want to major in Computer Science or Mathematics.

Output: A: 7 C: 5 D: 2 E: 6 F: 2 H: 2 I: 5 J: 1 L: 2 M: 4 N: 6 O: 9 P: 1 R: 5 S: 5 T: 9 U: 3 W: 2 Y: 2

325. Palindromes

Input a number, then find and output the nearest number to it that is a palindrome. If two palindromes are equally near, either may be output as the answer. A palindrome is a number whose digits are the same forward or backward.

Example

Input: Enter Number? 117
Output Palindrome : 121

Input: Enter Number? 8
Output: Palindrome : 8

326. Equation Solver

Write a program that given an expression will evaluate the expression and output the answer. The expression will contain one operation between two numbers (with one space on each side of the operator).

Input: 456 + 123
Output: 579

Input: 121 / 11
Output: 11

Input: 324 / 18
Output: 18

Input: 25 * 7
Output: 175

Input:	426 - 897
Output:	-471

327. Sequence Analyzer

Write a program that, given an increasing sequence of numbers (terminated by -1), determines the next number in the sequence. All sequences will be increased either at a constant rate or a constantly accelerating rate. At least 3 numbers will be input before the -1.

Example

Input:	? 2 ? 4 ? 6 ? 8 ? -1
Output:	Next Number : 10

Input:	? 1 ? 2 ? 4 ? 7 ? 11 ? -1
Output:	Next Number : 16

328. Bar Charts

Write a program that, given three numbers, creates a simple bar chart on the screen. The program should scale accordingly for the numbers given. The longest bar should be 40 characters long. Make sure that the numbers entered are all positive and in the range 1-1000. Put the number at the ends of the bars as shown below.

Example

Input:	Please enter three numbers for the bar chart: ? 10, 2, 5

Output:

```
|===================================== 10
|=====================================
|======== 2
|========
|==================== 5
|====================
```

Example

Input: Please enter three numbers for the bar chart:
? 100, 200, 175

Output:

```
|==================== 100
|====================
|==================================== 200
|====================================
|=============================== 175
|===============================
```

Example

Input: Please enter three numbers for the bar chart:
? 20, 0, 10

Output: Sorry, a number is out of range.

329. Finding Numbers

Hidden in a normal line of text will be some integers. Write a program that filters the text, finds the numbers, prints them out, and also prints their sum.

Example

Input: This 1s a234 te5t.

Output: Numbers: 1, 234, 5
Total: 240

330. Factorial Calulator

Write a program to output the factorials for the integers 1 through 10. For each factorial find and output its prime factorization.

N factorial is represented as N!, and is calculated as
N*(N-1)*(N-2)*...*1.
For example, 6 factorial = 6! = 6*5*4*3*2*1 and
4 factorial = 4! = 4*3*2*1. Also output the sum of all factorials found.

331. Basic Statistics

Write a program to input a set of numbers, then find and output the mean, median and mode of the set of numbers. The input will be in character mode. Trip the input with the character string FINISHED.

332. Palindrome Testing

A palindrome is a word, phrase, or sentence that reads the same from left to right as from right to left. Two simple examples are the words: PEEP and RADAR. Blanks are ignored in considering palindromes.

Write a program that will test a string of characters for being a palindrome. The string will be a maximum of 40 characters in length — all upper case with no punctuation.

Input: MADAM IM ADAM
Output: IS A PALINDROME

Input: ABRACADABRA
Output: IS NOT A PALINDROME

333. Selecting Numbers with Particular Characteristics

Write a program to input a set of numbers, then find and print the average of a subset of the numbers. Of the numbers read, consider only those that consist of four digits, and have no zeros in the four digits. The trip number should be 0.

Input:
1245
2046
1327
48321
0

Chapter 3

BASIC Programming

Lesson 1 Getting Started 185

1.1 The Basics of BASIC 185

1.2 Program Body 187

1.3 Program Variables 187

1.4 Assignment statement 189

1.5 Data Type 190

1.6 Mathematical Operators 191

Lesson 2 Read-Data and Input Statements 195

2.1 Data read through the INPUT statement 195

2.2 Data read through a READ/DATA statement 197

Lesson 3 Loops 200

3.1 General Information on Loops 200

3.2 Relational Operators 201

3.3 The WHILE/WEND loop 202

3.4 Loops using the FOR statement 205

Lesson 4 Decision Statements 209

4.1 If statements 209

4.2 If - Then - Else statements 210

Lesson 5 Arrays and the Dim Statement 214

5.1 Array Definition 214

5.2 Array Examples 216

Lesson 6 Two-Dimensional Arrays 219

6.1 Two-Dimensional Arrays Definition 219

6.2 Two-Dimensional Array Examples 220

Lesson 7 Functions 222

7.1 BASIC Functions 222

7.2 Random number generators 223

LESSON 1

BASIC
Getting Started

1.1 THE BASICS OF BASIC

A BASIC program is composed of a sequence of statements to be executed. The last statement in a BASIC program is the END statement. The END statement is an indicator that this is the last statement in the program.

Each statement begins with a unique statement label. The label or line numbers tell the computer the order in which the statement is to be executed. (NOTE: In some versions of BASIC statements will be executed in the order listed in the program and line numbers are not essential). For example:

```
100 S = 3 + 4
110 PRINT S
```

In the above program, line 100 would be executed and then line 110. Although you may number the lines in any sequential order you wish, it is important not to count by ones. That is, do NOT number your lines 10, 11, 12, 13, etc. You may need to go back and insert another statement between line 10 and line 11 and it would be impossible to do so without renumbering. It would be better to label them 10, 15, 20, etc.

Before beginning our study of BASIC, we will examine some short programs. Don't worry about understanding the details of these programs yet; it will all be explained as we go along.

```
5   REM Sample #1
10  REM "The REM will make this a comment statement"
20  print "My first BASIC program"
30  stop
40  end
```

The first line REM of this example is called a comment line. This statement is used to tell the programmer something about the program. The compiler (a program that takes the human-oriented program BASIC and writes an equivalent machine language program – binary) will not try to translate this statement to object code (binary or computer language code). The next line, print, tells the compiler to translate this statement to object code and when executed to print all information inside the quotes to the screen. The stop statement will be translated to object code and tell the compiler to stop executing the program when the stop statement is encountered. The end statement is optional and tells the compiler that this is physically the last statement in the program. If there are no more statements in the input stream the compiler will understand that the last statement has been entered.

Consider the following program:

```
5   REM      // Sample 2
10  print "Enter two numbers"
15  input n1, n2
20  sum = n1 + n2
25  print n1, "plus ", n2, " equals ", sum
30  stop
35  end
```

Note from the above program that BASIC does not require the programmer to declare variable names before using. The compiler will take each variable as found and allocate a memory position for that variable. Most versions of BASIC will also initialize the memory position with the value of 0. When the above program is executed it will ask the operator to Enter two numbers. The operator will enter the numbers separated with a comma – such as 15, 22. The number 15 will be stored in memory position allocated for n1 and 22 will be stored in the memory position allocated for n2. Line 20 commands the computer to add the two numbers that are stored in memory positions n1 and n2 and store the result in the memory position allocated for sum. Line 25 will cause the computer to print the information stored in memory positions allocated for n1, n2 and sum. The information enclosed in quotes "plus" and "equals' will also be printed to the screen. Most input in BASIC will be from the keyboard and output will be to the screen.

1.2 Program Body

The general structure of the program body for a BASIC program normally will start with a REM statement that describes the task the program is performing and will end with an END statement. Also, some BASIC interpreters or compilers do not require the programmer to label the statements. The statements will be executed in the order they appear in the program.

Example

```
REM the following program adds 4 and 7 and prints results
s = 4 + 7
print s
end
```

1.3 Program Variables

BASIC and most other common programming languages perform their calculations by manipulating items called variables. A variable is written as a string of letters and digits that begins with a letter. A variable allows the programmer to refer to variable names rather than the actual memory address. It is the task of the compiler to equate the variable name and the actual memory position at the time the program is changed or translated from the language BASIC to machine or binary language. Some sample names for BASIC variables are:

X Y Z SUM N1 N2 KELLY rate distance Time

Variables can hold numbers or other types of data. For now we will confine our attention to variables that hold only numbers. The data stored at the address assigned to a variable can be changed as the program is executed.

100 LET S = 3 + 4
110 PRINT S

In the above example, line 100 instructs the computer to add 3 and 4 and store the result in a location called S. Line 110 instructs the computer to print the value stored in location S. S is called a numeric variable because it is used to store a number. In BASIC, the LET statement is commonly used to assign some initial data to a variable. For example,

150 LET X = 1
160 LET AMOUNT = 500
170 LET RATE = .05
180 LET TAX = AMOUNT * RATE

What value will be stored in TAX after line 180 is executed? ________

The LET statement can also be used to assign string data to a variable. String data is data consisting of a group of characters rather than a number. For example,

100 LET nam$ = "Michael Jordan"
110 LET addres$ = "Chicago, Illinois"

causes the character string Michael Jordan to be assigned to the variable named nam$. Chicago, Illinois is assigned to **address$.** All string variables must end with $.

Correct the mistakes in the following program fragment:

10 LET a = 12.7
15 LET count = 10
20 LET nam = "john"
25 PRINT nam

1.4 Assignment Statement

The assignment operator in BASIC is = . The purpose of the operator is to assign a value to a memory position.

Example

c = 7

This statement will assign the value of 7 to the memory position labeled as c.

The symbol = is called the **ASSIGNMENT OPERATOR**, and this statement is called an **ASSIGNMENT STATEMENT**. There can be spaces between the equal sign and 7. BASIC is spoken of as a free format language as blank or white spaces can be used freely (c = 7). The assignment operator has no standard pronunciation but most people pronounce it "gets the value" or "is assigned". Whatever is on the left hand side of the operator gets the value of whatever the right hand side is or calculates to be. The left hand side of the assignment statement can only be a variable name. The above changes the value of what is stored in memory for c to the value of 7.

PROBLEM: What is the output produced by the following four lines (when correctly embedded in a complete program)?

```
X = 2
Y = 3
Y = X * 7
PRINT X, Y
```

ANSWER:

The following example is a program to print the letter L in magnified form:

```
rem prints a letter in magnified form
print "        **           "
print "        **           "
print "        **           "
print "        ******       "
```

```
print "          ******          "
stop
end
```

The **rem prints a letter in magnified form** is called a comment line. The rem at the beginning of the comment is necessary. Comments of this type can be placed throughout the program.
Examples of comments are:
rem an input statement follows
input a,b
rem an output statement follows
print a,b

PROGRAM #1: Write a BASIC program that will print your name on one line and your hometown on the next line.

PROGRAM #2: Write a program that will print your initials in magnified form.

1.5 Data Type

A **DATA TYPE** is a description of a category of data. Each variable can hold only one type of data. In BASIC the main data types are numeric (integer or float) and character. Integer data types are:
38 0 1 89 3987 -12 -5

Numbers that include a fractional part, such as the ones below, are of type float or real:
2.7192 0.098 -15.8 1000053.98

Character data types are
"This_is_character_data" , "John", "grade", "SCORE"

The variable names for numeric data is the standard variable – starts with the letter a through z, other characters can be a through z or 0 thru 9 with no special characters. Some BASIC processors will allow other characters in variable names – especially the underscore "_".
The variable name for character data ends with a $.

It is perfectly acceptable to have variables of more than one type in a program as illustrated below.

rem a sample program
c = 4 + 9
n$ = "My name is ___________________"
print c
print n$
stop
end

PROBLEMS:

1. **What is the output produced by the following three lines** (when correctly embedded in a program)? The variables are of type *integer*.
   X = 2
   X = X + 1
   PRINT X

2. **What is the output produced by the following?** The variables are of type char: (Be careful on this one - it is tricky!)
   REM Example
   A$ = "B"
   B$ = "C"
   C$ = A$;
   PRINT A$, B$, C$
   STOP
   END

1.6 Mathematical Operators

The mathematical operations that are available in BASIC and their symbols are given below:

OPERATION	SYMBOL	EXAMPLE
addition	+	A + B
subtraction	-	C - 14
multiplication	*	5 * B
division	/	A / B
raise to a power	^	A ^ B

Example of operator usage:

+ addition 3.14 + 2.9 (add 3.14 and 2.9)

- subtraction S - 35 (subtract 35 from variable S)

* multiplication 4.7 * 2 (multiply 4.7 by 2)

/ division H/10 (divide variable H by 10)

^ exponentiation 2^3 (raise 2 to the 3rd power -- means multiply 2 by itself 2 times)

Sometimes a statement contains more than one of these operations to be performed.

The order in which the operations are performed is:

1. exponentiation
2. multiplication or division (whichever comes first left to right)
3. addition or subtraction (whichever comes first)

This means that
10 PRINT 2 + 3 * 5 - 4

would multiply 3 by 5 first, then the addition and subtraction are performed left to right. So the first 2 is added to 15 to get 17, then 4 is subtracted from 17. Thus 13 is printed. What would be printed for each of the following lines?
10 PRINT 4 * 7 + 6 / 3 ____________
15 PRINT 5 + 10 / 5 ______________
20 PRINT 1 + 3 ^ 2 * 2 ____________

See if you were correct by typing the above lines using the BASIC language. Before you RUN the program add one more line:
25 END

Were you correct?

You have noticed that we have used the PRINT statement to display results. The PRINT statement can also be used to direct the computer to perform arithmetic calculations. The PRINT statement can also display messages or strings consisting of letters, numbers, and/or special symbols. For example,

50 PRINT "SCORES"

will cause the computer to display on the screen whatever is between quotation marks; therefore, the above statement will cause the computer to display:

SCORES

Remember, a PRINT statement containing quotation marks will display exactly the message enclosed between quotation marks. What will the following statements print?

10 PRINT 4 * 5 ____________

20 PRINT "4 * 5" ____________

Clear your workspace by using the FILE from the menu line. To check your results, type the above two lines into a BASIC language, followed by a line containing the END statement. Did you have the right answers?

The REM statement allows you to put comments or remarks in your programs. A REM statement does not translate to object code. However, it is useful for explaining your program to somebody reading it. You can also put remarks in your programs by using a single quotation mark (') in place of the word REM. This form of remark can be placed on a line following another statement, as in

100 LET INT = PRIN * RATE 'Calculate interest

Again clear your workspace. Now enter the following program:

```
100 REM *******SAMPLE PRINT PROGRAM*******
110 PRINT "Good afternoon, human."
115 PRINT "Punch my keys to find out"
120 PRINT "what I can do."
130 END
```

Run the program.

PROGRAM #3: Write a BASIC program that will read in two integers and will then output their sum, difference, and product. Use character data to label each output.

Lesson 2

Read-Data and Input Statements

2.1 Data Read Through the INPUT Statement

There are three ways of getting data into a program (assigning values to variables). You have already used one way when you used the assignment statement. For example,

100 TEST1 = 95
105 LET GRADE$ = "A"

Statement 100 assigns the value 95 to the numeric variable TEST1, and statement 105 assigns the character A to the string variable GRADE$. Note that the keyword LET is not used in line 100. Although using LET makes your intentions clear, it is not absolutely necessary to use LET in an assignment statement.

The second way we will learn to assign values to variables is with the INPUT statement. It works in the following way:

100 INPUT "What is your name"; N$
110 PRINT "Hello there, " ; N$
120 END

Line 100 causes the message "What is your name" to be printed on the screen, if a semicolon separated "What is your name" from N$ the computer would also print a question mark. The computer then waits for someone to type in a name. As soon as the name is entered, line 100 will assign that name to the variable N$. Line 100 contains both a prompt to tell the user what to type and a variable to be assigned the data that the user types.

Clear your workspace, type in the program, and run it. When the prompt appears on the screen, type in your name, followed by the ENTER key. What is printed on the screen?

Line 100 could be replaced by the following two lines:
100 PRINT "What is your name";
105 INPUT N$

In this case, statement 100 prints the prompt—What is your name—the semicolon keeps the cursor on the same line as the prompt. The statement 105 prints a question mark and waits patiently for the user to type some data; the data will be assigned to the string variable N$.

Move the cursor and edit line 100. Change it to the PRINT statement shown above and hit ENTER. Then type line 105. Now run the program again. Notice that the two statements on lines 100 and 105 accomplished the same thing as the INPUT statement did before.

What is the advantage of using INPUT statements over LET (or assignment) statements?

Why would someone use and INPUT statement rather than an assignment statement?_______________

PROGRAM #4: Write a program that will ask a user for his/her name and age. The computer will then respond by saying, Hello, ______, You do not look _____ years old. For example, when it asks for your name if you reply Michael, and when it asks for age if you reply 35, it should respond:

Hello, Michael.
You do not look 35 years old.

The following program is used to convert feet to inches.

100 ' A SIMPLE FEET TO INCHES CONVERSION
110 INPUT "HOW MANY FEET?";FEET
120 INCHES = FEET * 12
125 PRINT FEET; "FEET = ";INCHES; "INCHES"
130 END

2.2 Data Read through a READ/DATA Statement

The third way of getting data into a program is with the READ and DATA statements. The DATA statement is used to create a list of data, with each item separated by a comma. The data list may contain numbers and/or strings. The strings do not have to be in quotation marks. For example

100 DATA Michael Jordan, 35

has two items in its data bank: the string "Michael Jordan" and the number 35. The only way of removing data from the bank is with a READ statement.

50 READ nam$
60 READ age
100 DATA Michael Jordan,35
150 PRINT nam$,age

The above program demonstrates this nicely. When the computer executes line 50 it reserves space in memory for a string variable called nam$ and looks through the program for a string value to be assigned to it. It searches for a DATA statement and checks to see if the first thing in the DATA statement is a string variable. If it is, it makes the assignment (nam$ = Michael Jordan) and removes Michael Jordan from the data bank. When line 60 is executed, the computer reserves space in memory for a numeric variable called age and again searches for a DATA statement that will have a value to be assigned to it. When it encounters the DATA statement it checks to see if the first thing on its list is a numeric variable. It is, because 35 is now the first thing on the list, so it makes the assignment (age = 35), and deletes 35 from the bank. NOTE: The DATA statement does not have to come immediately after the READ statement. It may be anywhere in the program. You may use more than one DATA statement. After all the items in one DATA list are used up, the computer will go to the next DATA list. For example, line 100 above could have been replaced by the following two lines:

```
100 DATA Michael Jordan
105 DATA 35
```

The following program uses READ/DATA statements:

```
10  READ NAM$, CITY$, STATE$
15  PRINT NAM$
20  PRINT CITY$
25  PRINT STATE$
30  DATA George Clooney
35  DATA Hollywood
40  DATA California
50  END
```

PROGRAM #5: Change the above program so that it uses only one DATA statement:

The following program, ask for a name and two test scores and then calculates and prints the name and average score.

```
10  rem program to calculate the average grade from two grades
20  print "What is your name?:"
30  input name$
40  print "What are your test scores?:"
50  input test1, test2
60  average = (test1 + test2)/2
70  print name$, "  ", average
80  stop
90  end
```

In the above example we declared name$ as a string of characters. You may have noticed that the average was printed in a rather strange way. The reason it looks like this is because we have not specified how we would like decimal numbers to be printed.

PROGRAM #6: Write a BASIC program that will ask for a name and 3 test scores, and then print the person's name and average score.

PROGRAM #7: Write a program to convert hours and minutes to minutes only. Ask the user for the number of hours and the number of minutes, and then print the answer. For example, suppose the user's response for the number of hours is 3 and for the number of minutes is 10. The following message should be printed:
3 hours and 10 minutes equals 190 minutes

The next example computes the amount of interest that you would receive if you saved $100.00 in the bank for one year at an interest rate of 12 percent per year.

```
10 rem computes interest on $100 for one year at 12%
20 principal = 100
30 interest = principal * 0.12
40 print principal, "  ", interest
50 stop
60 end
```

PROGRAM #8: Write a program that asks the user for the amount of money he/she wants to invest at a rate of 7% per year, and then prints a message proclaiming the amount of interest earned in one year. For example, if the user responded that he has 200 dollars to invest, the computer will respond:
"You will earn $14 interest at the end of one year if you invest $200 with us at 7% interest."

LESSON 3

Loops

3.1 GENERAL INFORMATION ON LOOPS

In order to convert temperature from degrees Centigrade to degrees Fahrenheit, we just multiply the Centigrade temperatures by 9/5 and then add 32. The following is an example of a simple program that converts 100 degrees Centigrade to degrees Fahrenheit.

```
10 rem program to convert Centigrade to Fahrenheit
20 c = 100
30 rem formula for Fahrenheit
40 f = (c*9)/5. + 32.
50 print c, "  ",f
60 stop
70 end
```

Notice that this program only converts one value, 100, from Centigrade to Fahrenheit. It would be more useful and interesting if the program could calculate the Fahrenheit temperature for lots of different values for Centigrade; for example 100, 110, 120 ... etc. This could be accomplished by running the program for each Centigrade value. However, the logical way this is accomplished is by using a loop. There are two kinds of loops we will learn about: the **WHILE loop**, and the **FOR loop**. Before studying the loop structures we will first learn about relational operators.

3.2 Relational Operators

Relational operators are similar to mathematical operators. Each is a binary operator – operating on two numerical values, however, the result from the operation is a logical or Boolean value – True or False. The operators that can be used in a relational expression such as a WHILE loop and later for the control IF statement are:

= **equal**
< **less than**
> **greater than**
<> **not equal**
<= **less than or equal**
>= **greater than or equal**

For example, the way to use one of these in a WHILE loop is:
while(num1 < num2)

The next section will explain more about the WHILE statement. For now just understand that the loop will only work when num1 is less than num2.

Another use of the Relational Operators is in a comparison or control statement called the IF Statement. The IF statement will compare two items using the relational operators, and if the comparison is true, the statement(s) to the right will be executed; otherwise, the statement(s) to the right will be skipped. Below is the basic usage of the IF statement.
if(num1 < num2) then print "num1 is less than num2"

    -
    -
    -

The IF statement will be further explained in Chapter 4.

3.3 The WHILE/WEND Loop

The next example uses a **WHILE** loop to continuously calculate degrees Fahrenheit for new values of C. Each time through the loop, C is being incremented by 10. Thus we will be finding degrees Fahrenheit (F) for C = 100, 110, 120, 130. When will we stop? We will arbitrarily use 200 as our stopping criterion. Every loop must have a stopping criterion; otherwise you will be stuck in something known as an infinite loop. It is like being stuck in a revolving door with no way out. The loop starts with the **WHILE** statement and ends with the **WEND** statement. If the conditional expression, in this case C<=200 is true then the statements between the while and wend are executed. The wend statement sends control to the while statement and the relational expression is tested again. As long as the expression is true the 3 statements immediately following the while will be executed. When the expression becomes false then control is passed to the first statement after wend.

```
REM While loop example
10 C = 100
20 WHILE (C <=200)
30 F = (C*9)/5. + 32.
40 PRINT C, “  ” , F
50 C = C + 10
60 WEND
70 STOP
80 END
```

Sometimes it is necessary to count how many times a loop is to be executed. The following program goes through a loop 10 times. The variable COUNT is used to keep track of how many times the loop has executed. When COUNT becomes 10, the loop is exited. For example:

```
10 REM Print the numbers 1 through 10 using a WHILE/WEND loop
20 REM loop
30 LET COUNT = 1 ‘ initializes value of COUNT to 1
40 WHILE COUNT <= 10  ‘ conditions for continuing loop
50 PRINT COUNT
```

```
60 COUNT = COUNT + 1   ' adds one more to value of COUNT
70 WEND
80 END
```

Line 40 compares the value of COUNT to 10. If COUNT is < or = 10 then statements 50 and 60 (the ones between WHILE and WEND) are executed. When the computer reaches line 70, it returns to line 40 and checks to see whether it should go through the loop again. If line 40 evaluates to false (that is, if COUNT is greater than 10) then the program goes to the statement immediately following the WEND statement. In this case, it executes line 70, the STOP statement, and stops.

PROBLEM #9: Write a program that reads a list of student names and prints the name that comes first alphabetically.

Let's solve the problem together. If you were trying to find the alphabetically first name in a long list of names without using the computer, how would you do it? You would probably read down the list of names, one at a time, and remember only the name that was alphabetically first so far. If you read a name that was alphabetically before the one you were remembering, then you would remember the new name instead.

We can use this as a model for telling the computer how to solve the problem (This is called finding an ALGORITHM for the problem. An algorithm is simply a recipe for finding the solution.) We will tell the computer to read a list of names one at a time and to save the smallest (the one that comes first in alphabetical order) name it has processed so far in the variable SMALLNAME. Since we don't know how many names will be in the list, we will use the sentinel value "DONE" (a value that tells the computer that no more values will be read), since that should not be anyone's name. A sentinel value is often used to terminate a loop, especially if the number of input values is not known in advance. An outline or algorithm for our program will look like this:

Read the first name into NAME

Initialize SMALLNAME to NAME
WHILE NAME is not equal to "DONE"
START
If NAME is less than SMALLNAME then store it in SMALLNAME
Read the next name into NAME
END

PROGRAM #10: Write a program that continually asks the user for a name until the user says "DONE" and then prints out the smallest (alphabetically first) name. For example, if the user responded with the following names:
SALLY
JOE
KENNETH
ANNE
MABEL
ZYGMUND
BOBBY
DONE

the computer would respond with
The smallest name is ANNE.

If we know the number of data items to be processed beforehand, a counter can be used to control the **WHILE** loop. For example, we could change our algorithm to:
Ask the user how many names he wants to give and store this number in NUMNAMES

Read the number of names and store as NUMNAMES
Read the first name into NAME
Initialize SMALLNAME to NAME
Initialize COUNT to 1
WHILE COUNT is less than or equal to NUMNAMES
START

Read the next name into NAME
Store the smaller of NAME and SMALLNAME in SMALLNAME
Increase COUNT by 1 (COUNT = COUNT +1)
END

PROGRAM #11: Modify PROGRAM#10 so that it asks the user beforehand for the number of names to be processed. This time, do not use "DONE."

3.4 Loops using the FOR/NEXT Statement

The FOR/NEXT loop is handy to use when we know exactly how many times we need to execute a loop. The FOR and NEXT statements are always used as a pair of statements. Suppose we know that we want to go through a loop 10 times. Using a FOR loop we can do that as illustrated by the program below:

A program to print the numbers 1 through 10

```
10 REM Print the numbers 1 through 10 using a FOR loop
30 FOR COUNT = 1 TO 10 STEP 1
40 PRINT COUNT
50 NEXT COUNT
60 STOP
70 END
```

The variable COUNT is called the running variable and takes the initial value of 1. The block of statements between FOR and NEXT is then executed and COUNT takes on the value of 2 (since the initial value was 1 and the step size of 1 is added to count) and is checked against 10. If COUNT is still less than or equal to 10 the block is executed again. This process continues until COUNT is greater than 10 and then control is transferred to the STOP statement or the statement immediately following the NEXT statement. If the STEP in the FOR statement is missing then the step size by default will be 1. It is also possible to increment N by a value other than 1, use this form:

10 FOR N = 1 TO 5 STEP 2 'Counts by 2 each time
or
10 FOR N = 5 TO 1 STEP -1 'Goes backward by 1 each time

PROGRAM #12: Using a FOR loop, write a program that prints the number 1 - 10, along with their square and cube. An example of the Output: (Format the output to get a chart like this.)

NUMBER	SQUARE	CUBE
1	1	1
2	4	8
.	.	.
.	.	.
.	.	.
10	100	1000

PROGRAM #13: Write a program that prints your name 10 times. Use a FOR loop with a counter to keep track of the number of times the loop has executed.

PROGRAM #14: Write a program to input a student's name and three test scores. Print the name and average score. Continue this process until the name "END" is encountered. Hint: use the program that you wrote for program#10 and just make a few changes to it.

PROGRAM #15: Write a program to input a student's name and score that he/she received on their recent test, then calculate and print the class average for the test. Do not use a trip value to quit the loop, but assume there are 5 students in the class.

The next program uses a WHILE loop to find and print the sum of the integers 1 through 100:

```
10 rem sum the integers 1 through 100
20 sum = 0
30 num = 1
40 while (num <= 100)
50 sum = sum + num
60 num = num + 1
```

```
70  wend
80  print "The sum of first 100 integers is  ", sum
90  stop
100 end
```

The same program could be solved using a FOR statement as follows:

```
10  rem  sum the integers 1 through 100
20  sum = 0
40  for num = 1 to 100 step 1
50  sum = sum + num
70  next num
80  print "The sum of first 100 integers is  ", sum
90  stop
100 end
```

PROGRAM #16: Change the above program so that it finds and prints the sum of the odd integers 1 through 99. (Form the sum 1 + 3 + 5 +...+99)

Pretend that you are looking for a job for the month of July. Suppose that someone offers you a job that pays one cent for the first day, two cents for the second day, four cents for the third day, eight cents for the fourth day, etc. The amount of your pay is doubling each day. Would you take this job or one that offered you $1000 per day for the entire month? Before you answer, you may want to run the following program. It determines the day in which the day's pay for the first job first exceeds $10,000.

```
10 ' DETERMINES DAY OF MONTH THAT DAY'S PAY FIRST
20 ' EXCEEDS $10,000.
25 '
30  LET DAY = 1
40  LET DAYPAY = .01
50  WHILE DAYPAY < 10000
60  DAY = DAY + 1 ' go to the next day
70  DAYPAY = DAYPAY * 2 ' double the pay
80  WEND
```

```
90  PRINT "THE DAY IN WHICH PAY FIRST EXCEEDS $10,000 IS "; DAY
99  END
100 STOP
110 END
```

PROGRAM #17: Using the above program, change it so that it prints the total salary you will receive for the month of July. Hint: there are 31 days in July and you work all 31.

Lesson 4

Decision Statements

4.1 IF Statements

One of the most used constructions in the BASIC language is the IF statement. In its simplest form, it evaluates an expression and then proceeds on the basis of the result of that comparison. For example, the following program reads in a set of scores and counts the number of students that made an A. An A is considered to be 90 or above. A score of 0 is used as a trip value.

```
90  LET ACOUNT = 0 'ACOUNT is variable for number of As
95  READ SCORE
100 WHILE SCORE > 0
120 IF (SCORE >= 90) THEN ACOUNT = ACOUNT + 1
125 READ SCORE
130 WEND
135 PRINT "THERE WERE ";ACOUNT; " As."
140 DATA 98,45,17,90,91,87,34,99,100,0
150 STOP
160 END
```

How many times will the loop be executed? __________

What will be printed? __________

If you have more than one statement to be executed when the IF expression evaluates to true, you can separate them with a colon as line 120 shows:

```
90  LET ACOUNT = 0 'ACOUNT is variable for number of As
95  LET PASS = 0 'PASS is variable for number passing
100 READ SCORE
110 WHILE (SCORE > 0)
120 IF SCORE >= 90 THEN ACOUNT = ACOUNT + 1 :PRINT "CONGRATS"
125 READ SCORE
130 WEND
135 PRINT "THERE WERE ";ACOUNT; " As."
140 DATA 98,45,17,90,91,87,34,99,100,0
150 STOP
160 END
```

4.2 IF – THEN – ELSE Statements

Whenever you want one thing done when the IF expression evaluates to true and another thing done when it evaluates to false, it is handy to use the **IF -THEN - ELSE statement.** Here is a short program that asks the user to guess the number the computer is thinking. If the digit agrees with the one the program is trying to match (which is 6 in our case), the program prints "Right. Good job." If the digit is not 6 the program prints "Sorry, wrong number."

```
5  REM GUESS DIGIT PROGRAM
10 PRINT "I AM THINKING OF A DIGIT. WHAT IS IT?"
20 INPUT X
30 IF(X = 6) THEN PRINT "RIGHT. GOOD JOB"
40 ELSE PRINT "SORRY, WRONG NUMBER."
50 STOP
60 END
```

PROGRAM #18: Put the above program in a loop so that it will continue to play the game until the person guesses the digit. Have it count the number of guesses it takes. It should print a message to the user telling how many guesses it took him/her to get the correct digit.

(Hint: a WHILE /WEND loop seems to be needed here. Don't forget a counter.)

Suppose we need a program to count the number of students who are freshmen, sophomores, juniors, and seniors and we have a total of 10 students. This program accomplishes the job using the WHILE/ WEND loop and the control statement IF/THEN.

```
10  NFROSH = 0 ' initializes number of freshmen to 0
15  NSOPH = 0 ' initializes number of sophomores to 0
20  NJR = 0 ' initializes number of juniors to 0
25  NSR = 0 ' initializes number of seniors to 0
30  COUNT = 1 ' initializes count of students to 1
32  '
40  WHILE COUNT <= 10
42  INPUT "ENTER YOUR GRADE AS EITHER 9, 10, 11 OR 12";GRADE
45  IF GRADE = 9 THEN NFROSH = NFROSH + 1:COUNT =COUNT +1
55  IF GRADE = 10 THEN NSOPH = NSOPH + 1:COUNT =COUNT + 1
65  IF GRADE = 11 THEN NJR = NJR + 1:COUNT = COUNT + 1
75  IF GRADE = 12 THEN NSR = NSR + 1:COUNT = COUNT + 1
105 WEND
110 PRINT "THERE WERE";NFROSH; "FRESHMEN."
115 PRINT "THERE WERE" ;NSOPH; "SOPHOMORES."
120 PRINT "THERE WERE" ;NJR; "JUNIORS."
125 PRINT "THERE WERE" ;NSR; "SENIORS."
130 STOP
999 END
```

Notice that only one of lines 45 - 75 will be true, so only one of them will be executed each time through the loop. If the user enters some number other than 9, 10, 11, or 12, none of the IF - THEN statements will be executed. There can be as many IF/THEN statements as you wish.

The following program solves the same problem as above using the FOR/NEXT loop and the IF/THEN control statement.

```
10  NFR = 0
20  NSO = 0
30  NJR = 0
```

```
40  NSR = 0
50  FOR COUNT = 1 TO 10 STEP 1
60  PRINT "ENTER YOUR GRADE AS EITHER 9,10,11, OR 12."
70  INPUT GRADE
80  IF GRADE = 9 THEN NFR = NFR + 1
90  IF GRADE = 10 THEN NSO = NSO + 1
100 IF GRADE = 11 THEN NJR = NJR + 1
110 IF GRADE = 12 THEN NSR = NSR + 1
130 NEXT COUNT
140 PRINT "THERE WERE", NFR, " FRESHMEN."
150 PRINT "THERE WERE", NSO, " SOPHOMORES."
160 PRINT "THERE WERE", NJR, " JUNIORS."
170 PRINT "THERE WERE ", NSR, " SENIORS"
180 STOP
190 END
```

Run the program and try it out.

In the following program a company pays every employee $5.00 per hour. This program asks for name and number of hours worked. It then calculates and prints the total wages for the week.

```
10  ' PROGRAM TO CALCULATE EMPLOYEE'S PAY GIVEN
15  ' HOURS WORKED
30  INPUT "NAME PLEASE:",NAM$
35  INPUT "HOURS WORKED:",HOURS
40  PAYDUE = HOURS * 5
50  PRINT NAM$, HOURS, PAYDUE
60  STOP
99  END
```

PROGRAM #19: Write a program that pays an employee $5.00 per hour for all hours less than or equal to 40 and pays twice that amount for all hours over 40. For example, if you worked for this company last month for 52 hours you would have receive $5.00 per hour for 40 hours ($200) plus $10.00 per hour for 12 hours ($120) for a total of $320.

The next example demonstrates the selection and printing of 2 numbers in order of magnitude. It prints the numbers on one line, in order from low to high.

```
10 ' PROGRAM TO DEMONSTRATE THE SELECTION AND
15 ' PRINTING
20 ' OF NUMBERS IN ORDER OF MAGNITUDE
25 '
30 INPUT "A = " ;A
40 INPUT "B = " ;B
50 IF A < B THEN PRINT A, B
60 ELSE PRINT B, A
90 END
```

PROGRAM #20: Write a program to input three numbers, and then print all three numbers on one line in order from low to high.

PROGRAM #21: Write a program to determine how much fine you should pay for a speeding ticket. Assume the fine is computed as follows:

Amount over limit (miles/hour)	Fine
1 - 10	$10
11 - 20	$20
21 - 30	$25
31 - 40	$40
41 or more	$60

Your program should ask for both the speed limit and the driver's speed. It should then print.

THE FINE IS $_________

LESSON 5

Arrays and the Dim Statement

5.1 ARRAY DEFINITION

Suppose we wish to process grades for several classes of students. The number of students in each class will vary, but we wish to write a program that will calculate the average grade in the class and then find the number of grades less than the average. We cannot calculate the average until all the grades for the class are read. So we must save the grades and count the ones below average after the average is calculated.

Should we save each grade in a variable of a different name? This would lead to a long repetitious program. Fortunately, BASIC makes a solution to this problem straightforward through the use of arrays. The formal definition of an array is a set of elements stored in adjacent memory position.

An array is a variable that can contain more than one value of the same mode (integer, real, character). In order for BASIC to reserve the correct amount of space in memory for the variable, we tell BASIC the number of values we want the array to contain with a DIM (dimension) statement. The DIM statement is used to declare the name of the array and to state its size. If we neglect to tell BASIC the size of an array variable before using it, BASIC will usually default to a fixed size that is dependent on the BASIC being used. For QBASIC, the default is 10.

Arrays must appear in a DIM statement before using. It is best if they appear at the very beginning of a program. You can include more than one array variable in a DIM statement. For example, you might say:

```
10  DIM A(25), B(15)
```

This statement reserves 25 memory spaces for an array named A and 15 for an array named B. The first element of the array A is referenced as A(1) and the second element as A(2), etc.

As an example of array usage in BASIC, we could write a program to input values A(1), A(2), A(3), and A(4) and then sum these values as follows:

```
10  DIM A(4)
20  INPUT "PLEASE INPUT FOUR VALUES"; A(1), A(2), A(3), A(4)
30  LET S = A(1) + A(2) + A(3) + A(4)
40  PRINT "THE SUM IS"; S
50  STOP
60  END
```

The numbers 1, 2, 3, and 4 in lines 20 and 30 are called subscripts. We read A(1) as "A sub 1". It is possible to use a variable (or numeric expression) as a subscript in BASIC. We can therefore write A(N) in a program. If N has value 2 when the statement containing A(N) is reached, the variable A(2) will be used. This makes it possible to write a program that will accept any number (finite) of values that can be input when the program is run.

Here is an improved version of the previous program, making good use of an array called A.

```
10  DIM A(4)
15  ' READ NUMBER OF GRADES TO BE PROCESSED
20  READ N
30  ' READ THE GRADES FROM DATA STATEMENT
40  LET S = 0 ' initialize sum to 0
```

```
50  FOR I = 1 TO N
60  READ A(I)
70  LET S = S + A(I)
80  NEXT I
85  ' PRINT THE SUM OF THE GRADES
90  PRINT "THE SUM IS " ;S
100 DATA 4
110 DATA 65,14,70,90
115 STOP
120 END
```

When this program is run, N is given value 4 in the READ statement. Then 65 is read into A(1), 14 into A(2), 70 into A(3), and 90 into A(4). The variable S accumulates these values and will have value 239 after the fourth pass through the loop.

The simplicity of a loop like the above, which processes N variables, is the primary reason for the widespread use of arrays. If N was made 10 in the DATA statement and we dimension the array to size 10 in the DIM statement, then 10 values could be read into A and summed by the same program. Similarly, N could be 50 or 100 using the same program if we dimension the array A appropriately. Sometimes we dimension an array to the maximum size we think we shall ever need, and then use only part of it for any particular run.

5.2 Array Examples

The following program works with an array N. It inputs a sequence of numbers into N and then sums them. These numbers were used: 1, 23, -4.5, 16, 55, -33, 39.8, 49, 100, 50. The sum is 296.3

```
5   ' PROGRAM TO PRINT THE SUM OF A NUMBER LIST
10  DIM N(10)
15  LET S = 0 ' initialize sum to 0
20  FOR I = 1 TO 10
30  READ N(I) ' read next number on list
35  PRINT N(I) ' print it
40  S = S + N(I) ' add it to the sum
```

```
45 NEXT I
60 PRINT "SUM =";S
65 DATA 1,23,-4.5,16,55,-33,39.8,49,100,50
68 STOP
70 END
```

PROGRAM #22: Write a program to read numbers into an array, print them out, and then find the average of the numbers, and print that out also. Use the data from the previous example.

The following program finds the largest element in a list of numbers, and prints its position within the array.

Numbers: 33, 4, 16, 51, 11, 22, 41, 73, 66, 1
Largest: 73
Position: 8

```
10 ' PROGRAM TO FIND THE LARGEST ELEMENT IN A
15 'LIST OF NUMBERS
20 'AND ITS POSITION WITHIN THE LIST
25 'NUMBERS ASSUMED TO BE POSITIVE
30 DIM N(10)
35 LET LN = 0 ' initialize largest number, LN, to 0
40 FOR I = 1 TO 10
50 READ N(I)
60 PRINT N(I)
70 IF (N(I) > LN) THEN LN=N(I):P=I
110NEXT I
120PRINT "LARGEST: " ;LN
130PRINT "POSITION: " ;P
140DATA 33,4,16,51,11,22,41,73,66,1
150END
```

PROGRAM #23: Write a program to print the largest and the smallest element in a list of numbers and their positions within the list.

The next (and last) example is a program that uses an array to sort a list of numbers from highest to lowest.

```
10  'A PROGRAM TO SORT A LIST OF NUMBERS IN
15  'DESCENDING ORDER
20  'READ IN THE NUMBERS
22  DIM N(10)
25  FOR I = 1 TO 10
30  READ N(I)
35  PRINT N(I)
40  NEXT I
45  LET FLAG=1
50  WHILE (FLAG=1)
55  LET FLAG = 0 'indicates no changes have been made
60  FOR I = 1 TO 9
65  IF N(I) < N(I+1) THEN S=N(I):N(I)=N(I+1):N(I+1)=S:FLAG=1
70  'If N(I) is less than N(I+1) the two are swapped.
80  'Setting flag to 1 shows a swap has been made.
95  NEXT I
100 WEND
110 PRINT "THE SORTED LIST:"
115 FOR I = 1 TO 10
120 PRINT N(I)
125 NEXT I
130 DATA 12,4,34,1,23,45,21,17,16,3
180 STOP
199 END
```

PROGRAM #24: Write a program to sort a list of names in alphabetical order.

LESSON 6

Two-Dimensional Arrays

6.1 Two-Dimensional Arrays Definition

A two-dimensional array stores values in a table format instead of in a list. The DIM statement for a two-dimensional array gives the table a variable name and states the number of rows and columns the table contains. For example,

100DIM GRADES(10,4)

The above defines a two-dimensional array called GRADES so that it contains 10 rows and 4 columns. If a teacher has 10 students and gives 4 exams, the table can be used to store exam grades. Each row corresponds to a student and each column to an exam grade.

Suppose Jeremy Adams is student 1. Jeremy's grades are 87, 75, 92, and 95. His grades can be stored in the table with the following program:

```
100 DIM GRADES(10,4)
110 READ GRADES(1,1), GRADES(1,2), GRADES(1,3), GRADES(1,4)
120 DATA 87, 75, 92, 95
130 STOP
140 END
```

A simpler way to READ Jeremy's grades is with a FOR/NEXT loop:

```
100DIM GRADES(10,4)
110FOR EXAM = 1 to 4
120READ GRADES(1,EXAM)
130NEXT EXAM
140DATA 87, 75, 92, 95
150STOP
160END
```

6.2 Two-Dimensional Array Examples

You do not have to use one FOR/NEXT loop for each of the 10 students. Instead, you can use one FOR/ NEXT loop to keep track of the rows in the table, and another FOR/NEXT loop nested inside the first to keep track of the columns. For each row we want to read four grades—one grade per column. The following program will do the trick:

```
100DIM GRADES(10,4)
110FOR STUDENT = 1 to 10 'keep track of rows
120FOR EXAM = 1 to 4 'keep track of columns
130READ GRADES(STUDENT,EXAM)
140NEXT EXAM
150NEXT STUDENT
160DATA 87, 75, 92, 95
170DATA 82, 97, 89, 91
...
250STOP
260END
```

The inner FOR/NEXT loop is executed four times for each execution of the outer loop. So the table is filled row by row.

PROGRAM #25: Complete the DATA statements for the above program and modify the program (you define the additional grades) so that after all the grades are entered into the table, the program prints all four grades of each student. The output of the program might be something like:

Student#	Grade1	Grade2	Grade3	Grade4
1	87	75	92	95
2	82	97	89	91
.				
.				
.				

The following fragment of code would calculate the average exam grade for each of the 10 students using the exam grades from the table—this segment assumes the grades have already been stored in the array GRADES:

```
300 FOR STUDENT = 1 to 10
310 SUM = 0
320 FOR EXAM = 1 to 4
330 SUM = SUM + GRADES(STUDENT,EXAM)
340 NEXT EXAM
350 AVERAGE = SUM / 4
360 PRINT STUDENT,AVERAGE
370 NEXT STUDENT
```

PROGRAM #26: Modify PROGRAM #25 so that in addition to printing the grades of each student, the program also calculates and prints the student's average.

LESSON 7

Functions

7.1 BASIC Functions

BASIC has some built-in functions (special purpose programs) that come in quite handy. For example, the function SQRT finds the square root of a number. The following program segment shows how the function is called:

```
10 print sqrt(4)
20 print sqrt(25)
30 print sqrt(81)
40 print sqrt(100)
```

This would result in the following being printed:

```
2
5
9
10
```

Most programming languages have many pre-defined or built-in functions. All of the pre-defined functions are just special purpose programs, such as the sqrt function demonstrated above. These programs were written and stored with the compiler or translator and the systems programmer, the individual that loads the compiler, has the option of loading and storing these functions with the compiler at the time the compiler is loaded onto the computer.

Other similar functions are **SIN, COS, EXP, ALOG, ABS** and others. You may want to try each of these in a manner similar to the test case above for the SQRT function. These functions are for the sine, cosine, exponential—e to a power, natural logarithm and absolute value function. A library or set of pre-defined functions is normally supplied with the compiler.

PROGRAM #27: Write a program that finds the cube of a number. For example, the cube of 5 is 125 (5*5*5) and the cube of 2 is 8 (2*2*2). Test your program by printing a table of the numbers 1 through 10 with their cubes. It should look something like this: (Remember to format the output to get the chart.)

NUMBER	**CUBE**
1	1
2	8
3	27
.	.
.	.
.	.

PROGRAM #28: Write a program that finds the power of an integer. For example the 5th power of 2 is 32, since 2 to the fifth power = 2*2*2*2*2 = 32. Test your program.

7.2 Random Number Generators

Do you recall the program that has a user try to guess a number and answers whether the user guesses correctly or not? It would be more fun to run the program if a different number was selected by the program every time it was run. In order to write a program that can select such a number, we must understand the BASIC "random number generator". As a beginning, type in the following program and run it several times.

```
10 RANDOMIZE TIMER
20 FOR I = 1 TO 5
30 PRINT RND
40 NEXT I
50 END
```

Every time the program is run you will see five different decimal fractions between 0 and 1. The RANDOMIZE TIMER statement causes the random number generator, RND, to produce a different sequence of random numbers every time the program is run. If you omit line 10, RND will always give you the same sequence. Delete line 10 by typing 10 and pressing Enter, then run the program several times.

Usually we prefer to have integers instead of decimal fractions. An integer is a counting number like 1, 2, 3, and so forth. We can get random integers in any range we like by substituting for the A and B in the following statement.

```
25 X = INT(A * RND) + B
```

Since RND returns a number between 0 and 1, multiplying A * RND results in a number between 0 and A. In other words, the resulting number will be greater than 0 but less than A. It will also be a number that has a fractional part and we want an integer. So we have the BASIC function called INT change the number to an integer by chopping off the fractional part. INT will change 4.788597 to 4 and 51.000072 to 51. Now we will have a number in the range 0 to A - 1, including 0 and A - 1.

Suppose we want random integers between 1 and 100. Then we should use the statement

```
25 X = INT(100 * RND) + 1
```

If we want random integers between 5 and 10, we should multiply RND by 10-5+1 = 6. After multiplying by 6 we will have numbers between 0 and 6, but never a number that equals 6. Therefore, when we chop off the fractional part, we will have numbers between 0 and 5.

We then should add 5 to the number to slide the range of the numbers from 0 to 5 up to 5 to 10. So we should use the statement
25 X = INT(6 * RND) + 5

Clear your workspace and type the following program.

```
10  RANDOMIZE TIMER
20  INPUT "Want to try guessing my number"; ANS$
30  WHILE ANS$ = "y" OR ANS$ = "Y"
40  NUM = INT(100 * RND) + 1
50  PRINT "My number is between 1 and 100."
60  INPUT "Your guess"; GUESS
70  WHILE GUESS < > NUM
80  INPUT "Wrong!!!! Guess again"; GUESS
90  WEND
100 PRINT "Yes!!!!!! That's it!!!!!!"
120 INPUT "Want to play again"; ANS$
130 WEND
135 STOP
140 END
```

Now run the program.

I don't think a user would want to play this game a second time, do you? It is too difficult to guess the number when the program isn't giving you any clue as to which number to try next. Suppose we change the statements inside the WHILE - WEND loop that starts on line 70 so that if GUESS is smaller than NUM, the program says "Higher..." and if GUESS is greater than NUM, the program says "Lower..."

PROGRAM #29: Make the suggested change to the above program.

Now, if you play the game well, it should take you no more than seven guesses to guess the number that the program has generated.

PROGRAM #30: Write a program that will help you practice your multiplication tables. Generate two random numbers, A and B, between 0 and 12. Ask the user (yourself, when you are running the program!) to tell you the product of A and B. Then check his/your answer and either allow the user to try again, or congratulate the user. Put the code in a loop so the user can try as many problems as he/she wants. A sample problem might look like this:

Want to do another problem? Y

7 * 9 = ? 64

Sorry, try again.

7 * 9 = ? 63

That's correct!

CHAPTER 4

FORTRAN Programming

Lesson 1 Getting Started 229

1.1 FORTRAN Basics 229
1.2 Program Body 230
1.3 Program Variables 231
1.4 Assignment Statement 232
1.5 Data Type 234
1.6 Mathematical Operators 235

Lesson 2 Strings and Formatted Output 237

2.1 String Data Type 237
2.2 Formatted Output 238

Lesson 3 Loops 240

3.1 General 240
3.2 Relational Operators 241
3.3 The WHILE loop 242
3.4 The IF/GO TO loop 244
3.5 The DO loop 246

Lesson 4 More on Control and Decision Statements 250

4.1 If statements 250

4.2 If /Then/Else statements 251

Lesson 5 Arrays 255

5.1 Array Definition 255

5.2 Examples Involving Arrays 256

5.3 Sorting Algorithm 258

Lesson 6 Functions 259

6.1 Function Definition 259

6.2 Random Number Generators 262

Lesson 1

FORTRAN
Getting Started

1.1 FORTRAN Basics

Before beginning our study of FORTRAN, we will examine two short programs. Don't worry about understanding the details of these programs yet; it will all be explained as we go along.

```
C Sample program #1
C    my first FORTRAN program
        write(6,1)
1    format('1', 'My First FORTRAN Program')
     stop
     end
```

The first two lines of this example are called comment lines; they tell the compiler that these lines are for information purposes for the programmer and will not be compiled. The next line is an output line. The line with the label of 1 is called a format statement and along with the write statement will output the message 'My First FORTRAN Program'. The 6 in the **write(6,1)** tell the computer which output device to write the information. We will in our study assume the 6 refers to the monitor screen or CRT. The 1 in the **write** statement refers to the **format** statement. This statement tells the computer how to write the line. The '1' inside the **format** statement tell the computer to start a new page (or move to the top of the next page or top of screen) and then print the line 'My First FORTRAN Program'.

Statement labels such as the 1 above are used in FORTRAN mainly for cross referencing a statement. No two statements can have the same label, and the labels do not have to be in any particular sequential order.

1.2 Program Body

The program body can begin with the variable declaration, if there are variables to declare, and ends with the **end** (physically the last statement in a program) statement. Variables are simply names of memory position. The programmer assigns the variable names and can refer to the names rather than having to give the physical address in core of where the information is stored or is to be stored. The **write** and **stop** statements are the only executable statements in the example above. The stop statement tells the computer to stop execution the program. A FORTRAN program must contain at least one stop statements but can contain many. Executable statements are translated to object (binary code) before the program can be executed.

Execute the above program. After being successful with this program, save the program, and add another line to print this is fun. If all did not go well, REVISE the file and make any necessary changes.

Look at the following program:

```
C Sample program #2
      integer n1, n2, sum
      write(6,1)
1     format('Enter two numbers: ')
      read(5,2) n1,n2
2     format(i5,i5)
      sum = n1 + n1
      write(6,3) n1,n2,sum
3     format(1x, i5, 'plus', i5, 'equals', i8)
      stop
      end
```

1.3 Program Variables

FORTRAN and most other programming languages perform their calculations by manipulating things called **VARIABLES.** In a FORTRAN program a variable is written as a string of letters and digits that begins with a letter. Some sample names for FORTRAN variables are:
X, Y, Z, SUM, N1, N2, SALLY, RATE, DISTANCE, TIME

Variable names in FORTRAN, like most translating languages (languages that must first be converted to binary or object code before execution), will start with the character 'a' thru 'z', contain at most 8 characters, and contains no special characters. Special characters are characters other than 'a' thru 'z' or 0 thru 9. Some FORTRAN compilers will allow the character underscore (_) at positions other than the first.

FORTRAN variables are things that can hold numbers or other types of data. For now we will confine our attention to variables that hold only numbers. In FORTRAN, variables can be *declared* before they are used in the body of a program but this is not necessary. The **variables** can be declared at the beginning of the program, however, without declaring at the beginning of the program FORTRAN will consider variables starting with the character i,j,k,l,m,n as integer variable names and all others as float. If declared at the beginning of the program each declaration contains the type of the variable, followed by the variable name. All three variables in this **sample#2** program are integers. (A variable of type **INTEGER** can store whole numbers only.) If we want to allow decimals, we declare the numbers to be of type **real**. (Real or float variables contain decimal points.)

The first write statement in sample#2 program causes the following phrase to appear on the screen:
Enter two numbers

Suppose that in response to this, an obedient user enters two numbers on the keyboard, say 4, followed by 5, followed by pressing the

RETURN or ENTER key. The format statement for the **read(5,2) n1,n2** statement tells the programmer that each number will be entered in a **five column field.** The 'i' inside the format is used for integer data. For integers, numbers without decimals, the numbers must be right justified in the field. A proper input would appear as follows
____4____5

The next statement, called an INPUT statement, read(5,2) n1, n2 will read the input and the number 4 will be stored in variable n1 and 5 will be stored in n2. The number 5 in the **read(5,2)** refers to the physical device number; the 5 for most FORTRAN compilers refers to the keyboard and the 2 refers to a specification statement or format statement. The format statement will tell the computer how the data will appear on the line of input.

1.4 Assignment Statement

The next statement in our sample#2 program is:
sum = n1 + n2

The symbolism = is called the **ASSIGNMENT OPERATOR**, and this statement is called an **ASSIGNMENT STATEMENT**. There can be spaces between the equal sign and n1; FORTRAN is spoken of as a free format language and white spaces will be ignored. The assignment operator has no standard pronunciation but most people pronounce it *gets the value* or *is assigned*. Whatever is on the left hand side of the operator gets the value of whatever is on the right hand side. This changes the value of **sum** to the value of **n1** plus the value of **n2**. Finally, the **write(6,3)** statement, which is the OUTPUT statement, produces the output. The 6 in the output statement refers to the screen or CRT. The format statement:
3 format(1x, i5, ' plus ', i5, ' equals ', i8)

will generate the following to the CRT

____4 plus ____5 equals ________9

Enter and run the above program. Use the same procedure as before.

PROBLEM: What is the output produced by the following four lines (when correctly embedded in a complete program)? The variables are of type integer:

```
      integer x,y
      x = 2
      y = 3
      y = x * 7
      write(6,7) x,y
7     format(1x, i5,i5)
      stop
      end
```

ANSWER: ____________

PROGRAM #1: Write a FORTRAN program that will print your name on one line and your home town on the next line.

The following example is a program to print the letter L in magnified form:

```
C     Program start
C     prints a letter in magnified form
C
1     format(' ** ')
2     format(' ** ')
3     format(' ** ')
4     format(' ****** ')
5     format(' ****** ')
      write(6,1)
      write(6,2)
      write(6,3)
      write(6,4)
      write(6,5)
      stop
      end
```

PROGRAM #2: Write a program that will print your initials in magnified form.

1.5 Data Type

A DATA TYPE is a description of a category of data. Each variable can hold only one type of data. In our sample program all variables were of type *integer*. That means that their values must be a whole number such as:
38 0 1 89 3987 -12 -5

Numbers that include a fractional part, such as the ones below, are of type float or real:
2.7192 0.098 -15.8 1000053.98

The format specification for real numbers is f. A field is specified as follows f12.4. The f is used for real data and the 12 specifies the width of the field and 4 is used to specify that 4 places to the right of the decimal is desired. The number 12356.234 could be specified as follows:

f9.3 specifies a real field of 9 column with 3 places to the right of the decimal.

The *type* used for letters, or, more generally, any single symbol is **character.** Variables of this type are declared as follows:
character*1 x, y

A variable of type *character* can hold any character on the input keyboard. So, for example, **x and y** could hold any of the characters A, a, +, or 6.

It is perfectly acceptable to have variables of more than one type in a program. In such cases they are all declared at once following the format illustrated below:

```
C   different types or modes of data
    integer n1
    real time
    character initial
```

1.6 Mathematical Operators

The mathematical operations that are available in FORTRAN and their symbols are given below:

OPERATION	SYMBOL	EXAMPLE
addition	+	**A + B**
subtraction	-	**C - 14**
multiplication	*	**5 * B**
division	/	**A / B**
raise to a power	**	**A ** B**

Suppose memory positions A, B, and C have been declared as type integer and position A has the number 5 stored and position B has the number 12 stored. The statement used to add the two numbers and store their sum, 17, in memory position C would be

C = A + B

More complex mathematical expression could look as follows:

C = A / B + (3.6 + A * B) – B / 17.4

Mathematical operations are performed from left to right with division (/), and multiplication (*) taking precedence over addition (+), and subtraction (-). Grouping symbols can also be used to control the order of operations.

Consider the statement:

C = 3 + 8 / 2 – 5

The operation 8 / 2 would be performed first, giving 4, this 4 would then be added to 3 giving 7, and 5 would be subtracted from 7 giving 2.

In the statement C = (4 + 6) * 5 / 10; the 4 would be added to 6, giving 10, and then the 10 would be multiplied by 5, giving 50, and the 50 would be divided by 10 giving 5 which would be stored in memory position C.

PROBLEMS:

1. What is the output produced by the following four lines when correctly embedded in a program? The variable x is of type integer.

```
   x = 2
   x = x + 1
   write(6,4)x
4  format(1x, i5)
```

2. What is the output produced by the following? The variables are of type character (careful on this one – it could be tricky!)

```
   a = 'B'
   b = 'C'
   c = a
   write(6,7) a,b,c
7  format('1', 1x, a1, 1x, a1, 1x, a1)
   stop
   end
```

The '1' at the beginning of the format tell the computer to skip to the top of a new page or screen before printing the output. The '1x' in the format is used to skip one space between output items.

PROGRAM #3: Write a FORTRAN program that will read in two integers and will then output their sum, difference, and product.

Lesson 2

Strings and Formatted Output

2.1 String Data Type

Often we would like to store a whole word or combination of words in a variable rather than just a character. To do this in FORTRAN it is specified as follows:
Character *60 name

If we declare 'name' in this manner then it can store as much as 60 characters. The format specification for character data is 'a'. FORTRAN will let us work with character strings as follows.

```
c example using character data
      character*60 name
      integer test1, test2
      real average
      write(6,1)
1     format('What is your name?:')
      read(5,2) name
2     format(a)
      write(6,3)
3     format(1x, 'What are your test scores?:')
      read(5,4) test1,test2
4     format(2i5)
```

```
      average = (test1 + test2)/2
      write(6,5)name, average
 5    format(1x, a, 2x, f 8.2)
      stop
      end
```

In the above example we declared 'name' to be 60 characters in length. However, we could declare it to be of almost any length, for example, 25. The string type or array of characters will make more sense when we study arrays later on.

PROGRAM #4: Write a FORTRAN program that will ask for a name and 3 test scores and will print the person's name and average of the 3 scores.

PROGRAM #5: Write a program that will ask for a person's name and age and then respond with the statement:
"Hello, ______________. You do not look ___________ years old."

2.2 Formatted Output

Output can be formatted with the format statement. For example:

```
      write(6,2) a,b
 2    format(i10, i20)
```

The statement above allows 10 spaces for the value of 'a' and 20 spaces for the value of 'b'. Check out the following example:

```
C a program to convert feet to inches
      real feet,inches
      write(6,3)
 3    format('Enter number of feet:')
      read(5,1)feet
 1    format(f10.2)
      inches = feet * 12.0
      write(6,4) feet, inches
 4    format(f10.2, ' feet equal ', f12.4, ' inches')
```

The format for output allows 10 spaces for the value of feet, and there will be 2 digits after the decimal point. There are 12 total spaces for the value of inches, with 4 digits after the decimal point.

PROGRAM #6: Write a program to convert hours and minutes to minutes only. Ask the user for the number of hours and the number of minutes, and then print the answer. For example, suppose the user's response for the number of hours is 3 and for the number of minutes is 10. The following message should be printed:
3 hours and 10 minutes equals 190 minutes

The next example computes the amount of interest that you would receive if you saved $100.00 in the bank for one year at an interest rate of 12 percent per year.

```
C computes interest on $100 for one year at 12%
C
      real principl
      real interest
      principl = 100
      interest = principl * 0.12
      write(6,2) principl, interest
 2    format(f10.2,f10.2)
      stop
      end
```

PROGRAM #7: Write a program that asks the user for the amount of money he/she wants to invest at a rate of 7% per year and then prints a message proclaiming the amount of interest earned in one year. For example, if the user responded that he has 200 dollars to invest, the computer will respond:
"You will earn $14 interest at the end of one year if you invest with us."

LESSON 3

Loops

3.1 GENERAL

In order to convert temperature from degrees Centigrade to degrees Fahrenheit, we just multiply the Centigrade temperatures by 9/5 and then add 32. The following is an example of a simple program that converts 100 degrees Centigrade to degrees Fahrenheit.

```
C Centigrade to Fahrenheit
C
      integer c
      real f
      c = 100
C     formula for Fahrenheit from Centigrade
      f = (c*9)/5. + 32.
      write(6,2) c,f
2     format(i10, f10.2)
      stop
      end
```

Notice that this program only converts one value, 100, from Centigrade to Fahrenheit. It would be more useful and interesting to calculate the Fahrenheit temperature for lots of different values for Centigrade; for example 100, 110, 120, ... etc. This is accomplished by using a loop.

There are three kinds of loops we learn about: the **WHILE** loop, **DO** loop and the loop built with an **IF** and **GO TO**.

3.2 Relational Operators

The operators that can be used in a relational expression to assist in building a WHILE loop, or the control statement IF are:

.EQ. **equal**
.LT. **less than**
.GT. **greater than**
.NE. **not equal**
.LE. **less than or equal**
.GE. **greater than or equal**

For example, the way to use one of these in a WHILE loop is:
while(num1 .lt. num2)

Don't worry too much about understanding the **WHILE** statement now, that will be explained in the next section. Just understand that the loop will only work when num1 is less than num2. If num1 is less than num2 then the expression (num1.lt.num2) will be true.

Another use of the Relational Operators is in a comparison statement called the **IF** statement. The IF statement will compare two items using the Relational Operators, and if the comparison is true, the commands following the IF statement will be executed; otherwise, those commands will be skipped. Below is the basic usage of the IF statement.

```
   if(num1 .lt. num2) write(6,2)
2  format('num1 is less than num2')
```

The **IF** statement will be further explained in Chapter 4.

3.3 The WHILE Loop

The next example uses a **WHILE** loop to continuously calculate degrees Fahrenheit for new values of C. Each time through the loop, C is being incremented by 10. Thus we will be finding degrees Fahrenheit (F) for C = 100, 110, 120, 130,.., etc. When will we stop? How about stopping when C is 200? We will use this as our stopping criterion. Every loop must have a **stopping criterion**; otherwise you will be stuck in something known as an infinite loop. It is like being stuck in a revolving door with no way out. The following program demonstrates the use of the **WHILE** loop.

C program to demonstrate WHILE loop

```
C
      integer c
      real f
      c = 100
      while (c .lt. 200)
          f = (c*9)/5. + 32.
          write(6,2) c,f
2         format(i10, f10.2)
          c = c + 10
      endwhile
      stop
      end
```

In the line containing the WHILE statement, the value of c is compared to 200. If c is less than 200 the loop is executed. If c is equal to 200 the entire WHILE loop (the four statements between the while and endwhile) is skipped and the stop statement is executed.

PROBLEM: Write a program that reads a list of student names and prints the name that comes first alphabetically.

Let's solve the problem together. If you were trying to find the alphabetically first name in a long list of names *without* using the computer, how would you do it? You would probably read down the list of names, one at a time, and remember only the name that was alphabetically first so far. If you read a name that was alphabetically before the one you were remembering, then you would remember the new name instead.

We can use this as a model for telling the computer how to solve this problem (This is called finding an ALGORITHM for the problem. An **algorithm** is simply a recipe for finding the solution.) We will tell the computer to read a single name at a time and to save the *smallest* name it has processed so far in the variable **SMALLNAME.** Since we don't know how many names will be on the list, we will use the sentinel value 'DONE', since that should not be anyone's name. The sentinel value is used to exit us from the WHILE loop. An outline of our program will look like this:

Read the first name into NAME
Initialize SMALLNAME to NAME
WHILE NAME is not equal to 'DONE'
{
If NAME is less than SMALLNAME then store it in SMALLNAME
Read the next name into NAME
}

PROGRAM #8: Write a program that continually asks the user for a name until the user says 'DONE' and then prints out the smallest (alphabetically first) name. For example, if the user responded with the following names:

SALLY
JOE
KENNETH
ANNE
MABEL
ZYGMUND
BOBBY
DONE

then the computer would respond with
The smallest name is ANNE.

IF we know the number of data items to be processed beforehand, a counter can be used to control the **WHILE** loop. For example, we could change our algorithm to:

Ask the user how many names he wants to process – call this number NUMNAMES.
Read the first name into NAME
Initialize SMALLNAME to NAME
Initialize COUNT to 1
WHILE COUNT is less than or equal to NUMNAMES
{
Read the next name into NAME
Store the smaller of NAME and SMALLNAME in SMALLNAME
Increase COUNT by 1 (COUNT = COUNT +1)
}

PROGRAM #9: Modify PROG8 so that it asks the user beforehand for the number of names to be processed. This time, do not use 'DONE.'

3.4 The IF/GO TO Loop

The **IF/GO TO** loop works much the same way as the WHILE loop and a check can be made at the top of the loop or at the bottom of the loop to determine if more repetitions are needed. For example:

```
C IF/GO TO loop
      integer c
      real f
      c = 100
1     f= (c*9)/5. + 32.
      write(6,2) c, f
2     format(5x, i10, 5x, f10.2)
      c = c + 10
      if(c.lt.200) go to 1
      stop
      end
```

The **IF** statement is a conditional transfer of control statement. If the relational expression enclosed within the IF statement is true then the statement to the right of the IF is executed. Otherwise, the statement to the right is skipped and the statement under the IF is executed. The **GO TO 1** statement transfers control immediately to the statement with label 1 with no questions asked.

The following program inputs a student's name and two scores, then finds the average of the two scores, and prints the name and average score. The process is continued until the average of the scores is 0.0. The 0.0 is used as the sentinel value - a condition to terminate the loop.

```
C Program to print student name and average score
     character*60 name
     int score1, score2
     real average
1    write(6,2)
2    format(1x, 'What is your name?')
     read(5,4) name
4    format(1x, a60)
     write(6,5)
5    format(1x, 'Input your two scores, using the 2 I5 spacing.')
     read(5,7) score1,score2
7    format(i5,i5)
     average = (score1+score2)/2.0
     write(6,10) name, average
10   format(1x, a, 5x, f10.2)
     if(average .ne. 0.0) go to 1
     stop
     end
```

C Program to print student name and average score without printing the trip score.

```
     character*60 name
     int score1, score2
     real average
1    write(6,2)
2    format(1x, 'What is your name?')
```

```
      read(5,4) name
 4    format(a60)
      write(6,5)
 5    format(1x, 'Input your two scores.')
      read(5,7) score1,score2
 7    format(i5,i5)
      average = (score1+score2)/2.0
        if(average.eq.0.0)go to 22
      write(6,10) name, average
10    format(1x, a, 5x, f10.2)
      go to 1
22    stop
      end
```

Run the two programs with the following data:
Bonnie, 90,85
Elizabeth, 80,90
Beverly, 85,92
Dawn, 95,98
THATSALL, 0,0

3.5 The DO Loop

The DO loop is handy to use when we know exactly how many times we need to execute a loop. Suppose we wanted to go through the loop 5 times. Using a DO loop we can do that:

C Program demonstrating the DO loop

```
      integer count
      real number
C
      do 7 count=1, 5, 1
      write(6,2)
  2   format(1x, 'Give me a number, please.')
      read(5,4) number
  4   format(i5)
      write(6,6) number
```

```
  6 format(1x, 'Your number is:', i8)
    write(6,8)
  8 format(2x, 'Thank you for the numbers.')
  7 continue
C
    stop
    end
```

The variable COUNT is called the running variable and takes the initial value of 1. The block of statements which terminates with the CONTINUE statement is then executed. Control is passed back to the - do 7 Count = 1, 5, 1 - and COUNT is incremented by 1, and count takes on the value of 2 and is checked against 5. If COUNT is still less than or equal to 5 the block is executed again. This process continues until COUNT is greater than 5 and then control is transferred to the statement immediately following the statement with label 7—in this case the CONTINUE statement.

The CONTINUE statement is a place holder statement and in the example above is used to indicate the end of the block for the DO statement. Any executable, non-transfer of control statement can be used to end the DO loop.

PROGRAM #10: Write a program that prints your name 10 times. Use a DO loop with a counter to keep track of the number of times the loop has executed.

PROGRAM #11: Write another program to input a student's name and three test scores. Print the name and average score. Continue this process until the name 'END' is encountered. Hint: use the program that you wrote for program10 and just make a few changes to it.

PROGRAM #12: Write a program to input students' names and the score they received on their recent test, then calculate and print the class average for the test. Do not use a trip value to quit the loop, but assume there are 10 students in the class.

The next program finds and prints the sum of the integers 1 through 100:

C Program to find the sum of the integers 1 through 100

```
C
      integer sum, num
      sum = 0
      num = 1
      while (num .le. 100)
         sum = sum + num
         num = num + 1
      endwhile
      write(6,4) sum
4     format(2x, ' The sum of first 100 integers is: ', i8)
      stop
      end
```

The same program but using the DO loop rather than the WHILE loop.

C Program to find the sum of the integers 1 through 100

```
C
      integer sum, num
      sum = 0
      do 7 num = 1,100,1
         sum = sum + num
7     continue
      write(6,4) sum
4     format(2x, ' The sum of first 100 integers is: ', i8)
      stop
      end
```

PROGRAM #13: Change the above program so that it finds and prints the sum of the odd integers 1 through 99. (Form the sum 1 + 3 + 5 + ...+99)

Pretend that you are looking for a job for the month of July. Suppose that someone offers you a job that pays one cent for the first day, two cents for the second day, four cents for the third day, eight cents for the fourth day, etc. The amount of your pay is doubling each day. Would you take this job or one that offered you $1000 per day for the entire month? Before you answer, you may want to run the following program. It determines the day in which the day's pay for the first job exceeds $10,000. Assume that you work 30 of the 31 days for July.

```
C doubling pay each day
C
      integer day
      real daypay
      day = 1
      daypay = 0.01
      while (daypay .lt. 10000)
         day = day + 1
         daypay = daypay * 2
      endwhile
      write(6,2) day
2     format(1x, 'The day in which pay first exceeds $10,000 is:', i10)
      stop
      end
```

PROGRAM #14: Using the above program, change it so that it prints the total salary you will receive for the month of July. Again use the 30 workdays in July.

Lesson 4

More on Control and Decision Statements

4.1 IF Statements

One of the most used statements for control and decision in the FORTRAN language is the IF statement. In its simplest form, it evaluates an expression and then proceeds on the basis of the result of that comparison. For example, the following program reads in a set of scores and counts the number of students that made an A. An A is considered to be 90 or above. A sentinel value of 0 is used. This signals that no more data will follow and normally this is not a good data value—one to be included.

```
C Program to count number of A's
C
      integer account
      account = 0
      while
         read(5,1) score
         if(score . eq. 0) go to 7
1        format(i5)
         if (score .ge. 90) account = account + 1
      endwhile
7     write(6,4) account
4     format(1x, 'There were', 2x, i5, ' A scores. ')
```

```
      stop
      end
```

Use the following as input: 98 45 17 90 91 87 34 99 100 0

How many times will the loop be executed?

What will be printed?

If you have more than one statement to be executed and the IF expression evaluates to true, you can use the unconditional GO TO statement to designate the block to be executed.

4.2 IF/THEN/ELSE Statements

Whenever you want one thing done when the IF expression evaluates to true and another thing done when it evaluates to false, it is handy to use the **IF/THEN/ELSE** statement. Here is a short program that asks the user to guess the number the computer is thinking of. If the digit agrees with the one the program is trying to match (which is 6 in our case), the program prints "Right. Good job." If the digit is not 6 the program prints "Sorry, wrong number."

C program to illustrate the IF/THEN/ELSE statement

```
C
      integer x
      write(6,2)
2     format(1x, 'I am thinking of a digit. What is it?')
      read(5,1)x
1     format(i5)
      if (x .eq. 6) then
        write(6,3)
3     format(1x, 'Right. Good job.')
      else
        write(6,4)
4     format(1x, 'Sorry, wrong number.')
      endif
```

```
      stop
      end
```

Note that the IF/THEN/ELSE statement by itself does not form a loop.

PROGRAM #15: Put the above program in a loop so that it will continue to play the game until the person guesses the digit. Have it count the number of guesses it takes. It should print a message to the user telling how many guesses it took him/her to get the correct digit. Suppose we need a program to count the number of students who are freshmen, sophomores, juniors, and seniors in a class of 10 students. This program accomplishes that by combining IF/THEN/ELSE statements.

```
C count number of students in each class
C
      integer nfr,nso,njr,nsr,grade,count
      nfr = 0
      nso = 0
      njr = 0
      nsr = 0
      do 7 count = 1, 10, 1
        write(6,1)
1       format(1x, 'Enter your grade as either 9,10,11,or 12.')
        read(5,2)grade
2       format(i5)
        if (grade.eq.9) then
          nfr = nfr + 1
        else
        if (grade.eq.10) then
          nso = nso + 1
        endif
        if (grade.eq.11) then
          njr = njr + 1
        else
          if (grade.eq.12) then
          nsr = nsr + 1
```

```
      endif
7     continue
      write(6,10)nfr
10    format(1x, 'Number of freshmen.', i5)
      write(6,12)nso
12    format(1x, 'Number of sophomores.', i5)
      write(6,14)njr
14    format(1x, 'Number of juniors.', i5)
      write(6,16)nsr
16    format(1x, 'Number of seniors.', i5)
      stop
      end
```

Run the program and try it out.

In the following program a company pays every employee $5.00 per hour. This program asks for employee name and number of hours worked. It then calculates and prints the total wages for the week.

```
C Program to calculate the pay due an employee
C
      real hours, paydue
      character name(30)
      write(6,2)
2     format(1x, 'enter your name: ')
      read(5,1) name
1     format(a)
      write(6,3)
3     format(1x, 'enter hours worked:')
      read(5,5)hours
5     format(f5.2)
      paydue = hours * 5.00
      write(6,8) name, hours, paydue
8     format(1x, 'name: ', a, 3x, 'hours worked:', f7.2 , 3x, 'pay due', f8.2)
      stop
      End
```

PROGRAM #16: Write a program that pays an employee $5.00 per hour for all hours less than or equal to 40 and pays twice that amount for all hours over 40. For example, if you worked for this company last month for 52 hours you would receive $5.00 per hour for 40 hours (200 dollars) plus $10.00 per hour for 12 hours (120 dollars) for a total of 320 dollars.

PROGRAM #17: Write a program to determine how much fine you should pay for a speeding ticket. Assume the fine is computed as follows:

Amount over limit (miles/hour)	Fine
1 - 10	$10
2 - 20	$20
3 - 30	$25
4 - 40	$40
5 - >40	$60

Your program should ask for the speed limit and the driver's speed. It should then print

THE FINE IS $_________

PROGRAM #18: Using a DO loop, write a program that prints the number 1 - 10, along with their square and cube. An example of the Output: (Format the output to get a chart like this.)

NUMBER	SQUARE	CUBE
1	1	1
2	4	8
...		
...		
...		
10	100	1000

LESSON 5

Arrays

5.1 Array Definition

Suppose we wish to process grades for several classes of students. The number of students in each class will vary, but we wish to write a program that will calculate the average grade and then find the number of grades less than the average grade in the class. We cannot calculate the average until all the grades for the class have been entered. So we must save the grades and count the ones below average after the average is calculated.

Should we save each grade in a variable of different name? This would lead to a long repetitious program. Fortunately, FORTRAN lets us solve the problem in a very nice way using **ARRAYS**. An **ARRAY** is a data structure used for storing a collection of data items that are all of the same type. Usually, we first describe the structure of an array in an *array type declaration*. The array GRADE of 20 elements is declared as:
real GRADE(20) or dimension GRADE(20)

FORTRAN reserves 20 memory cells for the array GRADE; these memory cells will be adjacent to each other in memory. Each cell of GRADE will contain a single student's grade. We can use each one, just as we did variables, by calling it by its name. In the case of an array, it will be like this: GRADE(1) means the grade of the first student in the class. GRADE(20) will be the reference to grade 20.

To read the scores of students into the array GRADE, and then count the number of grades less than the average we would do this:

```
C Program to demonstrate the use of arrays
C
      real grade(20)
      integer i, count
      real average,sum
      do 7 i=1, 20, 1
         write(6,4)
3     format(1x, 'Please enter your score:')
         read(5,2)grade(i)
2        format(f5.0)
7     continue
C     Now to find the average
         sum = 0.
         do 9 i=1, 20, 1
9           sum = sum + grade(i)
         average = sum / 20.0
C     Count the number of grades less than the average
      count = 0
      do 15 i = 1, 20, 1
         if(grade(i) .lt. average) count = count + 1
15    continue
      write(6,22) count
22    format(1x, 'The number of grades less than the average is', i5)
      stop
      end
```

5.2 Examples Involving Arrays

PROGRAM #19: Change the above program so that it finds the average grade for a class of 10 students; then it prints each grade and whether it is "below average", "average", or "above average".

The following program finds the largest element in a list of 10 numbers, and prints the number of the cell where it was found (its position within the array).

```
C More on arrays
C
      integer n
      integer i, largest,position
C     input the first number and call it the largest number
      read(5,1) largest
    1 format(i5)
C     initially position 1 is the position of the largest number
      position = 1
C     read 9 more numbers and check each against the largest
      do 7 i=2, 10, 1
         read(5,1)n
         if (n .le. largest) go to 7
C     redefine the position of the largest and redefine the largest if
C     needed
         position = i
         largest = n
    7 continue
      write(6,12) largest
   12 format(1x, 'largest is ', i5)
      write(6,14) position
   14 format(1x, 'position is ', i5)
      stop
      end
```

PROGRAM #20: Write a program to print the smallest element in a list of numbers and its position within the list. (Be careful with this one; make sure you try it out).

PROGRAM #21: Write an interactive program that plays the game of HANGMAN. Hint: Let WORD be an array of characters. Read the characters of the word to be guessed into successive elements of the array WORD. The player must guess the letters that belong to WORD. The game ends when either all letters have been guessed correctly (player wins) or a specified number of incorrect guesses have been made (computer wins.) Use an array SOLUTION to keep track of the solution so far. Initialize SOLUTION to a string of symbols "*". Each time a letter in WORD is guessed, replace the corresponding "*" in SOLUTION with that letter and show it to the player before the next guess is made. Play several games to try it out.

Searching and sorting a list of numbers, names, etc. is a big topic in computer science. The following algorithm will illustrate how a list of numbers can be sorted from high element to low element. Code the algorithm and give it a try.

5.3 Sorting Algorithm

Input the numbers and store in the array called num. Assume there are 20 elements in the list.

1. Let sorted be a flag or indicator telling whether the list is sorted or not sorted. Sorted = 0 says the list is not sorted and sorted = 1 says the list is sorted.
2. Make sorted = 1
3. Make i (a pointer) = 2
4. Compare num(i) with num(i-1), if greater than see below, else skip below and go to 5.
   save = num(i-1)
   num(i-1) = num(i)
   num(i) = save
   sorted = 0
5. i = i + 1
6. Check i and if less than or equal 20 then branch to 4, else 7
7. Check sorted and if 0 branch to 2, else 8
8. Output the array num

PROGRAM #22: Code the above algorithm and test with the numbers 15, 22,33,44,55,66,77,88,12,11,9,8,7,6,5,4,3,17,19,20

LESSON 6

Functions

6.1 FUNCTION DEFINITION

FORTRAN has some built-in functions that come in quite handy. For example, the function SQRT finds the square root of a number. The following program segment shows how the function is called:

```
C built-in function, square root, demonstrated
2    format(i5)
     write(6,2) sqrt(4)
     write(6,2) sqrt(25)
     write(6,2) sqrt(81)
     write(6,2) sqrt(100)
C end of program segment
```

This would result in the following being printed:

```
2
5
9
10
```

Most programming languages have many pre-defined or built-in functions. All of the pre-defined functions are just special purpose programs, such as the sqrt function demonstrated above. These programs were written and stored with the compiler or translator and the systems programmer, the individual that loads the compiler, has the option of loading and storing these functions with the compiler at the time the compiler is loaded onto the computer.

Other similar functions are **SIN, COS, EXP, ALOG, ABS** and others. You may want to try each of these in a manner similar to the test case above for the SQRT function. These functions are for the sine, cosine, exponential - e to a power, natural logarithm and absolute value function. A library or set of pre-defined functions is normally supplied with the compiler.

Often, we need some functions other than the ones FORTRAN provides. In that case, we get to make our own. For example, suppose we wanted a function that would return the larger of two integers we gave it. We have to give the function a **name** and then define it for FORTRAN. Let's call it **LARGER.** We would define it like this:

```
function larger(first, second)
    if (first.gt. second) then
      larger = first
      return
    else
      larger = second
      return
    end
```

The first line may be a little confusing. We are telling FORTRAN that we are defining what is meant by the function LARGER. We are saying that we will give it two numbers and it should give us a number in return. The two numbers passed to this function are defined to be integers in the main or calling program. If we said in our program that x = larger(23,67), then the function we have written would assign x to be 67. Here is how it would look in the entire program.

In general to define a function in FORTRAN, use the form
function name of function (list of dummy arguments)

```
.
.
.
body
name of function = expression
return
end
```

```
C A program to illustrate the use of a user-defined function
      integer num1,num2,num3,num4,temp1,temp2,big
      write(6,2)
2     format(1x, 'Enter 4 numbers.')
      read(5,4)num1,num2,num3,num4
4     format(4i5)
      temp1 = larger(num1,num2)
      temp2 = larger(num3,num4)
      big = larger(temp1,temp2)
      write(6,7) big
7     format(1x, 'The largest number is', i5)
      stop
      end
C the function follows
      function larger(first, second)
      if (first.gt. second) then
         larger = first
         return
      else
         larger = second
         return
      end
```

PROGRAM #23: Write a function called CUBE that finds the cube of a number. For example, the cube of 5 is 125 (5*5*5) and the cube of 2 is 8 (2*2*2). Test your function by writing a program that makes a table of the number 1 through 10 with their cubes. It should look something like this: (Remember to format the output to get the chart.)

NUMBER	CUBE
1	1
2	8
3	27
..	
..	

PROGRAM #24: Write a function called POWER that finds the result when an integer is raised to a given power. For example POWER(2,5) should return 32, since 2 to the fifth power = 2*2*2*2*2 = 32. Test it out in a program.

6.2 Random Number Generators

Functions to generate *random numbers* are very common. Random number generators normally produce a sequence of real numbers between 0 and 1 that for all practical purposes appear to be random. Most random number generators start with an initial real value called a seed. The remainder of the random numbers are determined once the seed is specified. Here is a **pre-defined function** which is a random number generator:

randomize()
n = random(100)

The numbers generated are all between 0 and 99. The next function uses RANDOM but finds random numbers in whatever range you specify.

```
      integer n, range
      randomize()
      write(6,2)
2     format(1x, 'Enter the range.')
      read(5,4)range
4     format(i5)
      n = random(range)
```

Remember that when the above is executed the range of your random numbers will be between 0 and (range-1) and one random number is returned each time the function random is called.

Now that we have a random number generator, we can write some more interesting games. The number guessing game that we wrote back in program 15 can now be made more interesting.

PROGRAM #25: Write a guessing game program that will ask the user to guess a number. If the user is correct, the computer will respond with a nice message and tell the user how many guesses it took to guess the number. If the user is wrong, the computer will tell respond with HIGHER or LOWER and ask for another guess. This will continue until the correct number is entered. Change the program so that the user may select the range the integer will be in. Also, you might want to give the user a maximum number of guesses, in case the user keeps getting confused and never gets the right answer.

Chapter 5

PASCAL Programming

Lesson 1 Getting Started 267

1.1 Program Header 267
1.2 Program Body 267
1.3 Program Variables 268
1.4 Assignment Statement 269
1.5 Data Types 271
1.6 Mathematical Operators 272

Lesson 2 Strings and Formatted Output 274

2.1 String Data Type 274
2.2 Formatted Output 275

Lesson 3 Loops 277

3.1 General Information on Loops 277
3.2 Relational Operators 278
3.3 The WHILE Loop 279
3.4 The REPEAT / UNTIL Loop 281
3.5 The FOR Statement 282

Lesson 4 Decision Statements 286

4.1 IF Statements 286

4.2 IF /THEN/ELSE Statements 287

Lesson 5 Arrays 291

5.1 Array Defintion 291

5.2 Array Examples 293

Lesson 6 Functions 295

6.1 Function Basics 295

6.2 Random Number Generators 297

Lesson 1

PASCAL
Getting Started

1.1 Program Header

Before beginning our study of Pascal, we will examine two short programs. Don't worry about understanding the details of these programs yet; it will all be explained as we go along.

```
program sample1 (output);
begin
writeln('My first Pascal program');
end
```

The first line of this example is called the **PROGRAM HEADING.** It specifies the name of the program, which in this case is *sample1,* and also says that the program will produce some **OUTPUT**.

1.2 Program Body

The final three lines are called the **PROGRAM BODY**, and contain the **STATEMENTS** which will be executed by the computer. The program body consists of the word **BEGIN**, followed by some executable statements, followed by the word **END**. There is only one executable statement in this example. The **WRITELN** (pronounced write-line) statement will display the string "My first Pascal program" on the screen, when the program is executed. The ln on the end of write instructs the computer to start a new line for the next output item.

Create a file called sample1.pas and add some **control** lines at the top depending on the Pascal compiler you are using then execute or **RUN** the program.

Look at the following program:

```
program sample2 (input, output);
var
N1, N2, SUM : integer;
begin
writeln('Enter two numbers');
readln(N1, N2);
SUM := N1 + N2;
writeln(N1, 'plus', N2, ' equals ', SUM)
end.
```

1.3 Program Variables

Pascal and most other common programming languages perform their calculations by manipulating things called **VARIABLES.** In a Pascal program a variable is written as a string of letters and digits that begins with a letter. Some sample names for Pascal variables are:

X Y Z SUM N1 N2 SALLY rate distance Time

Pascal variables are things that can hold numbers or other types of data. Variable names are actually names of the computer's memory position where the information is stored. These names allow us to refer to familiar data such as RATE rather than give the actual memory position which will be a long binary number such as 1011100111111100. For now we will confine our attention to variables that hold only numbers. In Pascal all variables must be declared before they can be used in the body of a program. The **var** statement is used to declare these variables. Each declaration contains the name of the variable, followed by the type of the variable. All three variables in this sample2 program are integers. (A variable of type **INTEGER** can store whole numbers only.) If we wanted to allow decimals, we could declare the numbers to be of type **REAL**. (Real variables can store numbers with decimals.)

The lines between BEGIN and END contain the statements to be carried out by the computer. The semicolons at the ends of the statements are used to separate the statements. That is why the last statement is not followed by a semicolon; there is no subsequent statement that it needs to be separated from. Since BEGIN is not a program statement, there is no semicolon after it. Semicolons before END statements are optional.

The first statement in the body of the program causes the following phrase to appear on the screen:
Enter two numbers

Suppose that in response to this, an obedient user types two numbers on the keyboard, say 4, followed by a space, followed by a 5, followed by pressing the RETURN or ENTER key.

The next statement, called an **INPUT** statement,
readln(N1, N2);

tells the computer what to do with these numbers. This statement is an instruction to the computer to read the two numbers and store in memory positions referenced by the variables N1 and N2. It causes the value of the variable N1 to become equal to the first number typed in, 4, and the value of N2 to become equal to the second number typed in, 5.

1.4 Assignment Statement

The next statement in our sample2 program is:
SUM := N1 + N2;

The symbolism := is called the **ASSIGNMENT OPERATOR**, and this statement is called an **ASSIGNMENT STATEMENT**. There should be no space between the equal sign and the colon; they are treated as one symbol. The assignment operator has no standard pronunciation but most people pronounce it gets the value or is assigned. Whatever is on the left hand side of the operator gets the value of whatever is on the right hand side of the operator. This changes the value of number stored in the memory position called SUM to the value of the numbers stored in memory position N1 plus the value of the number stored in N2. Finally, the writeln statement, which is the **OUTPUT** statement, produces the output.

Now create a new file called sample2.pas and follow the same procedure as before to get the proper control lines at the top of the file. Type in sample2 and execute or RUN the program.

PROBLEM: What is the output produced by the following four lines (when correctly embedded in a complete program)? The variables are of type *integer*:

```
X := 2;
Y := 3;
Y := X * 7;
writeln(X, Y);
```

ANSWER:

PROGRAM #1: Write a Pascal program that will print your name on one line and your home town on the next line. Be sure to save the program before you execute it. Use the name prog1.pas when you create the file so it will be saved under that name.

The following example is a program to print the letter L in magnified form:

```
program LETTER (output);
(* prints a letter in magnified form *)
begin
writeln(' ** ');
writeln(' ** ');
```

```
writeln(' ** ');
writeln(' ****** ');
writeln(' ****** ');
end.
```

The (*prints a letter in magnified form*) is called a comment line and is used to assist the programmer or others to better understand the purpose of the program. Comment lines can be freely used within a program.

PROGRAM #2: Write a program that will print your initials in magnified form. Call this prog2.pas.

1.5 DATA TYPES

A DATA TYPE is a description of a category of data. Each variable can hold only one type of data. In our sample programs all variables have been of type integer. That means that their values must be a whole number such as:
38 0 1 89 3987 -12 -5

Numbers that include a fractional part, such as the ones below, are of type real:
2.7192 0.098 -15.8 1000053.98

To declare the variables x and y as float or real you will use the following declaration:
x,y : real;

The *type* used for letters, or, more generally, any single symbol is **CHAR**, which is short for character. Values of this type are declared as follows:
var X, Y : char;

A variable of type *char* can hold any character on the input keyboard. So, for example, X could hold any of the characters A, a, +, or 6.

It is perfectly acceptable to have variables of more than one type in a program. In such cases they are all declared at once following the format illustrated below:

var
N1, N2 : integer;
time : real;
initial: char;

1.6 Mathematical Operators

The mathematical operations that are available in Pascal and their symbol is given below:

OPERATION	SYMBOL	EXAMPLE
addition	+	**A + B**
subtraction	-	**C - 14**
multiplication	*	**5 * B**
division	/	**A / B**

Suppose memory positions A, B, and C have been declared as type integer and position A has the number 5 stored and position B has the number 12 stored. The statement used to add the two numbers and store their sum, 17, in memory position C would be:
C := A + B;

More complex mathematical expression could look as follows:
C := A / B + (3.6 + A * B) – B / 17.4;

Mathematical operations are performed from left to right with division (/), and multiplication (*) taking precedence over addition (+), and subtraction (-). Grouping symbols can also be used to control the order of operations.

Consider the statement:
C := 3 + 8 / 2 – 5;

The operation 8 / 2 would be performed first, giving 4, this 4 would then be added to 3 giving 7, and 5 would be subtracted from 7 giving 2. In the statement C := (4 + 6) * 5 / 10; the 4 would be added to 6, giving 10, and then the 10 would be multiplied by 5, giving 50, and the 50 would be divided by 10 giving 5 which would be stored in memory position C.

PROBLEMS:

1. What is the output produced by the following three lines (when correctly embedded in a program)? The variables are of type *integer*.

   ```
   X := 2;
   X := X + 1;
   writeln(X);
   ```

2. What is the output produced by the following? The variables are of type char: (Be careful on this one - it is tricky!)

   ```
   A := 'B';
   B := 'C';
   C := A;
   writeln(A, B, C);
   ```

PROGRAM #3: Write a Pascal program that will read two integers and will then output their sum, difference, and product.

LESSON 2

Strings and Formatted Output

2.1 STRING DATA TYPE

Often we would like to store a whole word or combination of words in a variable rather than just a character. To do this in some versions of Pascal it is necessary to define a new data type: **STRING**. We do it in the following way: (here string is just a set of characters).
name : string[1..80];

If we declare this type before we declare our variables we can use string as a type just like integer, real, and char. Turbo Pascal will let us do it as follows:

```
program CONVERSATION (input, output);
var
name : string[80];
test1, test2 : integer;
average : real;
begin
    writeln('What is your name?');
    readln(name);
    writeln('What are your test scores?');
    readln(test1, test2);
```

```
average := (test1 + test2)/2;
writeln(name, average)
end.
```

In the above example, we declared 'name' to be a string of 80 characters in length, but we could have declared it to be any number below that, 25 for example. The string type will make more sense when we study arrays later on. You may have noticed that the average was printed in a rather strange way. The reason it looks like this is because we have not specified how we would like decimal numbers to be printed. The next section deals with that topic.

PROGRAM #4: Write a Pascal program that will ask for a name and 3 test scores and will print the person's name and average.

PROGRAM #5: Write a program that will ask for a person's name and age and then respond with the statement:
"Hello, ______________. You do not look ___________ years old."

2.2 Formatted Output

Output may be formatted with the writeln statement. For example:
writeln(A:10, B:20, 'now':20);

allows 10 spaces for the value of A, 20 spaces for the value of B, and 20 spaces for the word 'now'. Check out the following example:

```
PROGRAM inch (input, output);
(* a program to convert feet to inches *)
VAR
feet, inches: real;
BEGIN
writeln('enter number of feet');
readln(feet);
inches :=feet * 12.0;
writeln(feet:4:1, ' feet equal ', inches:6:1, ' inches ');
END.
```

The writeln statement allows 4 spaces for the value of feet and includes 1 digit after the decimal point. There are 6 total spaces for the value of inches, with 1 digit after the decimal point.

PROGRAM #6: Write a program to convert hours and minutes to minutes only. Ask the user for the number of hours and the number of minutes and then print the answer. For example, suppose the user's response for the number of hours as 3 and for the number of minutes as 10. The following message should be printed:
3 hours and 10 minutes equals 190 minutes

The next example computes the amount of interest that you would receive if you saved $100.00 in the bank for one year at an interest rate of 12 percent per year.

```
PROGRAM bank (output);
(* computes interest on $100 for one year at 12% *)
VAR
principal : real;
interest : real;
BEGIN
principal := 100;
interest := principal * 0.12;
writeln(principal, interest)
END.
```

PROGRAM #7: Write a program that asks the user for the amount of money he/she wants to invest at a rate of 7% and then prints a message proclaiming the amount of interest earned in one year. For example, if the user responded that he has 200 dollars to invest, the computer will respond:
"You will earn $14 interest at the end of one year if you invest with us."

Lesson 3

Loops

3.1 General Information on Loops

In order to convert temperature from degrees Centigrade to degrees Fahrenheit, we just multiply the Centigrade temperatures by 9/5 and then add 32. The following is an example of a simple program that converts 100 degrees Centigrade to degrees Fahrenheit.

```
PROGRAM temperature(output);
VAR
C : integer;
F : real;
BEGIN
C := 100;
F := (C*9)/5. + 32; (* formula for Fahrenheit *)
writeln(C, F)
END.
```

Notice that this program only converts one value, 100, from Centigrade to Fahrenheit. It would be more useful and interesting to calculate the Fahrenheit temperature for lots of different values for Centigrade; for example 100, 110, 120, ... etc. This is accomplished by using a loop. There are three kinds of loops that we will learn about: the **WHILE** loop, the **REPEAT / UNTIL loop**, and the **FOR** loop.

3.2 Relational Operators

Before continuing with loops consider relational operators. Relational operators can be used in expressions normally found with the WHILE loop, and REPEAT/UNTIL loop:

OPERATORS:

= equal
< less than
> greater than
<> not equal
<= less than or equal
>= greater than or equal

These operators simply ask a question regarding two numbers – is one number equal to a second number, less than a second number, etc.

For example, the way to use one of these in a WHILE loop is:
while(num1 < num2) do

Don't worry too much about understanding the WHILE statement now, that will be explained in the next section. For now just understand that the loop will only work when num1 is less than num2.

Another use of Relational Operators is in a comparison statement called the IF/THEN statement. The IF/THEN statement will compare two items using one of the Relational Operators, and if the comparison is true, the commands following the IF/THEN statement or group of statement following the IF/THEN statement will be executed; otherwise, the statement or a group of statement will be skipped. Below is the basic usage of the IF/THEN statement.
if (num1 < num2) then   (* No Semicolon *)
writeln('num1 is smaller');

The IF/THEN statement will be further explained in Chapter 4.

3.3 The WHILE Loop

The next example uses a WHILE loop to continuously calculate degrees Fahrenheit for each new values of C. Each time through the loop, C is being incremented by 10. Thus we will be finding degrees Fahrenheit (F) for C = 100, 110, 120, 130,... When will we stop? How about stopping after C is 200? We will use this as our stopping criterion. Every loop must have a stopping criterion; otherwise you will be stuck in something known as an infinite loop. It is like being stuck in a revolving door with no way out. The following program demonstrates the use of the **WHILE** loop:

```
PROGRAM temperature(output);
VAR
C : integer;
F : real;
BEGIN
C := 100;
WHILE (C <=200) DO   (* notice no semicolon after word DO *)
   BEGIN
     F := (C*9)/5. + 32;
     writeln(C, F);
     C := C + 10   (* increment C by 10 each time through *)
   END;
END.
```

In the line containing the WHILE statement, the value of C is compared to 200. If C is less than or equal to 200 the compare statement is true, and the loop is executed. If C is greater than 200 the entire WHILE loop (the three statements between the BEGIN and END statements) is skipped.

PROBLEM: Write a program that reads a list of student names and prints the name that comes first alphabetically.

Let's solve the problem together. If you were trying to find the alphabetically first name in a long list of names without using the computer, how would you do it? You would probably read down the list of names, one at a time, and remember only the name that was alphabetically first so far. If you read a name that was alphabetically before the one you were remembering, then you would remember the new name instead.

We can use this as a model for telling the computer how to solve the problem (This is called finding an ALGORITHM for the problem. An **algorithm** is simply a recipe for finding the solution.) We will tell the computer to read a single name at a time and to save the smallest name it has processed so far in the variable **SMALLNAME**. Since we don't know how many names will be on the list, we will use the sentinel value 'DONE', since that should not be anyone's name. The sentinel value is used to eventually stop us from processing the WHILE loop. An outline of our program will look like this:

Read the first name into NAME
Initialize SMALLNAME to NAME
WHILE NAME is not equal to 'DONE' DO
BEGIN
    If NAME is less than SMALLNAME then store it in SMALLNAME
    Read the next name into NAME
END

PROGRAM #8: Write a program that continually asks the user for a name until the user says 'DONE' and then prints out the smallest (alphabetically first) name. For example, if the user responded with the following names

SALLY
JOE
KENNETH
ANNE
MABEL
ZYGMUND
BOBBY
DONE

then the computer would respond with
The smallest name is ANNE.

IF we know the number of data items to be processed beforehand, a counter can be used to control the **WHILE** loop. For example, we could change our algorithm to:

```
Ask the user how many names he wants to give and store
in NUMNAMES
Read the first name into NAME
Initialize SMALLNAME to NAME
Initialize COUNT to 1
WHILE COUNT is less than or equal to NUMNAMES DO
BEGIN
    Read the next name into NAME
    Store the smaller of NAME and SMALLNAME in
      SMALLNAME
    Increase COUNT by 1 (COUNT := COUNT +1)
END
```

PROGRAM #9: Modify PROG8 so that it asks the user beforehand for the number of names to be processed. This time, do **not** use 'DONE.'

3.4 The REPEAT / UNTIL Loop

The **REPEAT / UNTIL** loop works the same way as the WHILE loop except that the comparison (to determine whether or not to quit the loop) is not made until the end of the loop. For example:

```
BEGIN
C := 100;
REPEAT
    F := (C*9)/5. + 32;
    writeln(C, F);
    C := C + 10;
UNTIL C > 200;
END
```

Notice that a **BEGIN** and **END** is not needed with the **REPEAT / UNTIL** loop, as it was with the **WHILE** loop. Why not, do you suppose?

The following program inputs a student's name and two scores, and then prints the name and average score. The process continues until a name of THATSALL is given. THATSALL is used as the sentinel value. It is used as a condition to terminate the loop.

```
program GRADE (input, output);
var
name: string[80];
score1, score2 : integer;
average : real;
begin
writeln('what is your name?');
readln(name);
repeat
writeln('input your two scores, separated by a space.');
readln(score1, score2);
average:=(score1 + score2)/2.0;
writeln(name, average);
writeln('what is your name?');
readln(name);
until(name = 'THATSALL');
end.
```

Run the program with the following data:

Bonnie, 90,85
Elizabeth, 80, 90
Beverly, 85, 92
Dawn, 95, 98
THATSALL, 0, 0

3.5 The FOR Statement

The **FOR** loop is handy to use when we know exactly how many times we need to execute a loop. Suppose we know that we wanted to go through the loop 5 times. Using a FOR loop we can do that:

```
var
count : integer;
number : real;
```

```
begin
for count := 1 to 5 do
begin
    writeln('Give me a number, please.');
    readln(number);
    writeln('Your number is', number);
end;
writeln;
writeln('Thank you for the numbers.')
end.
```

The variable COUNT is called the running variable and takes the initial value of 1. The block of statements between begin and end is then executed and COUNT takes on the value of 2 and is checked against 5. If COUNT is still less than or equal to 5 the block is executed again. This process continues until COUNT is greater than 5.

PROGRAM #10: Write a program that prints your name 10 times. Use a FOR loop.

PROGRAM #11: Write a program to input a student's name and three test scores. Print the name and average score. Continue this process until the name 'END' is encountered. Hint: use the program that you wrote for prog10 and just make a few changes to it.

PROGRAM #12: Write a program to input students' names and score they received on recent test, then calculate and print the class average for the test. Do not use a trip value to quit the loop, but assume there are 5 students in the class. A FOR loop might be good here.

The next program finds and prints the sum of the integers 1 through 100:

```
program SUMINTEGERS(output);
var
sum,num : integer;
begin
sum := 0;
```

```
num := 1;
WHILE (num <= 100) DO
begin
    sum := sum + num;
    num := num + 1
end;
writeln('sum of first 100 integers is ',sum)
end.
```

PROGRAM #13: Change the above program so that it finds and prints the sum of the odd integers 1 through 99. (Form the sum 1 + 3 + 5 + ... +99)

Pretend that you are looking for a job for the month of July. Suppose that someone offers you a job that pays one cent for the first day, two cents for the second day, four cents for the third day, eight cents for the fourth day, etc. The amount of your pay is doubling each day. Would you take this job or one that offered you $1000 per day for the entire month? Before you answer, you may want to run the following program. It determines the day in which the day's pay for the first job first exceeds $10,000.

```
program job(output);
var
day:integer;
daypay : real;
begin
day := 1;
daypay := 0.01;
while (daypay < 10000) do
begin
    day := day + 1;
    daypay := daypay * 2;
end;
writeln('The day in which pay first exceeds $10,000 is',day);
end.
```

PROGRAM #14: Using the above program, change it so that it prints the total salary you will receive for the month of July. Hint: there are 31 days in July and you work all 31.

LESSON 4

Decision Statements

4.1 IF STATEMENTS

One of the most used CONTROL STATEMENTS in the Pascal language is the IF statement. In its simplest form, it evaluates an expression and then proceeds on the basis of the result of that comparison. For example, the following program reads in a set of scores and counts the number of students that made an A. An A is considered to be a score of 90 or above. A sentinel value of 0 is used. This signals that no more data will follow – here we would not expect 0 to be one of the scores.

```
program GRADEREPORT (input, output);
var
account, score : integer; (* account is the variable for number of A's *)
begin
account := 0;
REPEAT
    readln(score);
    IF (score >= 90) THEN account := account + 1;
UNTIL score = 0; (* trip on score of 0 *)
writeln('There were ', account, ' A scores. ')
end.
```

DATA
98 45 17 90 91 87 34 99 100 0

How many times will the loop be executed?

What will be printed out?

If you have more than one statement to be executed when the IF expression evaluates to true, you can use the BEGIN - END statements to designate the block to be executed.

4.2 IF / THEN / ELSE STATEMENTS

Whenever you want one thing done when the IF expression evaluates to true and another thing done when it evaluates to false, it is handy to use the **IF / THEN / ELSE** statement. Here is a short program that asks the user to guess the number the computer is thinking of. If the digit agrees with the one the program is trying to match (which is 6 in our case), the program prints "Right. Good job." If the digit is not 6 the program prints "Sorry, wrong number."

```
program Guess(input, output);
var
x : integer;
begin
writeln('I am thinking of a digit. What is it?');
readln(x);
IF (x = 6) THEN
    writeln('Right. Good job.')
ELSE
    writeln('Sorry, wrong number.')
end.
```

PROGRAM #15: Put the above program in a loop so that it will continue to play the game until the person guesses the digit. Have it count the number of guesses it takes. It should print a message to the user telling how many guesses it took him/her to get the correct digit.

Suppose we need a program to count the number of students who are freshmen, sophomores, juniors, and seniors in a class of 10 students. This program accomplishes that by combining IF and ELSE statements.

```
program classcount(input, output);
var
nfresh, nsoph, njr, nsr, grade, count : integer;
begin
nfresh := 0;
nsoph := 0;
njr := 0;
nsr := 0;
count := 1;
WHILE (count <= 10) DO
begin
    writeln('enter your grade as either 9,10,11,or 12.');
    readln(grade);
    IF (grade = 9) THEN
      nfresh := nfresh + 1
    ELSE IF (grade = 10) THEN
      nsoph := nsoph + 1
    ELSE IF (grade = 11) THEN
      njr := njr + 1
    ELSE IF (grade = 12) THEN
      nsr := nsr + 1
    ELSE
writeln('Please enter a 9,10,11, or 12. Try again.');
count := count + 1
end;
writeln('There were ', nfresh, ' freshmen.');
writeln('There were', nsoph, ' sophomores.');
writeln('There were ', njr, ' juniors.');
writeln('There were ', nsr, ' seniors.')
end.
```

Run the program and try it out.

In the following program a company pays every employee $5.00 per hour. This program asks for name and number of hours worked. It then calculates and prints the total wages for the week.

```
program WAGES (input, output);
var
hours, paydue : real;
name : string[25];
begin
    writeln('name:');
    readln(name);
    writeln('hours worked:');
    readln(hours);
    paydue := hours * 5.00;
    writeln(name, hours, paydue);
end.
```

PROGRAM #16: Write a program that pays an employee $5.00 per hour for all hours less than or equal to 40 and pays twice that amount for all hours over 40. For example, if you worked for this company last month for 52 hours you would receive $5.00 per hour for 40 hours (200 dollars) plus $10.00 per hour for 12 hours (120 dollars) for a total of 320 dollars.

PROGRAM #17: Write a program to determine how much fine you should pay for a speeding ticket. Assume the fine is computed as follows:

Amount over limit (miles/hour)	Fine
1 – 10	$10
11 – 20	$20
21 – 30	$25
31 – 40	$40
41 or more	$60

Your program should ask for both the speed limit and the driver's speed. It should then print :

THE FINE IS $________

PROGRAM #18: Using a FOR loop, write a program that prints the numbers 1 - 10, along with their square and cube. An example of the Output: (Format output to look like the chart below.)

NUMBER	SQUARE	CUBE
1	1	1
2	4	8
.		
.		
.		
10	100	1000

LESSON 5

Arrays

5.1 Array Definition

Suppose we wish to process grades for several classes of students. The number of students in each class will vary, but we wish to write a program that will calculate the average grade and then find the number of grades less than the average grade in the class. We cannot calculate the average until all the grades for the class have been entered. So we must save the grades and count the ones below average after the average is calculated.

Should we save each grade in a variable of a different name? This would lead to a long repetitious program. Fortunately, Pascal lets us solve the problem in a very nice way using **ARRAYS**. An **ARRAY** is a data structure used for storing a collection of data items that are all the same type. Usually, we first describe the structure of an array in an *array type declaration*. The array type **REALARRAY** is declared below followed by the declaration of array GRADE of type REALARRAY.

```
type
REALARRAY = array[1..20] of real;
var
GRADE : REALARRAY;
```

It was not necessary to define the type as we could have defined GRADE as an array as follows:
GRADE: array[1..20] of real;

If we have other real arrays of size 20 it may be best to define the REALARRAY through a type statement as above.

Pascal reserves 20 memory cells for the GRADEs; these memory cells will be adjacent to each other in memory. Each cell of GRADE may contain a single student's grade. We can use each one, just as we did with variables, by calling it by its name. In the case of an array, it will be like this: GRADE[2] means the grade of the second student in the class.

To read in the scores of students into the array GRADE, we would do this:

```
program CLASSAVERAGE(input, output);
var
GRADE : array[1..20] of real;
i,sum : integer;
average : real;
begin
for i:=1 to 20 do
begin
    writeln('Please enter your score:');
    readln(GRADE[i]);
end;
end.
```

To find the average of the class, we would change the main part of the program to this:

```
begin
sum:=0;
for i:=1 to 20 do
begin
    writeln('Please enter your score:');
    readln(GRADE[i]);
```

```
      sum:=sum + GRADE[i];
   end;
   average:=sum/20.0
   end;
```

5.2 Array Examples

PROGRAM #19: Change the above program so that it finds the average grade for a class of 10 students; then it prints each grade and whether it is "below average", "average", or "above average".

The following program finds the largest element in a list of numbers, and prints the number of the cell where it was found (its position within the array).

```
program largest(input, output);
type
list = array[1..10] of integer;
var
    n:list;
    i,largest,position:integer;
begin
    largest:=0;
    for i:=1 to 10 do
    begin
      readln(n[i]);
      if n[i] > largest then
    begin
      largest:=n[i];
      position:=i;
    end;
    end;
writeln('largest is', largest);
writeln('position is', position)
end.
```

PROGRAM #20: Write a program to print the smallest element in a list of numbers and its position within the list. (Be careful with this one, test all possible cases).

PROGRAM #21: Write an interactive program that plays the game of HANGMAN. Hint: Let WORD be an array of characters. Read the word to be guessed into successive elements of the array WORD. The player must guess the letters that belong to WORD. The game ends when either all letters have been guessed correctly (player wins) or a specified number of incorrect guesses have been made (computer wins.) Use an array SOLUTION to keep track of the solution so far. Initialize SOLUTION to a string of symbols – '*'. Each time a letter in WORD is guessed, replace the corresponding * in SOLUTION with that letter and show it to the player before the next guess is made. Play several games to try it out.

Searching an array of elements for a particular element and sorting a list to place in order lexicographically are large topics in computer science. Program #20 is an example of searching. To sort a list of elements (numbers) in order from largest number to smallest number consider the following algorithm:

1) Define or input the list of N numbers and store in an array
2) Search the list starting at the first element for the largest element and swap places with the largest element and the element in the first position
3) Search the list starting with the second element for the largest element and swap places with the new largest element and the element in the second position
4) Continue this process until you have considered the n-1st and nth element
5) Output the list—it should now be in order from largest element to smallest element

The above algorithm is spoken of as the selection algorithm or sort.

PROGRAM #22: Write a program, using the selection sort, to arrange a list of number in order from high number to low number.

LESSON 6

Functions

6.1 FUNCTION BASICS

Pascal has some built-in functions that come in quite handy. For example, the function SQRT finds the square root of a number. The following program segment shows how the function is called:

```
begin
writeln(sqrt(4));
writeln(sqrt(25));
writeln(sqrt(81));
writeln(sqrt(100));
end.
```

This would result in the following being printed:

```
2
5
9
10
```

Most programming languages, including Pascal, have many pre-defined or built-in functions. All of the pre-defined functions are just special purpose programs, such as the sqrt function demonstrated above. These programs were written and stored with the compiler or translator. The systems programmer, the individual that loads the compiler, has the option of loading and storing these functions with the compiler at the time the compiler is loaded onto the computer.

Other similar functions are **SIN, COS, EXP, ALOG, ABS** and others. You may want to try each of these in a manner similar to the test case above for the SQRT function. These functions are for the sine, cosine, exponential—e to a power, natural logarithm and absolute value function. A library or set of pre-defined functions is normally supplied with the compiler.

Often, we need some functions other than the ones Pascal provides. In that case, we get to make our own. For example, suppose we wanted a function that would return the larger of two integers we gave it. We have to give the function a name and then define it for Pascal. Let's call it LARGER. We would define it like this:

```
function larger (first,second:integer):integer;
begin
if first > second then
larger := first
else
larger := second
end;
```

The first line may be a little confusing. We are telling Pascal that we are defining what is meant by the function LARGER. We are saying that we will give it two integers (first and second); it should give us an integer in return. If we said in our program that **x:=larger(23,67)**, Pascal would call our pre-defined function and assign x to be 67. Here is how it would look in the entire program. Notice that we had to define the function before we got to the main body of the program.

```
program testlarger (input, output);
var
num1,num2,num3,num4,temp1,temp2,big : integer;
function larger (first,second:integer):integer;
begin
if first > second then
```

```
larger := first
else
larger := second;
end;
begin
writeln('Enter 4 numbers.');
readln(num1,num2,num3,num4);
temp1:=larger(num1,num2);
temp2:=larger(num3,num4);
big:=larger(temp1,temp2);
writeln('The largest number is',big)
end.
```

PROGRAM #23: Write a function CUBE that finds the cube of a number. For example, the cube of 5 is 125 (5*5*5) and the cube of 2 is 8 (2*2*2). Test your function by writing a program that makes a table of the numbers 1 through 10 with their cubes. It should look something like this: (format output as shown below):

NUMBER	CUBE
1	1
2	8
3	27
..	
..	
..	

PROGRAM #24: Write a function POWER that finds the power of an integer. For example POWER(2,5) should return 32, since 2 to the fifth power = 2*2*2*2*2 = 32. Test it out in a program.

6.2 Random Number Generators

Functions to generate *random numbers* are very common. Random number generators normally produce a sequence of real numbers between 0 and 1 that for all practical purposes appear to be random. Most random number generators start with an initial real value called a seed. Future random numbers are determined once the seed is specified. Here is Pascal's predefined function which is a random number generator:

```
randomize;
random(100);
```

The numbers generated are all between 1 and 99. The next function uses RANDOM but finds random numbers in whatever range you specify.

```
randomize;
writeln('Enter the range of your numbers.');
readln(range);
N := random(range);
```

'N' becomes the random number that the computer chooses for you between 1 and the range that was chosen.

Now that we have a random number generator, we can write some more interesting games. The number guessing game that we wrote back in program 15 can now be made more interesting.

PROGRAM #25: Write a guessing game program that will ask the user to guess a number. If the user is correct, the computer will respond with a nice message and tell her how many guesses it took her. If she is wrong, the computer will tell her HIGHER or LOWER and ask for another guess. This will continue until she gets it right. Change the program so that the user may select the range the integer will be in. Also, you might want to give the user a maximum number of guesses, in case the user becomes confused and never gets the right answer.

Chapter 6

C Programming

Lesson 1 Getting Started 301

1.1 Preprocessor Directives 301
1.2 Program Body 302
1.3 Program Variables 302
1.4 Assignment Statement 304
1.5 Data Types 305
1.6 Mathematical Operators 306

Lesson 2 Strings and Formatted Output 309

2.1 String Data Type 309
2.2 Formatted Output 310

Lesson 3 Loops 312

3.1 General Information on Loops 312
3.2 Relational Operators 313
3.3 The WHILE loop 313
3.4 The DO / WHILE loop 316
3.5 The FOR statement 317

Lesson 4 Decision Statements 320

4.1 IF statements 320

4.2 IF / ELSE statements 321

Lesson 5 Arrays 324

5.1 Array Definition 324

5.2 Array Examples 325

Lesson 6 Functions 328

6.1 Function Basics 328

6.2 Random Number Generators 331

Lesson 1

C
Getting Started

1.1 Preprocessor Directives

Before beginning our study of C, we will examine two short programs. Don't worry about understanding the details of these programs yet; they will all be explained as we go along.

```
#include <stdio.h> /* This directive is needed for C input and output */
void main()        // Sample 1
{
printf("My first C program \n");

}
```

The first line of this example is called the **PRE-PROCESSOR DIRECTIVE**; it tells the compiler to include routines necessary for input and output. The next line **VOID MAIN( )** is necessary for all C programs and is where execution starts. The **left brace {, and right brace}** will enclose the body of the program.

1.2 Program Body

The statements starting with the first brace {and ending with the last brace} are called the **PROGRAM BODY**, and contain the **STATEMENTS** which will be executed by the computer (i.e. the program body consists of the word {, followed by some executable statements, followed by the }). There is only one executable statement in this example. The **printf** (pronounced print f) statement displays the string "My first C program" on the screen. Including the **n** at the end of the enclosed line, *will not be printed but,* instructs the computer to start a new line for the next output item.

Execute the above program. After being successful with this program, save the program, and add another line to print **this is fun**. If all did not go well, **REVISE** the file and make any necessary changes.

Look at the following program:

```
void main() // Sample2
{
int N1, N2, SUM;
printf("Enter two numbers:");
scanf("%d%d",&N1,&N2);
SUM = N1 + N2;
printf("%d plus %d equals %d", N1,N2, SUM);
}
```

The above program will be explained as we continue our study of C programming.

1.3 Program Variables

C and most other common programming languages perform their calculations by manipulating things called **VARIABLES**. In a C program a variable is written as a string of letters and digits that begins with a letter. Some sample names for C variables are:

X Y Z SUM N1 N2 SALLY rate distance Time

C variables are things that can hold numbers or other types of data. For now we will confine our attention to variables that hold only numbers. In C all variables must be *declared* before they can be used in the body of a program. The **variables** are declared at the beginning of the program. Each declaration contains the type of the variable, followed by the *variable name*. All three variables in this sample2 program are integers. (A variable of type **INTEGER** can store whole numbers only.) If we wanted to allow numbers with decimals, we could declare the numbers to be of type **float.** (Real or float variables contain decimal points.)

The lines between {, and} contain the statements to be carried out by the computer. The semicolons at the ends of the statements are used to separate the statements. The semicolon is not necessary after the last statement since there is no subsequent statement that it needs to be separated from. Since {is not a program statement, there is no semicolon after it. A semicolon before} is optional.

The first statement in the body of the above program causes the following phrase to appear on the screen:
Enter two numbers:

Suppose that in response to this, an obedient user enters two numbers through the keyboard, say 4, followed by a space, followed by a 5, followed by pressing the RETURN or ENTER key.

The next statement, is called an **INPUT** statement,
scanf(...);

and tells the computer what to do with these numbers. This statement is an instruction to the computer to read the two numbers and store in memory positions N1 and N2. It causes the value of the variable N1 to become equal to the first number typed in, i.e.4, and the value of N2 to become equal to the second number typed in, i.e. 5.

1.4 Assignment Statement

The next statement in our sample2 program is:
SUM = N1 + N2;

The symbolism = is called the **ASSIGNMENT OPERATOR**, and this statement (**SUM = N1 + N2**) is called an **ASSIGNMENT STATEMENT**. There can be spaces between the equal sign and N1. C is spoken of as a free format language, which means that blank spaces are allowed and often used to make a statement easier to read. The assignment operator has no standard pronunciation but most people pronounce it *gets the value* or *is assigned*. The variable on the left hand side of the operator gets the value assigned to the variable or expression on the right hand side of the operator. In this statement SUM is assigned the value 9 which is the sum of 4 and 5, the values assigned to N1 and N2. Finally, the printf statement, which is the **OUTPUT** statement, produces the output. The %d and other symbols in the output statement are used to format, or arrange, the output and will be explained later.

Enter and run the above program. Use the same procedure as before and don't forget to include the pre-processor directive.

PROBLEM: What is the output produced by the following four lines (when correctly embedded in a complete program)? The variables are of type integer:
X = 2;
Y = 3;
Y = X * 7;
printf("%d %d\n", X, Y);

ANSWER:

PROGRAM #1: Write a C program that will print your name on one line and your home town on the next line. Be sure to Save and Execute it. Use the name prog1.C when you create the file so it will be saved under that name.

The following example is a program to print the letter L in magnified form:

```
void main()
/* prints a letter in magnified form */
{
printf(" ** \n");
printf(" ** \n");
printf(" ** \n");
printf(" ****** \n");
printf(" ****** \n");
}
```

The /* print a letter in magnified form */ is called a comment line. The /* at the beginning and end of a comment are necessary. Comments of this type can be extended on several lines. Another form of comment is the // Comment. Comments of this time cannot be extended over lines. The // comment can be placed at the end of any C statement or can be on a line by itself. The /* .... */ type of comment can be included within a statement.

Examples of comments are:

```
scanf("%d%d",&N1,&N2);        // this is an input statement
printf("Enter two numbers:");   /* this is an output statement */
```

PROGRAM #2: Write a program that will print your initials in magnified form.

1.5 Data Types

A DATA TYPE is a description of a category of data. Each variable can hold only one type of data. In our sample program all variables were of type *integer*. This means that the numbers they can store must be whole number such as:

38 0 1 89 3987 -12 -5

Numbers that include a fractional part, such as the ones below, are of type *float or real*:
2.7192 0.098 -15.8 1000053.98

To declare the variable x and y as float you will use the following declaration:
float x, y;

The *type* used for letters, or, more generally, any single symbol is **CHAR**, which is short for *character*. Values of this type are declared as follows:
char X, Y;

A variable of type char can hold any (**one**) character found on the input keyboard. So, for example, X when declared as char, could hold any of the characters A, a, +, or 6.

It is perfectly acceptable to have variables of more than one type in a program. In such cases they are all declared at once following the format illustrated below: (The order of variable declaration has no particular meaning)

```
{
int n1;
real time;
char initial;
}
```

1.6 Mathematical Operators

The mathematical operations that are available in C and their symbol is given below:

OPERATION	SYMBOL	EXAMPLE
addition	+	**A + B**
subtraction	-	**C - 14**
multiplication	*	**5 * B**
division	/	**A / B**
integer portion	%	**A % B**

Suppose memory positions A, B, and C have been declared as type integer and position A has the number 5 stored and position B has the number 12 stored. The statement used to add the two numbers and store their sum, 17, in memory position C would be
C = A + B;

More complex mathematical expression could look as follows:
C = A / B + (3.6 + A * B) – B / 17.4;

Mathematical operations are performed from left to right with division (/), and multiplication (*), and integer portion (%) taking precedence over addition (+), and subtraction (-). Grouping symbols can also be used to control the order of operations.

Consider the statement:
C = 3 + 8 / 2 – 5;

The operation 8 / 2 would be performed first, giving 4, this 4 would then be added to 3 giving 7, and 5 would be subtracted from 7 giving 2.

In the statement C = (4 + 6) * 5 / 10; the 4 would be added to 6, giving 10, and then the 10 would be multiplied by 5, giving 50, and the 50 would be divided by 10 giving 5 which would be stored in memory position C.

PROBLEMS:

1. What is the output produced by the following three lines (when correctly embedded in a program)? The variables are of type *integer.*

```
X = 2;
X = X + 1;
printf("%d\n",X);
```

2. What is the output produced by the following? The variables are of type char: (Be careful on this one — it is tricky! Also, note that we can assign a char variable a value through an input statement or an assignment statement, and note that the format specification for a char data value is %c)

```
A = 'B';
B = 'C';
C = A;
printf("%c %c %c \n", A, B, C);
```

PROGRAM #3: Write a C program that will read in two integers and will then output their sum, difference, and product.

Lesson 2

Strings and Formatted Output

2.1 String Data Type

Often we would like to store a whole word or combination of words in a variable rather than just a character. To do this in C it is necessary to define a new data type: STRING. We do it in the following way: (string is used to declare a set of characters).

string name;
char name[60];

If we declare this type before we declare our variables we can use 'name' as a set of characters just like integer, real, and char. C will let us do it as follows.

```
void main()
{
char name[60]; // we could have used string name in place of char
int test1, test2;
float average;
printf("What is your name?:");
scanf("%s", name);
printf("\n What are your test scores?:");
scanf("%d %d",&test1,&test2);
```

```
average = (test1 + test2)/2;
printf("\n %s %f \n",name, average);
}
```

In the above example we declared 'name' to be 60 characters in length. However, we could declare it to be of almost any length, for example, 25. The string type or array of characters will make more sense when we study arrays later on. You may have noticed that the average was printed in a rather strange way. The reason it looks like this is because we have not specified how we would like decimal numbers to be printed. The next section deals with that topic.

PROGRAM #4: Write a C program that will ask for a person's name and 3 test scores and will then print the person's name and average score.

PROGRAM #5: Write a program that will ask for a person's name and age and then respond with the statement:
"Hello, _______________. You do not look ___________ years old."

2.2 Formatted Output

Output can be formatted with the printf statement. For example:

```
printf("%10d %20d \n", A, B);
```

allows 10 spaces for the value of A, and 20 spaces for the value of B. Check out the following example:

```
void main();
/* a program to convert feet to inches */
{
float feet,inches;
printf("Enter number of feet:");
scanf("%f", &feet);
inches = feet * 12.0;
printf("%10.2f feet equal %12.4f inches\n", feet, inches);
}
```

The printf statement allows 10 spaces for the value of feet, and 2 digits after the decimal point. There are 12 total spaces for the value of inches, with 4 digits after the decimal point.

PROGRAM #6: Write a program to convert hours and minutes to minutes only. Ask the user for the number of hours and the number of minutes, and then print the answer. For example, suppose the user's response for the number of hours is 3 and for the number of minutes is 10. The following message should be printed:
3 hours and 10 minutes equals 190 minutes

The next example computes the amount of interest that you would receive if you saved $100.00 in the bank for one year at an interest rate of 12 percent per year.

```
void main()
/* computes interest on $100 for one year at 12% */
{
float principal ;
float interest ;
principal = 100;
interest = principal * 0.12;
printf(" %10.2f %10.2f \n", principal, interest);
}
```

PROGRAM #7: Write a program that asks the user for the amount of money he/she wants to invest at a rate of 7% per year and then prints a message proclaiming the amount of interest earned in one year. For example, if the user responded that he has 200 dollars to invest, the computer will respond:
"You will earn $14 interest at the end of one year if you invest with us."

LESSON 3

Loops

3.1 GENERAL INFORMATION ON LOOPS

In order to convert temperature from degrees Centigrade to degrees Fahrenheit, we just multiply the Centigrade temperatures by 9/5 and then add 32. The following is an example of a simple program that converts 100 degrees Centigrade to degrees Fahrenheit.

```
void main()
{
int C;
float F;
C = 100;
F = (C*9)/5. + 32.; /* formula for Fahrenheit */
printf("%10d %10.2f\n", C, F);
}
```

Notice that this program only converts one value, 100, from Centigrade to Fahrenheit. It would be more useful and interesting to calculate the Fahrenheit temperature for lots of different values for Centigrade; for example 100, 110, 120 ... etc. This is accomplished by using a loop. There are three kinds of loops that we learn about: the **WHILE loop,** the **DO/WHILE loop**, and the **FOR loop**.

3.2 Relational Operators

Before looking further at looping statements consider the relational operators that can be used in a relational expression such as a WHILE loop, a DO/WHILE loop, and a FOR loop:

== equal
< less than
> greater than
!= not equal
<= less than or equal
>= greater than or equal

An example of how to use one of these relational operators in a WHILE loop is:

while (num1 < num2)

Don't worry too much about understanding the WHILE statement as it will be explained in the next section. For now just understand that the loop will only work when num1 is less than num2.

Another use of the Relational Operators is in a comparison statement called the IF statement. The IF statement will compare two items using the Relational Operators, and if the comparison is true, the commands following the IF statement will be executed; otherwise, those commands will be skipped. Below is the basic usage of the IF statement.

IF(num1 < num2) /*No Semicolon*/
printf("num1 is less than num2");

The IF statement will be further explained in Chapter 4.

3.3 The WHILE Loop

The next example uses a WHILE loop to continuously calculate degrees Fahrenheit for new values of C. Each time through the loop, C is being incremented by 10. Thus we will be finding degrees Fahrenheit (F) for C = 100, 110, 120, 130, etc. When will we stop? How about stopping after C is 200? We will use this as our stopping criterion. Every loop must have a stopping criterion; otherwise, you will be stuck in something known as an infinite loop. It is like being stuck in a revolving door with no way out. The following program demonstrates the use of the **WHILE** loop:

```
void main()
{
int C ;
real F ;
C = 100;
while (C <=200) /* notice no semicolon after this statement */
    {
      F = (C*9)/5. + 32.;
      printf("%10d %10.2f \n", C, F);
      C = C + 10; /* increment C by 10 each time through */
    }
}
```

In the line containing the WHILE statement, the value of C is compared to 200. If C is less than or equal to 200 the loop is executed. If C is greater than 200 the entire WHILE loop (the three statements between the braces {and}) is skipped.

PROBLEM: Write a program that reads a list of student names and prints the name that comes first alphabetically.

Let's solve the problem together. If you were trying to find the alphabetically first name in a long list of names *without* using the computer, how would you do it? You would probably read down the list of names, one at a time, and remember only the name that was alphabetically first so far. If you read a name that was alphabetically before the one you were remembering, then you would remember the new name instead.

We can use this as a model for telling the computer how to solve the problem (This is called finding an ALGORITHM for the problem. An *algorithm* is simply a recipe for finding the solution.) We will tell the computer to read a single name at a time and to save the smallest name it has processed so far in the variable **SMALLNAME.** Since we don't know how many names will be on the list, we will use the sentinel value 'DONE', since that should not be anyone's name. The *sentinel value* is used to stop us from processing the WHILE loop. An outline of our program will look like this:

Read the first name into NAME
Initialize SMALLNAME to NAME
WHILE NAME is not equal to 'DONE'
{
    If NAME is less than SMALLNAME then store it in SMALLNAME
    Read the next name into NAME
}

PROGRAM #8: Write a program that continually asks the user for a name until the user says 'DONE' and then prints out the smallest (alphabetically first) name. For example, if the user responded with the following names:

SALLY
JOE
KENNETH
ANNE
MABEL
ZYGMUND
BOBBY
DONE

the computer would respond with
The smallest name is ANNE.

IF we know the number of data items to be processed beforehand, a counter can be used to control the **WHILE** loop. For example, we could change our algorithm to:

Ask the user how many names he wants to give and store in NUMNAMES
Read the number of names and store as NUMNAMES

```
Read the first name into NAME
Initialize SMALLNAME to NAME
Initialize COUNT to 1
WHILE COUNT is less than or equal to NUMNAMES
{
    Read the next name into NAME
    Store the smaller of NAME and SMALLNAME in SMALLNAME
    Increase COUNT by 1 (COUNT = COUNT +1)
}
```

PROGRAM #9: Modify PROG8 so that it asks the user beforehand for the number of names to be processed. This time, do **not** use 'DONE.'

3.4 The DO/WHILE Loop

The DO - WHILE loop works the same way as the WHILE loop except that the comparison (to determine whether or not to quit the loop) is not made until the end of the loop. For example:

```
void main()
{
C = 100;
do /* Remember, do not use upper case letters! */
{
F = (C*9)/5. + 32.;
printf("%10d %10.2f \n", C, F);
C = C + 10;
}
while (C <= 200);
}
```

The following program inputs a student's name and two scores, and then prints the name and average score. The process is continued until the average of the scores is 0.0. The 0.0 average is used as the sentinel value—condition to terminate the loop.

```
void main()
{
char name[60];
```

```
int score1, score2;
float average;
do
{
printf("What is your name?");
scanf("%s", name); // cannot have spaces in name
printf("Input your two scores, separated by a space.\n");
scanf("%d %d ",&score1,&score2);
average = (score1+score2)/2.0;
printf("%s %f", name, average);
}
while (average != 0.);
}
```

Run the program with the following data:

Bonnie, 90,85
Elizabeth, 80, 90
Beverly, 85, 92
Dawn, 95, 98
THATSALL, 0, 0

3.5 The FOR Statement

The FOR loop is convenient to use when you know exactly how many times you need to execute a loop. Suppose we know that we wanted to go through the loop 5 times. Using a FOR loop we can do that:

```
{
int count;
float number;
for (count=1; count <= 5; count = count + 1)
    {
      printf("Give me a number, please.");
      scanf("%d",&number);
      printf("Your number is %d",number, "\n");
    }
    printf("\n");
    printf("Thank you for the numbers.\n");
    }
```

The variable COUNT is called the running variable and takes the initial value of 1. The block of statements under the **for** statement is then executed and COUNT takes on the value of 2 and is checked against 5. If COUNT is less than or equal to 5 the block is executed again. This process continues until COUNT is greater than 5.

The language C provides **short cut methods** to add 1 or to subtract 1 from a memory position. Consider: count = count + 1 can be replaced by count++ or ++count; count = count - 1 can be replaced by count-- or --count .

PROGRAM #10: Write a program that prints your name 10 times. Use a FOR loop with a counter to keep track of the number of times the loop has been executed.

PROGRAM #11: Write another program to input a student's name and three test scores. Print the name and average score. Continue this process until the name 'END' is encountered. Hint: use the program that you wrote for prog10 and just make a few changes to it.

PROGRAM #12: Write a program to input students' names and the score they received on their recent test, then calculate and print the class average for the test. Do not use a trip value to quit the loop, but assume there are 5 students in the class.

The next program finds and prints the sum of the integers 1 through 100:

```
void main()
{
int sum, num ;
{
sum = 0;
num = 1;
while (num <= 100)
{
    sum = sum + num;
    num = num + 1;
```

```
}
printf("sum of first 100 integers is %d", sum);
}
```

PROGRAM #13: Change the above program so that it finds and prints the sum of the odd integers 1 through 99. (Form the sum 1 + 3 + 5 + ... +99)

Pretend that you are looking for a job for the month of July. Suppose that someone offers you a job that pays one cent for the first day, two cents for the second day, four cents for the third day, eight cents for the fourth day, etc. The amount of your pay is doubling each day. Would you take this job or one that offered you $1000 per day for the entire month? Before you answer, you may want to run the following program. It determines the day in which the day's pay for the first job first exceeds $10,000.

```
void main()
{
int day;
float daypay;
day = 1;
daypay = 0.01;
while (daypay < 10000)
{
    day = day + 1;
    daypay = daypay * 2;
}
printf("The day in which pay first exceeds $10,000 is %d" ,day);
}
```

PROGRAM #14: Using the above program, change it so that it prints the total salary you will receive for the month of July. Hint: there are 31 days in July.

LESSON 4

Decision Statements

4.1 IF STATEMENTS

One of the most used CONTROL STATEMENTS in the C language is the **IF** statement. In its simplest form, it evaluates an expression and then proceeds on the basis of the result of that comparison. For example, the following program **reads in a set of scores** and counts the number of students that made an A. An A is considered to be a score of 90 or above. A sentinel value of 0 is used. This signals that no more data will follow and normally this is not a good data value - one to be included.

```
void main()
{
int acount, score;/* acount is the variable for the number of A's */
acount = 0;
do
{
scanf("%d",&score);
if (score >= 90)
acount = acount + 1;
}
while (score != 0); /* trip on score of 0 */
printf("There were %d", acount, " A scores. ");
}
```

Use the following as input: 98 45 17 90 91 87 34 99 100 0

How many times will the loop be executed?

What will be printed out?

If you have more than one statement to be executed and the IF expression evaluates to true, you can use the braces { } to designate the block to be executed.

4.2 IF / ELSE STATEMENTS

Whenever you want one thing done when the IF expression evaluates to true and another thing done when it evaluates to false, it is handy to use the **IF - ELSE** statement. Here is a short program that asks the user to guess the number the computer is thinking. If the input agrees with the one the program is trying to match (which is 6 in our case), the program prints "Right. Good job." If the digit is not 6 the program prints "Sorry, wrong number."

```
void main()
{
int x ;
printf("I am thinking of a digit. What is it?");
scanf("%d", &x);
if (x == 6)
printf("Right. Good job.");
else
printf("Sorry, wrong number.");
}
```

PROGRAM #15: Put the above program in a loop so that it will continue to play the game until the person guesses the digit. Also, count the number of guesses it takes. It should print a message to the user telling how many guesses it took him/her to get the correct digit.

Suppose we need a program to count the number of students who are freshmen, sophomores, juniors, or seniors in a class of 10 students. This program accomplishes that by combining IF and ELSE statements.

```
void main()
{
int nfr,nso,njr,nsr,grade,count;
nfr = 0;
nso = 0;
njr = 0;
nsr = 0;
count = 1;
while (count <= 10)
{
    printf("enter your grade as either 9,10,11,or 12.");
    scanf("%d", &grade);
    if (grade == 9)
      nfr = nfr + 1;
    else if (grade == 10)
      nso = nso + 1;
    else if (grade == 11)
      njr = njr + 1;
    else if (grade == 12)
      nsr = nsr + 1;
      count = count + 1;
}
printf("There were %d freshmen.", nfr);
printf("There were %d sophomores.", nso);
printf("There were %d juniors", njr);
printf("There were %d seniors", nsr);
}
```

Run the program and try it out.

In the following program a company pays every employee $5.00 per hour. This program asks for name and number of hours worked, and then calculates and prints the total wages for the week.

```
void main()
{
float hours, paydue ;
char name[30];
```

```
printf("enter your name: ");
scanf("%s",name);
printf("hours worked:");
scanf("%f", &hours);
paydue = hours * 5.00;
printf("%s %7.2f %8.2f", name, hours, paydue);
}
```

PROGRAM #16: Write a program that pays an employee $5.00 per hour for all hours less than or equal to 40 and pays twice that amount for all hours over 40. For example, if you worked for this company last month for 52 hours you would receive $5.00 per hour for 40 hours (200 dollars) plus $10.00 per hour for 12 hours (120 dollars) for a total of 320 dollars.

PROGRAM #17: Write a program to determine how much fine you should pay for a speeding ticket. Assume the fine is computed as follows:

Amount over limit (miles/hour)	Fine
11 – 20	$20
21 - 30	$25
31 – 40	$40
41 or more	$60

Your program should ask for both the speed limit and the driver's speed. It should then print

THE FINE IS $________

PROGRAM #18: Write a program that prints the number 1 - 10, along with their square and cube. An example of the Output: (Format the output to get a chart like this.)

NUMBER	SQUARE	CUBE
1	1	1
2	4	8
.	.	.
.	.	.
.	.	.
10	100	1000

Lesson 5

Arrays

5.1 Array Definition

Suppose we wish to process grades for several classes of students. The number of students in each class will vary, but we wish to write a program that will calculate the average grade and then find the number of grades less than the average grade in the class. We cannot calculate the average until all the grades for the class have been entered. So we must save the grades and count the ones below average after the average is calculated.

Should we save each grade in a variable of different name? This would lead to a long repetitious program. Fortunately, C lets us solve the problem in a very nice way using **ARRAYS**. An **ARRAY** is a data structure used for storing a collection of data items that are all the same type. Usually, we first describe the structure of an array in an *array type declaration*. The array GRADE of 20 elements is declared as

float grade[20];

The 20 elements of grade are referenced as grade[0], grade[1], ...grade[19]. C reserves 20 memory cells for the GRADEs; these memory cells will be adjacent to each other in memory. Each cell of GRADE may contain a single student's grade. We can use each one, just as we did variables, by calling it by its name. In the case of an array, it will be like this: grade[1] means the grade of the second student in the class.

To read the scores of students into the array GRADE, we would do this:

```
void main()
{
float grade[20];
int i, sum ;
float average;
for (i=0; i< 20; ++i)
{
printf("Please enter your score:");
scanf("%f", &grade[i]);
}
}
```

To find the class average, we would change the main part of the program to this:

```
sum = 0;
for (i=0; i<20; ++i)
{
printf("Please enter your score:");
scanf("%f", &grade[i]);
sum = sum + grade[i];
}
    average = sum / 20.0;
```

5.2 Array Examples

PROGRAM #19: Change the above program so that it finds the average grade for a class of 10 students; then print each grade and tells whether it is "below average", "average", or "above average".

The following program finds the largest element in a list of numbers, and prints the number of the cell where it was found (its position within the array).

```
void main()
{
int n[10];
int i,largest,position;
largest = 0;
for (i=0; i<10; ++i)
{
scanf("%d", &n[i]);
if (n[i] > largest)
{
largest = n[i];
position = i;
}
}
printf("largest is %d", largest);
printf("position is %d", position);
}
```

PROGRAM #20: Write a program to print the smallest element in a list of numbers and its position within the list. (Be careful with this one, test all possible cases.)

PROGRAM #21: Write an interactive program that plays the game of HANGMAN. Hint: Let WORD be an array of char. Read the word to be guessed into successive elements of the array WORD. The player must guess the letters that belong to WORD. The game ends when either all letters have been guessed correctly (player wins) or a specified number of incorrect guesses have been made (computer wins.) Use an array SOLUTION to keep track of the solution so far. Initialize SOLUTION to a string of symbols "*". Each time a letter in WORD is guessed, replace the corresponding "*" in SOLUTION with that letter and show it to the player before the next guess is made. Play several games to try it out.

Searching an array of elements for a particular element or sorting a list to place in order lexicographically are large topics in computer science. Program #20 is an example of searching. To sort a list of elements (numbers) in order from largest number to smallest number consider the following algorithm:

1. Define or input the list of N numbers and store in an array
2. Search the list starting at the first element for the largest element and swap places with the largest element and the element in the first position
3. Search the list starting with the second element for the largest element and swap places with the new largest element and the element in the second position
4. Continue this process until you have considered the n-1st and nth element
5. Output the list—it should now be in order from largest element to smallest element

The above algorithm is spoken of as the selection algorithm or sort.

PROGRAM #22: Write a program, using the selection sort, to arrange a list of number in order from high number to low number.

LESSON 6

Functions

6.1 FUNCTION BASICS

C has some built-in functions that come in quite handy. For example, the function SQRT finds the square root of a number. The following part of a program shows how the function is called:

```
{
printf("%10d\n", sqrt(4));
printf("%10d\n", sqrt(25));
printf("%10d\n", sqrt(81));
printf("%10d\n", sqrt(100));
}
```

This would result in the following being printed:

```
2
5
9
10
```

Most programming languages have many pre-defined or built-in functions. All of the pre-defined functions are just special purpose programs, such as the sqrt function demonstrated above. These programs were written and stored with the compiler or translator and the systems programmer, the individual that loads the compiler, has the option of loading (or not loading) these functions with the compiler at the time the compiler is loaded onto the computer.

Other similar functions include **SIN, COS, EXP, LN, LN10, POW, FABS, ABS,** and there are others. You may want to try each of these in a manner similar to the test cases above for the SQRT function. These functions are for the sine, cosine, exponential—e to a power, natural logarithm, common logarithm, a number raised to a power, absolute value of a float number and the absolute value of an integer. A library or set of pre-defined functions is normally supplied with the compiler. Be careful with the POW function—you will find that it has two arguments.

A library or set of pre-defined functions is normally supplied with the compiler.

Often, we need some functions other than the ones C provides. In that case, we get to make our own. For example, suppose we wanted a function that would return the larger of two integers we gave it. We have to give the function a *name* and then define it for C. Let's call it **LARGER.** We would define it like this:

```
int larger(int first, int second)
{
int la;
if (first > second)
la = first;
else
la = second;
return(la);
}
```

The first line may be a little confusing. We are telling C that we are defining what is meant by the function LARGER. We are saying that we will give it two integers and it should give us an integer in return. If we said in our program that **x = larger(23,67)**, C would assign x to be 67. Here is how it would look in the entire program:

```
int larger(int, int);
void main()
{
int num1,num2,num3,num4,temp1,temp2,big ;
printf("Enter 4 numbers.");
scanf("%d %d %d %d ", &num1,&num2,&num3,&num4);
temp1 = larger(num1,num2);
temp2 = larger(num3,num4);
big = larger(temp1,temp2);
printf("The largest number is %d", big);
}
int larger (int first, int second)
{
int la;
if (first > second)
la = first;
else
la = second;
return(la);
}
```

Notice that we had to define the function before we got to the main body of the program. The method of defining a function in this manner is spoken of as defining the **function prototype**. This would not be necessary if we had placed the actual function before the main program.

PROGRAM #23: Write a function CUBE that finds the cube of a number. For example, the cube of 5 is 125 (5*5*5) and the cube of 2 is 8 (2*2*2). Test your function by writing a program that makes a table of the numbers 1 through 10 with their cubes. It should look something like this: (Remember to format the output to get the chart.)

NUMBER	CUBE
1	1
2	8
3	27
.	.
.	.
.	.

PROGRAM #24: Write a function POWER that finds the power of an integer. For example POWER(2,5) should return 32, since 2 to the fifth power = 2*2*2*2*2 = 32. Test it out in a program.

6.2 Random Number Generators

Functions to generate **random numbers** are very common. Random number generators normally produce a sequence of real numbers between 0 and 1 that for all practical purposes appear to be random. Most random number generators start with an initial real value called a seed. Subsequent random numbers are determined once the seed is specified. Here is a function which is a random number generator:

```
randomize();
n = random(100); /* You need to #include <stdlib.h> */
```

The numbers generated are all between 0 and 99. The next function uses RANDOM but finds random numbers in whatever range you specify.

```
int n, range;
randomize();
printf("Enter the range.");
scanf("%d", &range);
n = random(range);
```

The above sequence will define random numbers in the range between 0 and (range-1).

Now that we have a random number generator, we can write some more interesting games. The number guessing game that we wrote back in program 15 can now be made more interesting.

PROGRAM #25: Write a guessing game program that will ask the user to guess a number. If the user is correct, the computer will respond with a nice message and tell the user how many guesses it took. If the guess is wrong, the computer will output HIGHER or LOWER and ask for another guess. This will continue until the user gets it right. Change the program so that the user can select the range the integer will be in. Also, you might want to give the user a maximum number of guesses, in case the user becomes confused and never gets the right answer.

Chapter 7

C++ Programming

Lesson 1 Getting Started 335

1.1 Preprocessor Directives 335
1.2 Program Body 335
1.3 Program Variables 336
1.4 Assignment Statement 337
1.5 Data Types 339
1.6 Mathematical Operators 340

Lesson 2 Strings and Formatted Output 342

2.1 String Data Type 342
2.2 Formatted Output 343

Lesson 3 Loops 346

3.1 General Information on Loops 346
3.2 Relational Operators 347
3.3 The WHILE loop 347
3.4 The DO/WHILE loop 350
3.5 The FOR statement 351

Lesson 4 Decision Statements 354

4.1 If Statements 354

4.2 If / Else Statements 355

Lesson 5 Arrays 359

5.1 Array Definition 359

5.2 Array Examples 360

Lesson 6 Functions 363

6.1 Function Basics 363

6.2 Random Number Generators 366

Lesson 7

C++
Getting Started

1.1 Preprocessor Directives

Before beginning our study of C++, we will examine two short programs. Don't worry about understanding the details of these programs yet; it will all be explained as we go along.

```
#include <iostream.h> /*This directive is needed for C++ input and
  output*/
void main()          // Sample 1
    {
cout << "My first C++ program" << endl;
    }
```

The first line of this example is called the **PRE-PROCESSOR DIRECTIVE**; it tells the compiler to include routines necessary for input and output. The next line **VOID MAIN**( ) is necessary for all C++ programs and is where execution starts. The **left brace** {, and **right brace** } will enclose the body of the program.

1.2 Program Body

The statements starting with the left brace {, and ending with the right} brace are called the **PROGRAM BODY** and contain the **STATEMENTS** which will be executed by the computer. The program body consists of the word {, followed by some executable statements, followed by the}. There is only one executable statement in this example. The **cout** (pronounced c out) statement displays the string "My first C++ program" on the screen. The "**endl**" on the end of the line, *will not be printed. Even though it will not be printed it instructs* the computer to start a new line for the next output item.

Execute the above program. After being successful with this program, save the program, and add another line to print "**this is fun**". If all did not go well, **REVISE** the file and make any necessary changes. Save the file and continue.

Look at the following program:

```
void main()        // Sample 2
   {
 int N1, N2, SUM;
cout << "Enter two numbers:";
cin >> N1 >> N2;
SUM = N1 + N2;
cout << N1 << "plus" << N2 << "equals" << SUM; }
```

1.3 Program Variables

C++ and most other common programming languages perform their calculations by manipulating items called **VARIABLES**. In a C++ program, variable names are written as a string of letters and digits that begins with a letter. Some sample names for C++ variables are:
X Y Z SUM N1 N2 KELLY rate distance Time

Numbers or other types of data can be associated with C++ variables. For now we will confine our attention to variables that hold only numbers. In C++ all variables must be **declared** before they can be used in the body of a program. The **variables** are declared at the beginning of the program. Each declaration contains the type of the variable, followed by the **variable name**. All three variables in this sample 2 program are of type integer. (A variable of type **INTEGER** can store whole numbers only.) If we wanted to allow decimals, we could declare the numbers to be of type **float**. (Real or float variables contain decimal points.) The programmer must be aware of declaring variables as integer or as float as the data they represent are stored differently in the computer's memory. The performance of arithmetic is also different on integer variables and float variables.

The lines between {and} contain the statements to be carried out by the computer. The semicolons at the ends of the statements are used to separate the statements. The semicolon is not necessary after the last statement since there is no subsequent statement that it needs to be separated from. Since {and} are not program statements, there is no semicolon after them. A semicolons before } is optional.

The first statement in the body of the program (Sample 2) causes the following phrase to appear on the screen:
Enter two numbers

Suppose that in response to this, an obedient user enters two numbers on the keyboard, say 4, followed by a space, followed by a 5, followed by pressing the RETURN or ENTER key (Data input will be separated by one or more blank spaces).
The next statement, called an **INPUT** statement,
cin >>...;

tells the computer what to do with these numbers. This statement is an instruction to the computer to read the two numbers and store in memory positions allocated for N1 and N2. It causes the memory position allocated for the variable N1 to become equal to the first number typed in, i.e.4, and the memory for N2 to become equal to the second number typed in, i.e. 5.

1.4 Assignment Statement

The next statement in our sample 2 program is:
SUM = N1 + N2;

The symbol = is called the **ASSIGNMENT OPERATOR**, and this statement is called an **ASSIGNMENT STATEMENT**. There can be spaces between the equal sign and N1 as C++ is a free format language and blank spaces or white spaces are ignored. The assignment operator has no standard pronunciation but most people pronounce it *"gets the value"* or *"is assigned"*. The memory position on the left hand side of the operator gets the value of what is on the right hand side of the operator. This changes the value of what is stored in memory for SUM to the value of what is stored in N1 plus the value of what is stored in N2. Finally, the cout statement, which is the OUTPUT statement, produces the output.

Enter and run the above program. Use the same procedure as before. Do not forget to include the pre-processor directive.

PROBLEM: What is the output produced by the following four lines (when correctly embedded in a complete program)? The variables are of type **integer**:

```
X = 2;
Y = 3;
Y = X * 7;
cout << X << Y;
```

ANSWER:

PROGRAM #1: Write a C++ program that will print your name on one line and your hometown on the next line. Be sure to Save and then Run or Execute it. Use the name prog1.cpp when you create the file so it will be saved under that name.

The following example is a program to print the letter L in magnified form:

```
void main()

/* prints a letter in magnified form */
  {
   cout << "    **    " << endl;
```

```
    cout << “    **     ” << endl;
    cout << “    **     ” << endl;
    cout << “    ******  ” << endl;
    cout << “    ******  ” << endl;
  }
```

The /* **print a letter in magnified form** */ is called a comment line. The /* at the beginning and */ at the end of a comment is necessary. Comments of this type can be extended on several lines. Another form of comment is the // Comment. Comments of this time cannot be extended over lines. The // comment can be placed at the end of any C++ statement or can be on a line by itself. The /* .... */ type of comment can be included within a statement.

Examples of comments are:
cin>>a>>b; // this is an input statement
cout<<a<<b; /* this is an output statement */

PROGRAM #2: Write a program that will print your initials in magnified form. Call this prog2.cpp.

1.5 Data Types

A **DATA TYPE** is a description of a category of data, and each variable in a data type can represent only one data element of given type. In our sample program all variables were of type integer. That means that the numbers they represent must be whole number such as:
38 0 1 89 3987 -12 -5

Numbers that include a fractional part, such as the ones below, are of type float or real:
2.7192 0.098 -15.8 1000053.98

To declare the variable x and y as float you will use the following declaration:
float x,y;

The type used for letters, or, more generally, any single symbol is **CHAR**, which is short for character. Values of this type are declared as follows:
char X, Y;

A variable of type *char* can hold any (**one**) character on the input keyboard. Therefore, X could hold any of the characters A, a, +, or 6. It is perfectly acceptable to have variables of more than one type in a program. In such cases they are all declared at once following the format illustrated below:

```
    {
int n1;
float time;
char initial;
    }
```

1.6 Mathematical Operators

The mathematical operations that are available in C++ and their symbol are given below:

OPERATION	SYMBOL	EXAMPLE
addition	+	**A + B**
subtraction	-	**C - 14**
multiplication	*	**5 * B**
division	/	**A / B**
integer portion	%	**A % B**

Suppose memory positions A, B, and C have been declared as type integer and position A has the number 5 stored and position B has the number 12 stored. The statement used to add the two numbers and store their sum, 17, in memory position C would be
C = A + B;

More complex mathematical expression could look as follows:
C = A / B + (3.6 + A * B) – B / 17.4;

Mathematical operations are performed from left to right with division (/), and multiplication (*), and integer portion (%) taking precedence over addition (+), and subtraction (-). Grouping symbols can also be used to control the order of operations.

Consider the statement:
C = 3 + 8 / 2 – 5;

The operation 8 / 2 would be performed first, giving 4, this 4 would then be added to 3 giving 7, and 5 would be subtracted from 7 giving 2.

In the statement C = (4 + 6) * 5 / 10; the 4 would be added to 6, giving 10, and then the 10 would be multiplied by 5, giving 50, and the 50 would be divided by 10 giving 5 which would be stored in memory position C.

PROBLEMS:

1. What is the output produced by the following three lines if they are correctly embedded in a program, and the variables are of type integer?
   X = 2;
   X = X + 1;
   cout << X;

2. What is the output produced by the following? The variables are of type char: (Be careful on this one - it is tricky!)
   A = 'B';
   B = 'C';
   C = A;
   cout << A << B << C;

PROGRAM #3: Write a C++ program that will read in two integers and will then output their sum, difference, and product.

LESSON 2

Strings and Formatted Output

2.1 STRING DATA TYPE

Often we would like to store a whole word or combination of words in a variable rather than just one character. To do this in C++ it is necessary to define a new data type: STRING. We can do this in either of the following ways: (string is used to declare a set of characters).

```
string name;
char name[60];
```

If we declare this type before we declare our variables we can use "name" as a set of characters just like integer, real, and char. C++ will let us do it as follows:

```
void main()
    {
char name[60];
int test1, test2;
float average;
cout << "What is your name?:";
cin >> name;
cout << endl << "What are your test scores?:";
cin >> test1 >> test2;
```

```
average = (test1 + test2)/2;
cout << endl << name << " "<< average;
    }
```

In the above example we declared name to be 60 characters in length (a maximum of 59 characters as one character is used as an end of string marker). However, we could declare it to be of almost any length, for example, 25. The string type or array of characters will make more sense when we study arrays later on. You may have noticed that the average was printed in a rather strange way. The reason it looks like this is because we have not specified how we would like decimal numbers to be printed. The next section deals with that topic.

PROGRAM #4: Write a C++ program that will ask for a name and 3 test scores, and will print the person's name and average score.

PROGRAM #5: Write a program that will ask for a person's name and age and then respond with the statement:
"Hello, _______________. You do not look ___________ year old."

2.2 Formatted Output

The output for integer, float, and character data can be controlled by formatting. You can specify the field width through the setw( ) function as well as the number of places to the right of the decimal point through the setprecision function. To use the following formatting function, you must include the library file:
#include <iomanip.h>

The output statement:
cout << setw(10) << 100 << setw(10) << 50 << setw(10) << 25;
Would produce:
_ _ _ _ _ _ _ 100 _ _ _ _ _ _ _ _ _ 50 _ _ _ _ _ _ _ _ _ 25

cout << setw(3) << 78634;
OUTPUT: 78634

```
cout << setprecision(3) << setw(10) << 765.432;
OUTPUT: ___765.432

cout << setprecision(4) << setw(10) <<.00456;
OUTPUT: ______.0046
```

Check out the following example:

```
void main()
/* a program to convert feet to inches */
{
float feet, inches;
cout << "Enter number of feet:";
cin >> feet;
inches = feet * 12.0;
cout << setw(8) << feet << "feet equal "<< setw(8) << inches;
cout <<" inches" << endl;
}
```

PROGRAM #6: Write a program to convert hours and minutes to minutes only. Ask the user for the number of hours and the number of minutes, and then print the answer. For example, suppose the user's response for the number of hours is 3 and for the number of minutes is 10. The following message should be printed:
3 hours and 10 minutes equals 190 minutes

The next example computes the amount of interest that you would receive if you saved $100.00 in the bank for one year at an interest rate of 12 percent per year.

```
void main()
/* computes interest on $100 for one year at 12% */
{
float principal ;
float interest ;
principal = 100;
interest = principal * 0.12;
cout << principal << " "<< interest << endl;
}
```

PROGRAM #7: Write a program that asks the user for the amount of money he/she wants to invest at a rate of 7% per year and then prints a message proclaiming the amount of interest earned in one year. For example, if the user responded that he has 200 dollars to invest, the computer will respond:
"You will earn $14 interest at the end of one year if you invest with us."

Lesson 3

Loops

3.1 General Information on Loops

In order to convert temperature from degrees Centigrade to degrees Fahrenheit, we just multiply the Centigrade temperatures by 9/5 and then add 32. The following is an example of a simple program that converts 100 degrees Centigrade to degrees Fahrenheit.

```
void main()
{
int C;
float F;
C = 100;
F = (C*9)/5. + 32.;      /* formula for Fahrenheit */
cout << C << " "<<F ;
}
```

Notice that this program only converts one value, 100, from Centigrade to Fahrenheit. It would be more useful and interesting to calculate the Fahrenheit temperature for lots of different values for Centigrade; for example 100, 110, 120, ... etc. This is accomplished by using a loop. There are three kinds of loops that we learn about: the **WHILE loop**, the **DO/WHILE loop**, and the **FOR loop**. Before studying the loop structure we will learn about relational operators.

3.2 Relational Operators

The relational operators that can be used in a relational expression such as a WHILE loop, a DO/WHILE loop, and a FOR loop are:
== equal
< less than
> greater than
!= not equal
<= less than or equal
>= greater than or equal

An example of how to use one of these relational operators in a WHILE loop is:
while(num1 < num2)

Don't worry too much about understanding the **WHILE** statement now, that will be explained in the next section. For now just understand that the loop will only work when num1 is less than num2.

Another use of the Relational Operators is in a comparison or a control statement called the **IF statement.** The IF statement will compare two items using Relational Operators, and if the comparison is true, the commands following the IF statement will be executed; otherwise, those commands will be skipped. Below is the basic usage of the IF statement.

```
if(num1 < num2) /*No Semicolon*/
cout << "num1 is less than num2";
```

The IF statement will be explained in more detail in Chapter 4.

3.3 The WHILE Loop

The next example uses a **WHILE** loop to continuously calculate degrees Fahrenheit for new values of C. Each time through the loop, C is being incremented by 10. Thus we will be finding degrees Fahrenheit (F) for C = 100, 110, 120, 130. When will we stop? We will arbitrarily use 200 as our stopping criterion. Every loop must have a stopping criterion;

otherwise you will be stuck in something known as an infinite loop. It is like being stuck in a revolving door with no way out. The following program demonstrates the use of the **WHILE** loop:

```
void main()
 {
int C ;
float F ;
C = 100;
while (C <=200) /* notice no semicolon after statement */
  {
F = (C*9)/5. + 32.;
cout << C << "  "<< F;
C = C + 10;  /* increment C by 10 each time through */
  }
 }
```

In the line containing the WHILE statement, the value of C is compared to 200. If C is less than or equal to 200 the loop is executed, i.e. all statement under the WHILE and between the left brace and the right brace {and}. If C is greater than 200 the entire WHILE loop is skipped - the three statements under the WHILE and between the {and}.

PROBLEM: Write a program that reads a list of student names, and prints the student name that comes first alphabetically.

Let's solve the problem together. If you were trying to find the alphabetically first name in a long list of names without using the computer, how would you do it? You would probably read down the list of names, one at a time, and remember only the name that was alphabetically first so far. If you read a name that was alphabetically before the one you were remembering, then you would remember the new name instead.

We can use this as a model for telling the computer how to solve the problem (This is called finding an ALGORITHM for the problem. An **algorithm** is simply a recipe for finding the solution). We will tell the computer to read a list of names one at a time and to save the *smallest* (the one that comes first in alphabetical order) name it has processed so far in the variable **SMALLNAME**. Since we don't know how many names will be in the list, we will use the ***sentinel value*** "DONE" (a value that tells the computer that no more values will be read), since that should not be anyone's name. A sentinel value is often used to terminate a loop, especially if the number of input values is not known in advance. An outline of our program will look like this:

Read the first name into NAME
Initialize SMALLNAME to NAME
WHILE NAME is not equal to "DONE"
{
If NAME is less than SMALLNAME then store it in SMALLNAME
Read the next name into NAME
}

PROGRAM #8: Write a program that continually asks the user for a name until the user says "DONE" and then prints out the smallest (alphabetically first) name. For example, if the user responded with the following names:

SALLY
JOE
KENNETH
ANNE
MABEL
ZYGMUND
BOBBY
DONE

then the computer would respond with:
The smallest name is ANNE.

If we know the number of data items to be processed beforehand, a counter can be used to control the **WHILE** loop. For example, we could change our algorithm to:

Ask the user how many names he wants to give and store this number in NUMNAMES

```
Read the first name into NAME
Initialize SMALLNAME to NAME
Initialize COUNT to 1
WHILE COUNT is less than or equal to NUMNAMES
   {
  Read the next name into NAME
  Store the smaller of NAME and SMALLNAME in SMALLNAME
  Increase COUNT by 1 (COUNT = COUNT +1)
   }
```

PROGRAM #9: Modify PROG8 so that it asks the user beforehand for the number of names to be processed. This time, do **not** use "DONE."

3.4 The DO/WHILE Loop

The **DO/WHILE** loop works the same way as the WHILE loop except that the comparison (to determine whether or not to quit the loop) is not made until the end of the loop. We say it is a post-test loop and the While Loop is a pre-test loop. For example:

```
void main()
{
  float C, F;
  C = 100;
  do      /* Remember, do not use upper case letters! */
    {
      F = (C*9)/5. + 32.;
      cout << "\n"<< C<< "  " << F ;
      C = C + 10;
    }
  while (C <= 200);
      }
```

The following program inputs a student's name and two scores and then prints the name and average score. The process is continued until the average of the scores is 0.0. The 0.0 average is used as the *sentinel* value—a condition to terminate the loop.

```
void main()
    {
char name[60];
int score1, score2;
float average;

do
  {
  cout << "What is your name?";
  cin >> name;       // cannot have spaces in name
  cout << "Input your two scores, separate the two by a space." << endl;
  cin >> score1 >> score2;
  average = (score1+score2)/2.0;
  cout << name << "  " << average;
    }
while (average != 0);
    }
```

Run the program with the following data:

Bonnie, 90,85
Elizabeth, 80, 90
Beverly, 85, 92
Dawn, 95, 98
THATSALL, 0, 0

3.5 The FOR Statement

The FOR loop is convenient to use when the number of times a loop is to be executed is known in advance. Suppose we know that we want to go through a loop 5 times. Using a FOR loop we can easily do that:

```
int count;
float number;
for (count=1; count <= 5; count = count + 1)
    {
    cout << "Give me a number, please.";
    cin >> number;
```

```
cout << “Your number is ” << number << endl;
}
cout << “Thank you for the numbers.” << endl;
```

The variable COUNT is called the running variable and takes the initial value of 1. The block of statements is then executed and COUNT takes on the value of 2 and COUNT is checked against 5. If COUNT is less than or equal to 5 the block is executed again. This process continues until COUNT is greater than 5.

The language C++ provides **short cut methods** to add 1 or to subtract 1 from a memory position. Consider: count = count + 1 can be replaced by count++ or ++count; count = count - 1 can be replaced by count-- or --count.

PROGRAM #10: Write a program that prints your name 10 times. Use a FOR loop with a counter to keep track of the number of times the loop has executed.

PROGRAM #11: Write a program to input a student's name and three test scores. Print the name and average score. Continue this process until the name "END" is encountered. Hint: use the program that you wrote for prog10 and just make a few changes to it.

PROGRAM #12: Write a program to input a student's name and score that they received on their recent test, then calculate and print the class average for the test. Do not use a trip value to quit the loop, but assume there are 5 students in the class.

The next program finds and prints the sum of the integers 1 through 100:

```
void main()
  {
 int sum, num ;
 sum = 0;
 num = 1;
 while (num <= 100)
```

```
    {
    sum = sum + num;
    num = num + 1;
    }
  cout << "The sum of first 100 integers is  " << sum;
  }
```

PROGRAM #13: Change the above program so that it finds and prints the sum of the odd integers 1 through 99. (Form the sum 1 + 3 + 5 +...+99)

Pretend that you are looking for a job for the month of July. Suppose that someone offers you a job that pays one cent for the first day, two cents for the second day, four cents for the third day, eight cents for the fourth day, etc. The amount of your pay is doubling each day. Would you take this job or one that offered you $1000 per day for the entire month? Before you answer, you may want to run the following program. It determines the day in which the day's pay for the first job first exceeds $10,000.

```
void main()
  {
int day;
float daypay;
 day = 1;
   daypay = 0.01;
   while (daypay < 10000)
  {
    day = day + 1;
    daypay = daypay * 2;
  }
cout << "The day in which pay first exceeds $10,000 is  " << day;
  }
```

PROGRAM #14: Using the above program, change it so that it prints the total salary you will receive for the month of July. Hint: there are 31 days in July.

LESSON 4

Decision Statements

4.1 IF STATEMENTS

One of the most used CONTROL STATEMENTS in the C++ language is the **IF** statement. In its simplest form, it evaluates an expression and then proceeds on the basis of the result of that evaluation. For example, the following program **reads in a set of scores** and counts the number of students that made an A. An A is considered to be a score of 90 or above. A sentinel value of 0 is used. This signals that no more data will follow and normally this is not a good data value – here we would not expect 0 to be one of the scores.

```
void main()
   {
int acount, score; /* acount is the variable for the number of A's */
acount = 0;
do
  {
  cin >> score;
  if (score >= 90)
acount = acount + 1;
   }
while (score != 0);    /* trip on score of 0 */
cout << "There were  " << acount << "  A scores.";
   }
```

Use the following as input:
98 45 17 90 91 87 34 99 100 0

How many times will the loop be executed?

What will be printed out?

If you have more than one statement to be executed when the IF expression evaluates to true, you can use the braces { } to designate the block to be executed.

4.2 IF / ELSE STATEMENTS

Whenever you want one thing done when the **IF** expression evaluates to true and another thing done when it evaluates to false, it is handy to use the **IF - ELSE statement.** Here is a short program that asks the user to guess the number the computer is thinking. If the digit agrees with the one the program is trying to match (which is 6 in our case), the program prints "Right. Good job." If the digit is not 6 the program prints "Sorry, wrong number."

```
void main( )
   {
int x ;
cout << "I am thinking of a digit.  What is it?";
cin >> x;
if (x = = 6)
     cout << "Right. Good job.";
else
    cout << "Sorry, wrong number.";
   }
```

PROGRAM #15: Put the above program in a loop so that it will continue to play the game until the person guesses the digit. Have your program count the number of guesses it takes. It should print a message to the user telling how many guesses it took him/her to get the correct digit.

Suppose we need a program to count the number of students who are freshmen, sophomores, juniors, and seniors in a class of 10. This program accomplishes that by combining IF and ELSE statements.

```
void main( )
   {
int nfr,nso,njr,nsr,grade,count;
nfr = 0;
nso = 0;
njr = 0;
nsr = 0;
count = 1;
while (count <= 10)
  {
     cout << "Enter your grade as either 9,10,11,or 12.";
     cin >> grade;
    if (grade = = 9)
      nfr = nfr + 1;
    else if (grade == 10)
      nso = nso + 1;
    else if (grade == 11)
      njr = njr + 1;
    else if (grade == 12)
      nsr = nsr + 1;
    count = count + 1;
     }
   cout << "There were  " << nfr << "  freshmen."<<endl;
   cout << "There were  " << nso << "  sophomores."<<endl;
   cout << "There were  " << njr << "  juniors."<<endl;
   cout << "There were  " << nsr << "  seniors";
   }
```

Run the program and try it out.

In the following program a company pays every employee $5.00 per hour. This program asks for name and number of hours worked. It then calculates and prints the total wages for the week.

```
void main()
  {
float hours, paydue ;
char name[30];
cout << "Enter your name: ";
cin >> name;
cout << "hours worked:";
cin >> hours;
paydue = hours * 5.00;
cout << name<< " " << hours << " " << paydue;
  }
```

PROGRAM #16: Write a program that pays an employee $5.00 per hour for all hours less than or equal to 40 and pays twice that amount for all hours over 40. For example, if you worked for this company last week for 52 hours you would receive $5.00 per hour for 40 hours (200 dollars) plus $10.00 per hour for 12 hours (120 dollars) for a total of 320 dollars.

PROGRAM #17: Write a program to determine how much fine you should pay for a speeding ticket. Assume the fine is computed as follows:

Amount over limit (miles/hour)	Fine
1 - 10	$10
11 - 20	$20
21 - 30	$25
31 - 40	$40
41 or more	$60

Your program should ask for both the speed limit and the driver's speed. It should then print:
THE FINE IS $__________

PROGRAM #18: Write a program that prints the numbers 1 through 10, along with the square and cube of the number.

An example of the output: (Format the output to get a chart like this.)

NUMBER	SQUARE	CUBE
1	1	1
2	4	8
.	.	.
.	.	.
.	.	.
10	100	1000

LESSON 5

Arrays

5.1 Array Definition

Suppose we wish to process grades for a class of several students. The number of students in each class will vary, but we wish to write a program that will calculate the average grade and then find the number of grades less than the average grade in the class. We cannot calculate the average until all the grades for the class have been entered. So we must save the grades and count the ones below average after the average is calculated.

Should we save each grade in a variable of different name? This would lead to a long repetitious program. Fortunately, C++ lets us solve the problem in a very nice way using **ARRAYS**. An ARRAY is a data structure used for storing a collection of data items that are all the same type (an array stores items in adjacent memory positions). Usually, we first describe the structure of an array in an **array type declaration**. The array GRADE of 20 elements is declared as
float grade[20];

C++ reserves 20 memory cells for the GRADEs; these memory cells will be adjacent to each other in memory. Each cell of GRADE will contain a single student's grade. We can use each cell, just as we used variables, by calling it by its name. The elements are stored in the array GRADE as GRADE[0], GRADE[1], ... GRADE[19]. GRADE[0] means the grade of the first student in the class, and GRADE[1] means the grade of the second student in the class, etc.

To read in the scores of students into the array GRADE, we would do this:

```
void main()
 {
float grade[20];
int i, sum ;
float average;
  for (i=0; i< 20; ++i)
   {
   cout << "Please enter your score:";
   cin >> grade[i];
   }
  }
```

To find the average grade of the class, we would change the main part of the program to this:

```
sum = 0;
for (i=0; i<20; ++i)
  {
cout << "Please enter your score:";
cin >> grade[i];
sum = sum + grade[i] ;
average = sum / 20.0; }
```

5.2 Array Examples

PROGRAM #19: Change the above program so that it finds the average grade for a class of 10 students; then it prints each grade and whether it is "below average", "average", or "above average".

The following program finds the largest element in a list of numbers, and prints the number of the cell where it was found (its position within the array).

```
void main()
   {
int n[10];
int i, largest, position(0); // will initialize the position as 0

largest = 0;
for (i=0; i<10; ++i)
  {
cin >> n[i];
if (n[i] > largest)
   {
largest = n[i];
position = i;
    }
  }
cout << "largest is  " << largest<<endl;
cout << "position is " << position;
  }
```

PROGRAM #20: Write a program to print the smallest element in a list of numbers and its position within the list. (Be careful with this one, test all possible cases.)

PROGRAM #21: Write an interactive program that plays the game of HANGMAN. Hint: Let WORD be an array of characters. Read the characters of the word to be guessed into successive elements of the array WORD. The player must guess the letters that belong to WORD. The game ends when either all letters have been guessed correctly (player wins) or a specified number of incorrect guesses have been made (computer wins). Use an array SOLUTION to keep track of the solution so far. Initialize SOLUTION to a string of symbols "*". Each time a letter in WORD is guessed, replace the corresponding "*" in SOLUTION with that letter and show it to the player before the next guess is made. Play several games to try it out.

Searching an array of elements for a particular element or sorting a list to place in order lexicographically are large topics in computer science. Program #20 is an example of searching. To sort a list of elements (numbers) in order from largest number to smallest number consider the following algorithm:

1) Define or input the list of N numbers and store in an array
2) Search the list, starting at the first element, for the largest element and swap places with the largest element and the element in the first position
3) Search the list starting with the second element for the largest element and swap places with the new largest element and the element in the second position
4) Continue this process until you have considered the n-1st and nth element
5) Output the list – it should now be in order from largest element to smallest element

The above algorithm is spoken of as the selection algorithm or sort.

PROGRAM #22: Write a program, using the selection sort, to arrange a list of number in order from high number to low number.

LESSON 6

Functions

6.1 FUNCTION BASICS

C++ has some built-in functions (special purpose programs) that come in quite handy. For example, the function SQRT finds the square root of a number. The following part of a program shows how the function is called:

```
  {
cout << sqrt(4)<<endl;
cout << sqrt(25)<<endl;
cout << sqrt(81)<<endl;
cout << sqrt(100)<<endl;
  }
```

This would result in the following being printed:

2
5
9
10

Most programming languages have many pre-defined or built-in functions. All of the pre-defined functions are just special purpose programs, such as the sqrt function demonstrated above. These programs were written and stored with the compiler or translator and the systems programmer, the individual that loads the compiler, has the option of loading and storing these functions with the compiler at the time the compiler is loaded onto the computer.

Other similar functions are **SIN, COS, EXP, LN, LN10, POW, FABS, ABS** and others. You may want to try each of these in a manner similar to the test cases above for the SQRT function. These functions are for the sine, cosine, exponential - e to a power, natural logarithm, common logarithm, a number raised to a power, absolute value of a float number and the absolute value of an integer. Be careful with the POW function – you will find that it has two arguments.

A library or set of pre-defined functions is normally supplied with the compiler.

Often, we need some functions other than the ones C++ provides. In that case, we get to make our own. For example, suppose we wanted a function that will return the larger of two integers we give it. We have to give the function a ***name*** and then define it for C++. Let's call it **LARGER**. We would define it like this:

```
int larger(int first, int second)
   {
int la;
if (first > second)
la = first;
else
la = second;
return(la);
   }
```

The first line may be a little confusing. We are telling C++ that we are defining what is meant by the function LARGER. We are saying that we will give it two integers and it should give us an integer in return. If we said in our program that **x = larger(23,67)**, C++ should assign x to be 67. Here is how it would look in the entire program.

```
int larger(int, int);
void main()
   {
int num1,num2,num3,num4,temp1,temp2,big ;
 cout << "Enter 4 numbers.";
 cin >> num1 >> num2 >> num3 >> num4;
 temp1 = larger(num1,num2);
 temp2 = larger(num3,num4);
 big = larger(temp1,temp2);
 cout << "The largest number is  " << big;
   }

int larger (int first,int second)
  {
int la;
if (first > second)
 la = first;
   else
 la = second;
return(la);
   }
```

Notice that we had to define the function before we reached the main body of the program. The method of defining a function in this manner is spoken of as defining the **function prototype**. This would not be necessary if we had placed the actual function before the main program.

PROGRAM #23: Write a function CUBE that finds the cube of a number. For example, the cube of 5 is 125 (5*5*5) and the cube of 2 is 8 (2*2*2). Test your function by writing a program that makes a table of the numbers 1 through 10 with their cubes. It should look something like this: (Remember to format the output to get the chart.)

NUMBER	CUBE
1	1
2	8
3	27
.	.
.	.
.	.

PROGRAM #24: Write a function POWER that finds the power of an integer. For example POWER(2,5) should return 32, since 2 to the fifth power = 2*2*2*2*2 = 32. Test it out in a program.

6.2 Random Number Generators

Functions to generate random numbers are very common. Random number generators normally produce a sequence of real numbers between 0 and 1 that for all practical purposes appear to be random. Most random number generators start with an initial real value called a seed. Other random numbers are determined once the seed is specified. Here is a function in C++ which is a random number generator:

```
randomize();
n = random(100); /* Include #include <stdlib.h> */
```

The numbers generated are all between 0 and 99. The next function uses RANDOM but finds random numbers in whatever range you specify.

```
int n, range;
randomize();
cout << "Enter the range.";
cin >> range;
n = random(range);
```

The above sequence will define random numbers in the range between 0 and (range -1).

Now that we have a random number generator, we can write some more interesting games. The number guessing game that we wrote back in program 15 can now be made more interesting.

PROGRAM #25: Write a guessing game program that will ask the user to guess a number (integer). If the user is correct, the computer will respond with a nice message and tell how many guesses it took. If the user is wrong, the computer will tell the user HIGHER or LOWER and ask for another guess. This will continue until the user gets it right. Change the program so that the user can select the range the integer will be in. Also, you might want to give the user a maximum number of guesses, in case the user becomes confused and never gets the right answer.

www.ingramcontent.com/pod-product-compliance
Lightning Source LLC
Chambersburg PA
CBHW051222050326
40689CB00007B/766

* 9 7 8 0 6 1 5 8 7 2 7 7 3 *